MIDDLEWARE AND CLOUD COMPUTING

Oracle Fusion Middleware on Amazon Web Services and Rackspace Cloud

Dr. Frank Munz

cloudbook.munzandmore.com

MIDDLEWARE AND CLOUD COMPUTING
By Frank Munz

ISBN: 978-0-9807980-0-5
Published by: munz & more publishing
Printing History: January 2011/ First Edition

© 2011 Dr. Frank Munz. All rights reserved.

Notice of Rights

All rights reserved. No part of this book may be reproduced, stored in a retrieval system, or transmitted in any form or by any means, without the prior written permission of the copyright holder, except in the case of brief quotations embedded in critical articles or reviews.

Notice of Liability

The author and publisher have made every effort to ensure the accuracy of the information herein. However, the information contained in this book is sold without warranty, either express or implied. Neither the author and publisher, nor its dealers or distributors will be held liable for any damages caused either directly or indirectly by instructions contained in this book, or by the software or hardware products described herein.

Trademarks

Trademark Notice rather than indicating every occurrence of a trademarked name as such, this book uses the names only in an editorial fashion and to the benefit of the trademark owner, with no intention of infringement of the trademark.

Contents

1	Introduction	1
2	Cloud Computing	5
2.1	Definition and Features	5
	Cloud Computing Definition	6
	Public Clouds	6
	Private Clouds	7
	Hybrid Clouds	8
	Features	8
2.2	Service Models	9
	Infrastructure as a Service	9
	Platform as a Service	10
	Software as a Service	11
	XaaS and HuaaS	14
2.3	Cloud Computing Applications	15
	Freshbooks	17
	Animoto	18
	99designs	19
3	Amazon Web Services	21
3.1	Elastic Compute Cloud	21
	Setting Up an Account	22
	Amazon Machine Images	23
	Selecting an AMI	26
	EBS- and S3-backed AMIs	27
	Selecting an Instance Type	28
	Starting an EC2 Instance	31
	Instance Addressing	34
	Elastic IP Addresses	34
	Getting Access to the Instance	35
	Amazon Linux	38

		Other AMI Offerings	39
		EC2 Tools	41
		EC2 Command-Line	41
		EC2 Instance Pricing	44
		Reducing Costs	47
	3.2	Amazon Cloud Storage	50
		Instance Storage	50
		Elastic Block Storage	51
		Starting an EBS-backed Windows Instance	53
		Simple Storage Service	55
		S3 Tools	56
	3.3	Creating Your Amazon Machine Image	62
	3.4	EC2 Command-Line Example	65
		Starting an Ubuntu Desktop EBS Image	65
		Resizing an Instance	67
		Creating Images, Snapshots and Volumes	68
	3.5	AWS Cloud Services	69

4		**Rackspace Cloud**	**71**
	4.1	Rackspace Cloud Servers	71
		Signing up for Rackspace Cloud and Files	71
		Cloud Support and Service	73
		Locations	73
		Machines and Pricing	74
		Addressing Cloud Servers	76
		Starting a Rackspace Cloud Instance	76
		Connecting to a UNIX Desktop	78
		Adding a Desktop with NX to a Linux Server Image	80
		Creating a Rackspace Server Image	82
		REST Access to Cloud Servers	82
	4.2	Rackspace Cloud Files	87
		Features	87
		Limelight	88
		Cloud Files APIs	89

		REST Access to Cloud Files	89
		Tools for Cloud Files	92

5 SOA and Oracle Fusion Middleware — 95

5.1 Service Oriented Architecture — 95
- The Big Picture in Layers — 95
- Service Implementation — 96
- Service Virtualization — 97
- Service Orchestration — 99
- Governance — 99

5.2 Oracle Fusion Middleware — 101
- SOA Suite — 102
- Service Component Architecture — 102
- Development Environments — 103

5.3 Oracle WebLogic Server — 104
- Basics and Terminology — 104
- WebLogic Cluster — 107
- Oracle Coherence — 109

5.4 Oracle Service Bus — 110
- OSB versus OESB/Mediator — 110
- Oracle Service Bus — 110
- Proxy and Business Services — 111
- Location Transparency — 112
- Content Based Routing — 112
- Message Transformation and System Integration — 112
- Protocols — 113
- Architecture — 113

5.5 Oracle BPM / WebCenter — 114
- Design Time — 116
- Runtime — 116
- Architecture — 116

5.6 Oracle Service Registry — 116
- Architecture — 117

5.7 Oracle Enterprise Repository — 117

Architecture 118

6 Designing for the Cloud 119
6.1 Design Principles 119
Designing for Availability 119
Designing for Scalability 120
6.2 IaaS Platform Choice 120
EC2 and Rackspace Cloud Server 121
Instance Storage 123
Cloud Storage 123
Conclusion 124
6.3 AMI Design 125
S3 vs. EBS AMIs 125
User Data and Startup Scripts 127
runurl 128
Configuration Model 129
Provisioning of Oracle Software 130
Security 131
Cleaning Up before Creating an Image 132
6.4 Architecture Blueprint 132
Distributed WLS Application 132
Middleware Features and AWS Services 134
Middleware in the Cloud 134

7 Cloud Databases 135
7.1 Oracle Database AMI 135
Oracle Provided AMIs 135
Custom AMIs 136
Oracle VM with Database on AWS 136
7.2 AWS SimpleDB 136
Tools 137
Costs 138
7.3 AWS Relational Database Service 139
Creating an RDS Instance 139

		Backup and Maintenance	141
		Instance Management	143
		RDS Pricing	148
	7.4	WebLogic with RDS	151
		Configuring a WLS Data Source	151
		Verifying the RDS Connectivity	154
	7.5	Multi Data Sources	154
		Oracle Real Application Cluster (non-Cloud)	154
		Oracle RAC in the Cloud?	156
		Multi Data Sources with RDS	157
	7.6	Conclusion	158

8 Cloud Management _____ 161

	8.1	File System	161
		WebLogic Domains and File Systems	161
		Shared File Systems in the Cloud	162
		WebLogic Domains Using a Local File System	162
	8.2	Provisioning of Distributed Domains	163
		Provisioning the Admin Server	163
		Provisioning a Domain with Managed Servers	163
	8.3	Oracle Licensing	164
	8.4	Backups	165
		Data	165
		AMIs	166
	8.5	Disaster Recovery	167
	8.6	RightScale Cloud Management	168
		Usage	168
		RightImages	169
		MultiCloud Images	169
		ServerTemplates	169
		Deployments	170
		Running a Deployment	172
		Cost Report and Prediction	173
		Summary	174

9 Availability — 175

9.1 Availability Basics — 175
- Decoupling Systems — 175
- Elastic IPs — 176
- Availability Zones — 176

9.2 Clustering WebLogic — 176
- Clustering in the Cloud — 177
- AWS Cloud — 177
- Rackspace Cloud — 178
- Multicast Testing — 178

9.3 Distributed JMS — 179
- Scalability — 179
- Availability — 180

9.4 Whole-server Migration — 181
- Classic Non-Cloud Environment — 181
- Whole-server Migration on EC2 — 182
- Whole-server Migration on Rackspace Cloud Servers — 182
- Conclusion — 183

9.5 Service Migration — 183
- Classic Non-Cloud Environment — 183
- Service Migration in the Cloud — 184

9.6 WebLogic JTA — 184

9.7 AWS Simple Queue Service — 184
- Features — 185
- Usage — 185
- Conclusion — 186
- Pricing — 187

9.8 Overload Protection — 188
- WebLogic Overload Protection and OFM — 190
- WebLogic Administration Port — 190
- Workmanager Capacity Constraint — 191
- Maximum Queue Length — 191
- Maximum Thread Poolsize — 191
- Maximum Heap and Panic Setting — 192

Restricting the Number of HTTP sessions	192
JMS quota	193
Specifying a Blocking Send Policy on JMS Servers	193
JMS Message Buffer Size	193
Maximum Number of JDBC Database Connections	195

10 Scalability — 197

10.1 Basics — 197
- Granularity — 197
- Horizontal Scalability — 197
- Vertical Scalability — 198
- Resource Ceilings — 199
- User Experience Metric — 200
- Economy and Procurement — 200
- Capacity Planning — 201

10.2 Load Balancing — 202
- DNS Round Robin — 203
- Hardware Load Balancers — 204
- WebLogic Proxy Plugin Servlet — 205
- WebLogic Web Server Plugin — 206
- HAProxy — 206
- AWS Elastic Load Balancing — 208
- Load Testing Load Balancers: HAProxy and ELB — 217

10.3 AWS Auto Scaling — 219
- AWS Auto Scaling Overview — 219
- Auto Scaling Installation — 220
- Usage Example — 221
- Description Commands Example — 225
- Remove Auto Scaling Example — 226
- Fixed Size Cloud — 228

10.4 Content Distribution Network — 228
- Content Distribution Networks — 228
- AWS CloudFront — 230
- CloudFront Usage — 231

	CloudFront Pricing	235
	CloudFront with WebLogic Server	235
	More CDN Use Cases	236

11 Monitoring — 237

11.1	Overview	237
11.2	WebLogic Scripting Tool	239
	JMX Basics	239
	WebLogic MBeans	240
	Monitoring with WLST	241
11.3	WebLogic Diagnostic Framework	244
	Collected Metrics	244
	Watches and Notifications	245
	Instrumentation	246
	Dashboard	249
11.4	JMX4Perl and JMXShell	250
	JMX without Java	250
	REST based JMX Monitoring	251
	JMX Shell j4psh	252
11.5	AWS CloudWatch	253
	Basics	253
	Installation	255
	Usage	255
11.6	AWS Simple Notification Service	259
	Usage	260
	SNS APIs	263
	SNS versus SQS	264
	Integration with SQS	264
	Integration with Oracle Service Bus	264
	Pricing	265
11.7	Misc Tools	266
	RRD Tool	266
	Ganglia	267
	Hyperic	268

		Nagios	268
		Oracle Enterprise Manager Grid Control	269

12 Oracle VM — 271

12.1	Oracle Virtualization	271
	Sun Ray	271
	Oracle VM Virtual Box	271
	Oracle VM	272
12.2	Oracle WebLogic Virtual Edition	273
	Oracle JRockit Virtual Edition	273
	Oracle Virtual Assembly Builder	275
12.3	Oracle VM on AWS	275
	Licensing	276

Bibliography — 277

Alphabetical Index — 279

About this book

I started writing this book on a cold and snowy day in February 2010. The timing was perfect: Amazon Web Service was stable and proven technology and some of my customers had begun to prick up their ears when I name-dropped "cloud computing". After a rather hectic 2009, I finally had a couple of more relaxed weeks to further investigate some advanced aspects of cloud computing. I am particularly interested in middleware and scalable applications and have spent most of my professional life working for and on behalf of the top middleware vendors. This is why I would like to help you to grasp the potential of cloud computing and then show you how to efficiently run Oracle Fusion Middleware within the cloud.

The time has come to use clouds. Often, using the cloud will be really simple. I feel it is important to understand how to use cloud computing and how to add this useful and exciting technology to your toolbox. But first, let's tune out all of the buzzwords and ignore all the marketing hype that wants us to believe that cloud computing will be the answer to all our problems.

This book aims to fill the gap between the official (and sometimes lean) information available from the key cloud players and from other, more general books about web architectures in the cloud.

Furthermore, this book comes with an opinion - my opinion, which is *not* the opinion of any of the vendors. More often than not, computer books are written by the product managers of multi-billion dollar companies. Whereas the one you are holding in your hands is completely independent. You can expect a critical analysis and to learn about features and showstoppers.

This book contains many suggestions. You can only call yourself an architect and design your cloud architecture if you know the alternatives. I will also cite additional (and sometimes open source) products and tools. So, in addition to explaining and critically reviewing Oracle's technology for the cloud, you could also consider this book to be an approach to running the key products of Oracle middleware efficiently in the cloud, without having to buy the complete product stack.

I set several weeks aside in order to form my own critical and independent view about cloud computing - a view that I would like to share with you.

Finally, my goal was always to write a pragmatic, down-to-earth, short and crisp book. I am convinced this will keep a high signal-to-noise ratio. But don't worry, you will still encounter links to tons of relevant material and documentation.

In the writing of this book, neither financial support nor influence was taken from any of the vendors or from any other company.

Munich, Germany and Manly, Australia,

December 2010.

Audience of this Book

I like to think that there is something in this book for everyone with an interest in cloud computing, middleware in general or scalable application architectures.

A large chunk of the book deals with Oracle's technology, yet most concepts are also applicable to other middleware solutions. Even if you decide to replace WebLogic with the free Glassfish application server (which incidentally is now part of the Oracle product family), most of the underlying design principles explained here will still be helpful.

In any case, this book is certainly most suitable for a technical audience with at least some experience in distributed systems and WebLogic server.

There isn't much content in this book about the life-changing and social aspects of cloud computing that would serve you well at a cocktail party (unless you go to really dull parties).

About the Author

Dr. Frank Munz is an expert in middleware and distributed computing. He earned a Ph.D. with summa cum laude in computer science from the Technische Universität München for his work on distributed computing and medical imaging in brain research. He published more than 20 peer reviewed scientific papers.

Frank has over 15 years experience working for and on behalf of top middleware vendors and consultancies such as ConSol, Sun, BEA, TIBCO and Oracle, throughout Europe and Australia as a software architect, project manager and developer. In 2007 Frank founded munz & more - a cutting-edge consultancy focusing on Oracle middleware and cloud computing. Based on over a decade of teaching experience with the big vendors, and its limitations, Frank is offering his own high-end training program now.

He loves to talk about features and showstoppers and frequently speaks at conferences all over the world.

When Frank is not working, he enjoys travelling in Southeast Asia, skiing in the Alps, tapas in Spain, and scuba diving in Australia.

Organization of Material

The book is organized into 13 chapters.

Chapter 1 introduces cloud computing.

Chapter 2 introduces a critical and proper definition of cloud computing, public, private and hybrid clouds, and why SaaS is not cloud computing. The first chapter also gives some examples of real applications running in the cloud.

Chapter 3 teaches the basics of Amazon Web Services, the biggest and most important provider of cloud computing services. At the end of this chapter you will find references to advanced AWS topics such as services for load balancing, content distribution networks, relational database services and others.

Chapter 4 introduces the Rackspace Cloud and Rackspace Cloud Files. Rackspace is a smaller but very appealing competitor to Amazon's offering.

Chapter 5 provides an easy to understand yet detailed explanation of service oriented architecture and the overwhelming Oracle product stack. This chapter is not about the cloud. It serves as a stand-alone introduction to Oracle Fusion Middleware, and teaches the WebLogic server foundations necessary for the following chapters.

Chapter 6 explains how to choose the right cloud computing platform provider. It introduces an architectural blueprint of a distributed WebLogic domain in the Amazon cloud, including all the cloud services such as EBS, S3, SimpleDB, relational database service, elastic load balancing, and availability zones.

Chapter 7 walks you through the database options in the cloud: AMIs provided by Oracle, AWS SimpleDB, AWS relational database services. Also, WebLogic JDBC in the cloud and multi-data sources are explained.

Chapter 8 covers cloud management issues: from the question of local or shared file systems, to the provisioning of distributed WebLogic instances, to the RightScale management platform.

Chapter 9 discusses strategies for availability in the cloud. Topics include: clustering in clouds, distributed JMS, whole-server migration, service migration, user-defined singletons, AWS simple queue service, and WebLogic overload protection.

Chapter 10 discusses the steps necessary to provide scalability, including horizontal and vertical scalability, load balancing options, AWS auto scaling, and content distribution networks.

Chapter 11 is about monitoring. Topics include the WebLogic scripting tool, WebLogic Diagnostic Framework, JMX4Perl, AWS simple notification service, and AWS CloudWatch. Common tools such as RRD, Hyperic, Nagios, and Oracle Enterprise Manager are introduced.

Chapter 12 explains Oracle VM and how to use Oracle VM based templates in the Amazon cloud.

Links and References

To make your life easier, I am providing all links mentioned in this book on the following site. I recommend to bookmark the site now so you can conveniently click on the links later instead of typing them into your browser:

`http://cloudbook.munzandmore.com`

Note: These are links from third-party companies. No responsibility is taken for their content.

Conventions Used

All statements about costs are as accurate as possible. Prices are accurate as of November 2010. Be aware that costs change and companies often lower their fees.

Unless otherwise indicated, the prices shown are for Amazon Web Services in Europe.

As it is common, computer output or command-lines are set `in typewriter font`.

Acknowledgement

Thanks! Everyone agrees that writing is a notoriously lonely task, yet acknowledgements are usually long. While writing "Middleware and Cloud Computing", I met some extraordinary folks and some of them have become good friends.

Lots of people supported me in writing this book, without whom you'd be holding a very different publication in your hands. Needless to say, all remaining errors are mine.

Berthold Maier from Oracle believed in my idea to write an "Oracle Cloud Computing" book from the very first minute I met him. Berthold, I appreciate your precise and insightful feedback over many coffees at SFCS, as well as the generous encouragement that kept me going.

Christian Kücherer from Zühlke, and Klaus Pfreundner from Bosch, are the best technical editors I can imagine. Sincerely. Many thanks to both of you!

Klaus sent me daily updates after commuting - so all train delays worked in favor of this book (I guess there were many). His comments lead to many helpful conclusions throughout the book.

Imagine! This cloud computing book was even proof-read in the clouds. I couldn't stop Christian from taking a printout of the book with him on his off-road trip to the arid outback of Australia. He read it on his flight from Munich to Alice Springs. Hope you took plenty of water, Christian!

Oliver Stavljanin created the design for the book cover. A lot of people did a fantastic job proofreading this book, which helped make the text more aesthetically pleasing.

Cameron Nouri, Michael Ferranti, and Mike Welsh patiently answered my questions about the Rackspace Cloud. Chris Addis from RightScale established some very useful contacts, provided a RightScale account for testing, as well as valuable feedback. Willy Tarreau surprised me with a long, detailed email, full of fabulous technical feedback one Sunday morning. Willy, your comments add value to more than just the HAProxy section. Cheers!

Werner Vogels, CTO of Amazon, replied to one of my emails, thanks! I can only assume the CTO of Oracle would do the same.

Thank you Nico, for explaining to me over Skype, that at some point even the best book has to be finished, period ☺. It's done now! And there were many, many others. Abi, Adria, Andrew, Lisa, Mike, etc. Many thanks to you as well!

Comments and Feedback

I would love to have your feedback. Please send any comments, bug reports, broken links, and suggestions regarding this book to cloudbook@munzandmore.com. At my discretion, I am considering offering an exclusive munz & more coffee mug for the three most helpful pieces of feedback I receive within the next twelve months! *Coffee mug*

For technical articles and updates on forthcoming events, such as workshops and conferences, feel free to have a look at my web site or subscribe to my mailing list: *Newsletter*

http://www.munzandmore.com/newsletter

I would also like to invite you to take a look at my blog, which covers everything from WebLogic to Oracle Service Bus to Cloud Computing: *Blog*

http://www.munzandmore.com/blog

1 Introduction

"It is not tolerable that the therapy of critically ill patients, e.g. those with brain tumours, is delayed simply because our computers are too slow.", said Prof. Dr. P. Bartenstein, Head of the Nuclear Medicine Department, Ludwig-Maximilians-Universität München, and my former boss.

This conversation took place in 1998. I was just out of university, interested in supercomputers, functional imaging and brain research, and distraught by my boss's comment. Back then, I was doing a research project in computer science, trying to run better algorithms to improve the quality of highly sophisticated medical imaging scanners. These scanners measure in three dimensions and, over time, the slightest change in heart or brain function. They can also detect tumors in cancer patients.

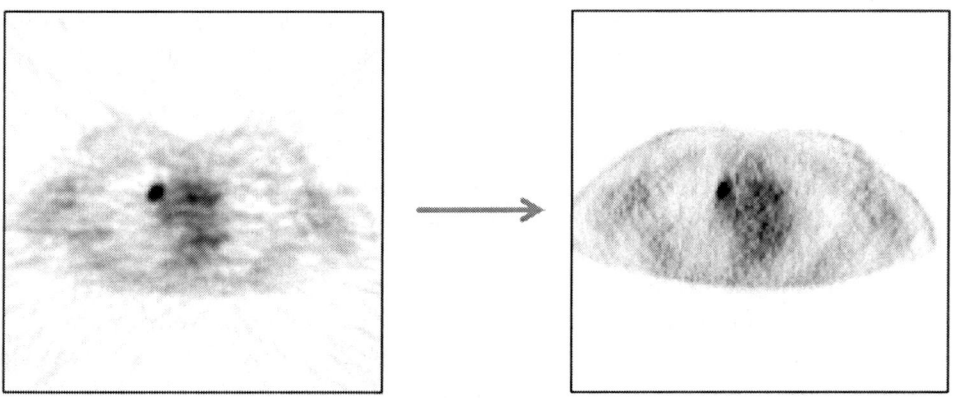

Figure 1: Normal Image (left) and Compute-Intensive Algorithm (right)

We already had algorithms that produced better images that doctors could potentially use to detect even the smallest of tumors. However, we couldn't use them for all patients because it took up to three whole days of processing to produce the images, even on the clinic's newest and biggest UNIX workstation. Have a look at Figure 1 to see how the image quality improved with the compute-intensive algorithms. *12 years ago*

Unfortunately, we were always short on RAM and in need of CPUs with more power. However, after almost three years, we managed to get funding for a Linux cluster and used it to run new algorithms for the clinical data.

... and now?   Now, more than 10 years later, research is *still* hungry for bigger computers. Researchers still dream of bigger machines than the ones they can actually afford.

Clouds   Over this same period, the situation has nevertheless changed dramatically. Nowadays, you can set up an online account with a cloud provider, submit your credit card details, and just a few clicks later run the software of your choice on any number of machines. If you require a lot of resources, machines are available with 8 cores and 68 GByte of RAM. Such a machine will cost you less than $3 US per hour at the Amazon cloud. The smallest machine only costs a few cents *and* is still capable of running a web application.

HPC   There is even a special class of machines in the cloud that is ideally suited to high performance computing (HPC). This HPC class of machines provides 23 GB of main memory, two Intel Xeon X5570, quad-core Nehalem processors, low latency and full bisection 10 Gbps bandwidth between instances.

The medical imaging example above does of course raise a number of other questions: on the one hand, we are all aware of data protection acts that regulate the transmission of patient records. On the other, everyone always insists on the best possible diagnosis. Certainly for scientific studies (and once sensitive data has been removed), cloud computing can be a cost effective way to achieve further improvements from more sophisticated compute-intensive algorithms.

I guess some of you may be thinking "what's with all this talk about medical research and computers which are never big enough?" Are you nervously flipping back to the cover of this book, double-checking if it really says "Middleware" in the title?

I assume you're beginning to understand the implications of the above for your business. At the moment, your business is probably more similar to mine i.e. your computers are used for developing applications, integrating complex systems, or running web and application servers, rather than for processing medical data for cutting pieces out of other people's brains or rewiring their clogged coronary blood vessels. Yet, everyone still has the desire for cheaper, easier and quicker access to computing capacity.

Ideally, you find the thought of cloud computing fascinating. Maybe you are attracted to the idea of launching machines in the cloud yourself? My advice: just do it! A proof of concept for cloud computing is generally a bargain. Running your own application on computers in different parts of the world takes only a few clicks and the cloud provider will even guarantee a service level agreement (SLA) for the availability of these resources.

Perhaps you are now considering using the cloud for some extensive load testing? In the cloud you can request as much CPU cores, main memory and disk space as you need. Finally, you could even test your application with that particular heap setting of 50 GByte about which you always dreamed.

All of this is within easy reach!

2 Cloud Computing

I would like to start this chapter with a proper definition of cloud computing and then go on to explore key characteristics and features of public, private and hybrid clouds. We will also look at the three different service models and analyze the economy of clouds. At the end of the chapter, I will provide some real-life examples of successful applications currently running in the cloud.

2.1 Definition and Features

It is amazingly difficult to find an all-encompassing definition of cloud computing. A group of researchers from Berkeley (those who typically coin terms and come up with snappy definitions), admitted that they could not agree on an exact definition of the service model described in a research paper:

http://www.eecs.berkeley.edu/Pubs/TechRpts/2009/EECS-2009-28.pdf

There are definitions from the National Institute of Standards and Technology (NIST) in the US, the obligatory summary on Wikipedia and you can find a definition in several books including George Reese's classic book "Cloud Architectures". Although all of them contribute to the overall picture of cloud computing, to date there is still no common agreement amongst scholars.

Let me expand on my point: I have two problems with almost all the definitions I have come across in other books or research papers.

Firstly, I don't like to include applications which are running in the cloud in the definition of what the cloud is; these are simply new kinds of applications. They don't characterize the cloud. On the contrary, the cloud is what enables them. Cloud computing is what enables the creation of new kinds of applications based on a new business model without any capital expenditure (CAPEX) for computing resources.

Secondly, I strongly believe that we should distinguish between general *features* of cloud computing and the *specific characteristics* which *uniquely define* what cloud computing is.

Cloud characteristics

For example, electricity will power cloud computing over forthcoming decades. Yet we could not possibly include electricity in the definition of cloud computing.

If this sounds far-fetched, then I'd like to remind you that even Gartner includes "Internet Technologies", such as URLs, HTTP, IP and REST, as part of its definition of cloud computing. See the press release entitled, "Five Attributes of Cloud Computing".

Now, doesn't 'Internet technology' mean exactly the same as 'electricity' in the example above? My phone, my printer and my car navigation system are all using 'Internet technologies'. Even the TV that I just bought has an IP address. 'Internet technologies' are so commonplace, that I feel there is no point including them in the definition of cloud computing. To read the whole press release, go to the following URL:

http://www.gartner.com/it/page.jsp?id=1035013

Cloud Computing Definition

4 Criteria The question remains: what characterizes a cloud? In my opinion, there are four important criteria that characterize cloud computing:

(1) When using a cloud, you *consume resources as services*. These resources are typically CPUs, disks, main memory and network bandwidth. However, they can also be a cluster of Java EE application servers, a BPM tool, a firewall or a load balancer.
(2) You either pay for the cloud *per use*, or you get charged back. Under special circumstances, these services can also be provided free of charge.
(3) Clouds offer *rapid elasticity*: resources are quickly scalable.
(4) Working with the cloud is *self service*. There is an API and a tool to request new services.

You often read about CAPEX becoming operational expenditure (OPEX) for cloud computing. This is certainly the case for public clouds such as Amazon Web Services or Rackspace Cloud, but not really for private clouds. Let me introduce the different cloud types and then return to our discussion of the features of cloud computing at a later stage.

Public Clouds

A compelling feature of public clouds is the lack of upfront payment. In other words, instead of buying expensive computers and storage for your project, installing and patching the operating system, hooking it up to the network, hiring sysadmins, paying the bill for data center rental, electricity, cooling, the security guy at the entrance and so on - you simply pay a small fee for the actual time you use the desired infrastructure in a public cloud.

In other words, using a public cloud is similar to outsourcing, while at the same time, being more than *just* outsourcing. Somebody else owns the IT-infrastructure, but unlike traditional outsourcing, where you're bound to a monthly or yearly contract, with public clouds you only pay for *actual* usage.

Private Clouds

Private clouds require your company to buy a stack of computer at the outset. So, all of a sudden you are back to CAPEX. Yet you are still running a cloud that fulfills all of the four criteria mentioned in the definition above.

Interestingly enough, there are ways to use the same API for public and private clouds: the private cloud could be running on Eucalyptus and using the same command-line tools as the public Amazon compute cloud. The White House named it "a top emerging technology player" – take a look at their web site:

http://open.eucalyptus.com

Think of the benefits: users can request instances for load testing, builds, regression testing, version control, number crunching, training or demos, whenever they want. In fact, apart from the financial investment, the private cloud is very similar to the public cloud - it just happens to be on the other side of your corporate firewall.

By the way, this is the reason why, in my opinion, having no "upfront commitment" or CAPEX should not be included among the criteria that define cloud computing.

Time for another analogy: private clouds are somehow less exciting than public clouds. Private clouds are like owning your own restaurant. You go to a restaurant because you fancy that special pizza and unique vintage wine. You only go there for the meal and that's the only thing that you want to pay for; you don't want to hire a chef and rent a wine cellar or buy the whole place. Yet this '100% purchase' is exactly what you do when you buy machines, rent a datacenter etc. in order to set up a private cloud.

Interestingly, some of the big companies do have their own restaurants. These larger companies are also the places where private clouds make sense. They are large enough for the hardware investment to make sense.

Since such companies are a prime target for software vendors like Oracle, HP or IBM, you now understand why these software vendors claim the importance of private clouds. For millions of other companies (and sometimes also for the ones mentioned above), public or hybrid clouds are more exciting, since there is no CAPEX.

Hybrid Clouds

Hybrid clouds extend the private network and computing infrastructure into a public cloud via virtual private networks (VPN). They blend the public cloud into your local network.

I am sure we will see an increasing number of hybrid clouds in the future, since they combine the zero investment benefit of public clouds, with the convenience of having cloud instances that belong to your own network.

Coming back to the restaurant example above, hybrid clouds blend the restaurant into your home. It is 'virtually' there, but is 'actually' at some other location. You don't have to leave the house. It only takes a quick phone call and 30 minutes later that fantastic pizza and wine are delivered straight to your door. The restaurant food arrives conveniently on your doorstep, in the same way that the hybrid cloud appears to be a part of your local network.

Features

I'd now like to talk about additional features. The following section on service models explains some of these in more detail.

- Clouds use virtualization. Compared to the virtualization-only techniques such as Oracle VM, VMWare ESX, Virtual Box, Xen or KVM, clouds also provide pay per use services and offer a self-service option.
- Clouds are accessible via the network, or as Gartner puts it, they use 'Internet technology'.
- Clouds require monitoring for the services provided. Interestingly enough, clouds often provide monitoring themselves.
- Clouds enable new business models.

In the following comment, Werner Vogels (CTO of Amazon) summarized what is interesting and new about clouds and why they are changing the way we think about IT: *"with the cloud comes unconstrained thinking and willingness to tinker and experiment without worrying too much about cost"*.

2.2 Service Models

The NIST published a cloud computing definition which illustrates a layered delivery model. Layers one (infrastructure as a service) and two (platform as a service), are self-explanatory, the third layer (software as a service), leads to a great deal of confusion. Let's have a look at each one, starting with the lowest layer; infrastructure as a service.

Infrastructure as a Service

The medical imaging case I mentioned in the introduction, is a good example of Infrastructure as a Service (IaaS).

IaaS enables you to rent computer infrastructure, such as multi-processor machines and disk space and network bandwidth, as a service for a certain period of time.

With an IaaS model, you are in full control and have the highest amount of flexibility: you decide which operating system you want to use. You can install a .NET environment, a Java EE application server, Ruby on Rails, or any other framework you need, and then deploy your application on top. If you need a database, go for it. If you need an LDAP server, you can also add it to your cloud environment in the same way as you would to any other middleware product.

The term "service" implies that these computing resources come with a pay-per-use model. This is correct. You only pay for the resources that you use and for as long as you use them. It is scalable on-demand: if you need more resources, you just request them. If you need less, you release them and halt payment.

Economy of scale, to put it bluntly, is the underlying principle of the supermarket sector. Since an IaaS provider buys tremendous amounts of CPUs, it can resell disks and network bandwidth at competitive rates. The model is based on the assumption that not everyone is using the resources at the same time, and that based on statistical fluctuations, there is always enough demand. The Berkeley researchers cited above call this effect "statistical multiplexing". *Economy of Scale*

All IaaS providers use virtualization techniques such as Xen or KVM to virtualize their computing infrastructure and to sell slices of it. Currently, Xen is more established, but KVM is now a part of the Linux kernel. Both technologies support multi-processors (SMPs) and live migration. *Virtualization*

Virtualization offers many advantages. First, virtualization increases utilization of the physical hardware. For a typical Java EE application, the server utilization is often surprisingly low. Using virtualization techniques, one physical machine can deploy several virtual machines. Increased utilization of fewer, bigger, and consolidated machines results in less power consumption, a lower administration overhead and therefore, increased savings.

I expect the trend to continue to make virtualization an increasingly widespread hardware feature. Have a look at the newest Sun or HP machines: they can be partitioned at runtime.

Platform as a Service

The NIST defines Cloud Platform as a Service (PaaS) as *"The capability provided to the consumer [is] to deploy onto the cloud infrastructure consumer-created or acquired applications created using programming languages and tools supported by the provider"*.

The idea of platform as a service is to develop or deploy your application in the cloud based on some underlying platform. The key question is what exactly is this platform typically provided by the PaaS provider? There are three variations. PaaS can be one of the following:

- An API you program against plus a runtime environment.
- A complete framework with a distributed file system, a distributed database, algorithms for distributed processing, etc.
- A platform containing pre-installed infrastructure such as an Java EE application server, a BPM tool or a service bus.

Google App Engine
For example, Google App Engine is a platform as a service offering, so called because you are programming your application against the App Engine's Java Servlet, JDO and JPA APIs. Programming against PaaS provided APIs is just one way of thinking about PaaS. For more details about Google App Engine have a look at their site:

`http://code.google.com/appengine`

Framework
An interesting example of a more extensive framework as PaaS is the Apache Hadoop project. Hadoop is an open-source implementation of frameworks for reliable, scalable, distributed computing and data storage.

See `http://hadoop.apache.org` for further details.

The best known among the Hadoop sub-projects are:

- HBase, a scalable and distributed database (now a top level Apache project).
- HDFS, a distributed file system with high throughput.
- MapReduce, an implementation of the map-reduce algorithm for the distributed processing of large data sets.

Neither Amazon nor Rackspace offer Hadoop as a service, yet Amazon does offer an implementation of the map reduce algorithm.

Yet another way of doing PaaS is to use Oracle Fusion Middleware in the compute cloud. In this case, the platform consists of the middleware components such as Oracle Business Process Management, Service Bus or WebLogic Server. The platform can be provided by Oracle, or you can install it yourself. Using middleware in the cloud as PaaS is certainly part of the focus of this book.

Middleware

This book is not only teaching you how to use the Oracle middleware as PaaS in the cloud, but also how to create such a platform in the cloud yourself. We begin by looking into the details of IaaS, then go on to cover the issues of PaaS as well.

In the end, you will be able to run cloud instances with pre-installed middleware components with the versions that you need, independently from the subset provided by Oracle.

With a PaaS model, you control your application and your data. The platform itself, including the underlying operating system, is delivered by the PaaS provider, which could be Oracle, the cloud provider or even yourself.

Software as a Service

We are now approaching a more exciting topic. How many times have you heard "*Cloud computing is the new revolution. Google's Gmail is cloud computing...*" ? Unfortunately, even normal newspapers are full of articles raving about cloud computing, emphasizing the idea of using applications without installation and hosting your data in some remote place that lacks description.

This is not cloud computing. At least it is not what I think cloud computing is and I am in good company with this opinion. Larry Ellison, the CEO of Oracle, was disgruntled when asked in an interview about cloud computing. You can enjoy one of his famous interviews on YouTube at the following URL: http://www.youtube.com/watch?v=8UYa6gQC14o and another one, with audio only, at http://www.youtube.com/watch?v=0FacYAI6DY0.

I agree with Larry. Do you remember that web mail was around long before Gmail ever existed? This was way before anybody was talking about cloud computing. Older readers may remember that the Internet did not start with Google.

A main part of the confusion comes from the wrong idea that software as a service (SaaS) is cloud computing. Actually, the situation is a bit confusing because there are at least two conflicting definitions for SaaS.

Wikipedia Definition

Sticking to the Wikipedia definition, which can be found at the following site `http://en.wikipedia.org/wiki/Software_as_a_service`, SaaS is a model of software deployment over the Internet:

"With SaaS, a provider licenses an application to customers as a service on demand, through a subscription or a "pay-as-you-go" model. SaaS is also called 'software on demand.' SaaS vendors develop, host, and operate software for customer use. Rather than purchase the hardware and software to run an application, customers need only a computer or a server to download the application and Internet access to run the software".

Now, don't get me wrong. SaaS is the right idea. In the future, we should see more and more applications offered as a service via the Internet. Newer technologies such as rich Internet client applications (RIA) using JavaFX, AJAX frameworks, and other technologies, improve user interfaces for Internet based applications that resemble desktop applications.

However, SaaS is only a broad concept and is not linked to a particular infrastructure technology. The SaaS concept is certainly the right approach, because zero-installation applications are attractive.

On the other hand, this definition of SaaS is so vague, that most web applications qualify as SaaS. Some even argue that web applications are indistinguishable from SaaS - I don't disagree based on the definition above.

The most prominent example of SaaS is SalesForce.com - but did you ever think of Amazon's bookshop as SaaS? If I charged money for my blog (don't worry, I won't), does that qualify as SaaS as well?

NIST Definition

Here is another definition of SaaS provided by the NIST, which states the following about Software as a Service: *"The capability provided to the consumer is to use the provider's applications running on a cloud infrastructure. The applications are accessible from various client devices through a thin client interface such as a web browser (e.g., web-based email)."*

Based on the NIST definition, a cloud infrastructure is the prerequisite for SaaS. Yet this doesn't sound right. Imagine I provided a multi-tenant, web-based tax advisory software with an AJAX GUI, which would help you to complete your tax declaration for a small usage fee. Contrary to everybody's belief, this application only qualifies as real SaaS if it is running on a cloud infrastructure.

If you still have doubts about this definition, think about my personal blog running on a public cloud. Does it qualify a SaaS? It does! It's more than a few static pages: it's an application implemented on top of a framework, displaying information with the possibility of adding comments, you only need the Internet to run it (there is no need to download a client) and it is running in the cloud.

For the rest of this book I will stick to the Wikipedia definition where SaaS is defined as a concept for software provisioning. Although this software will ideally run in the cloud, it doesn't necessarily have to. With this definition, software that was considered as SaaS, because it is provided over the Internet, can keep its SaaS sticker even if it is not running in the cloud.

There are areas where SaaS seems to be taking off. Microsoft Docs from Facebook can be used to create and share documents. Google is offering the zero-installation office suite Google Docs. There are also areas where SaaS has failed to deliver until now. Millions of people install tax advisory software year after year and use it just once.

CLOUD COMPUTING AND SAAS

With SaaS you only control your data - the application, the platform and the operating system is provided for you.

You can implement SaaS on top of cloud computing infrastructure.

Using cloud computing for SaaS certainly has many advantages, but cloud computing is not a necessary precondition for SaaS.

The most exciting idea is certainly the concept of real software as a service. The software is composed of reusable services hosted in the cloud, the same way as in a non-cloud service oriented architecture. These services are integrated and virtualized by a service bus in the cloud and orchestrated by a workflow system in the cloud. Have a look at the underlying principles and components of a service oriented architecture discussed in chapter 5 of this book.

XaaS and HuaaS

Increasingly, everything is referred to as a service (XaaS) which includes "Service as a Service" and "Human as a Service" - interestingly enough more often at conferences than in newsgroups or in user group conferences where people are solving real problems.

Service as a Service
"Service as a Service" is a buzzword often explained with barely convincing examples: Outsourcing the HR department of a company is one such example. Forcing employees who travel a lot to use a travel agency service instead of being able to book their own flights is another example.

In my opinion, none of these examples are related to important technical or architectural issues of cloud computing - apart from being questionable measures for a company.

Human as a Service
Amazon's Mechanical Turk implements the idea of Human as a Service (HuaaS), also known as *crowdsourcing*.

With crowdsourcing, anybody can complete a Human Intelligence Task (HIT) for a small remuneration. At the time of writing, only 7 out of 1,700 entries have a remuneration of more than $10. Two typical examples on the Mechanical Turk list are the tagging of 5,000 jewelry images with appropriate keys (you cannot assign tags such as "gold", "jewelry" etc.) which gets you $0.02 per HIT, and the verification of 2,000 restaurant and hotel phone numbers in India for $0.07 per HIT.

Amazon charges a 10% commission on top of what a crowdsourcing company has paid for a HIT. The minimum commission charge is $0.005 per HIT.

Since the Mechanical Turk has an API, developers can leverage it to include low cost human intelligence directly in their business processes. In any case, they should take into account possible delays, and consider some kind of quality management.

Why not check if you can make some money off the HITs at:

https://www.mturk.com

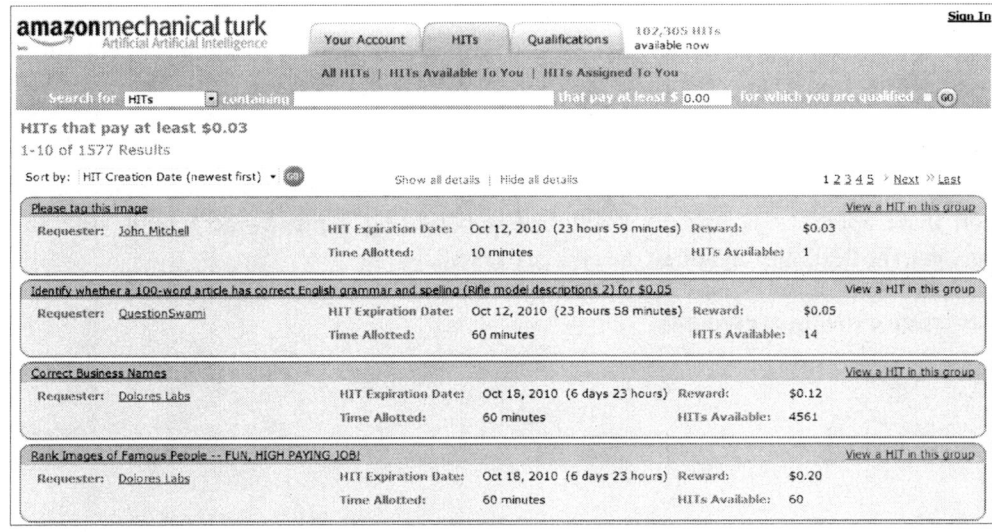

Figure 2: Amazon Mechanical Turk

2.3 Cloud Computing Applications

After conference presentations and my workshops, delegates often ask me if I have any examples of real-life applications running in the cloud. Well, I think it is a well-acknowledged fact that the cloud is a compelling environment for a broad range of usage scenarios:

- The cloud is a fantastic training environment. Create your own images with your customized training environment and start as many of them as you need for running a training course. I love to run my own workshops in the cloud. Starting an image in the cloud is much preferable to ordering real hardware. It's cheaper, it saves me from carrying, installing and configuring boxes, and best of all, I can use these images at anytime, anywhere in the world.
- You can use additional resources for one-time trials, testing, etc. by adding a hybrid cloud to your network either via VPN technology or by directly using a public cloud.
- The cloud is a great environment for large jobs that would take months or years in your data center. In the cloud, 300 machines for one day cost the same as one machine for 300 days. For large scale problems that can be run as a distributed application, the cloud helps you to reduce the time for solving them because you can use any number of machines simultaneously.

Okay, but what about real companies? Real applications? Yes, they exist. Obviously, you can use the cloud instead of any classical web hosting company for running your enterprise website or personal blog. The cloud is a superset of your web hosting.

On the other hand, there are applications that use cloud specific services such as cloud storage, auto scaling, load balancing, monitoring, notification, and queuing. You couldn't run these applications using a traditional web hosting company because it lacks the services, the flexibility and often the capacity as well.

Let me give you three examples.

Freshbooks

The Toronto based company, Freshbooks, is one of the leading online invoicing and bookkeeping companies. They use the Rackspace Cloud and Rackspace Cloud Files. Freshbooks aims to provide small and medium businesses, consultants, and freelancers with a fast, cost-effective and easy way to create a polished image for their business, offering professional web-based invoicing and expense and time tracking services. Over 1,000,000 users send invoices by email or ground mail and take advantage of features including recurring billing, employee timesheets and project management features.

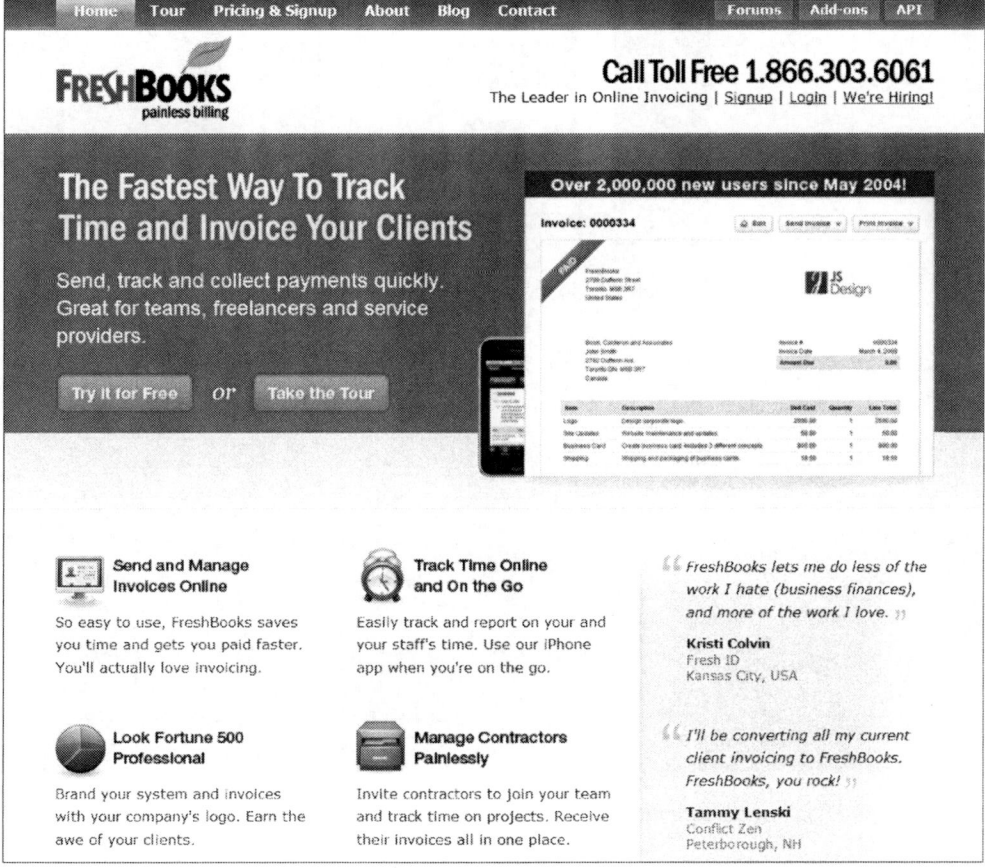

Have a look at their web site at:

http://www.freshbooks.com

Animoto

Another real-company example is the video production company Animoto. They use the AWS cloud for rendering high quality videos with great effects. All you need to do is upload your photos and videos from your digital camera.

Animoto does the rendering in the cloud instead of you having to buy and install video editing software and then blocking your home computer for several days.

Figure 3: Cloud Application: Animoto

Take a look at their web site and try a 30-second video for free at:

http://animoto.com

99designs

Another great example is 99designs. The cover design of this book was done in the AWS cloud by 99designs. You simply post your design brief to a community of almost 90,000 designers signed up to 99designs. Those who are interested can submit their designs and you pick the one you like most. You could get your business cards designed in the cloud, and they also design logos, web sites, icons and even t-shirts.

In September 2010, 99designs paid over $600,000 to their designers. Indeed, when I submitted the design brief there were over 500 other open projects. For my contest 25 designers submitted over 200 entries. Take a look below to see some examples of what the cover might have looked like.

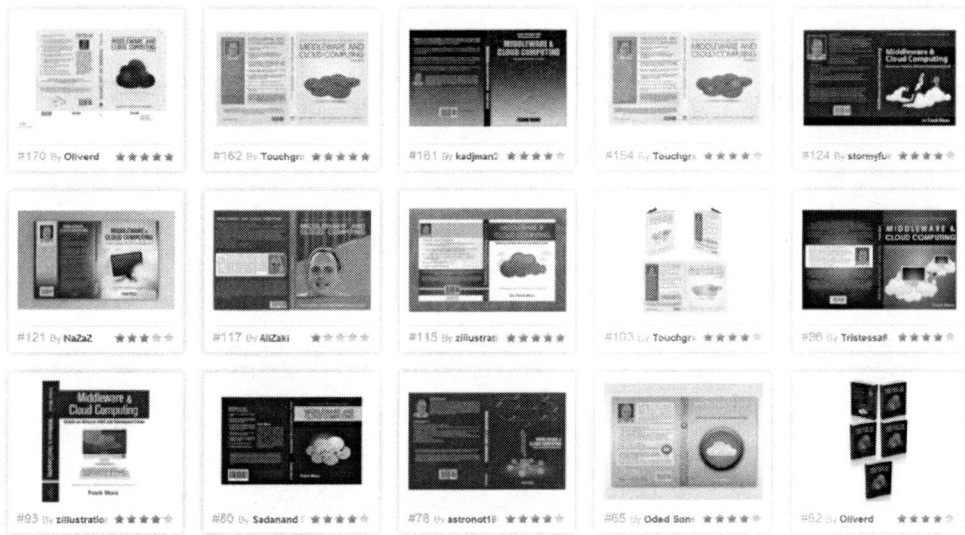

Figure 4: Cloud Application: 99designs Contest for this Book Cover

Check out their web site at:

http://99designs.com

3 Amazon Web Services

Interestingly enough, the most well known infrastructure as a service offering comes from Amazon.com, a company that was founded as an online bookshop by Jeff Bezos in his garage. Amazon is America's largest online retailer and in addition to selling books about cloud computing, like this one, they also offer a variety of cloud computing services. If this combination seems strange, it might help to know that Jeff has a Ph.D. in computer science from Princeton, so maybe the evolution from selling books to selling virtual computers was inevitable?

Isn't it just an online bookshop?

So why was the name "Amazon Web Services" (AWS) given to this offering? Simple: Amazon was involved with cloud computing long before a cool name for it was coined.

Technically, you can in fact access Amazon's cloud services using SOAP or REST web services, so the naming isn't too inappropriate after all. AWS uses these web services to implement a user-programmable data center. Software architects use the same protocols and standards to design a service oriented business architecture.

3.1 Elastic Compute Cloud

Amazon is best known for its elastic compute cloud (EC2). Amazon's EC2 lets you start your own computer instances in Amazon's data center. Such an instance is not a dedicated, real computer, but rather a virtual machine running an Amazon Machine Image (AMI). With one AMI, you can start as many instances as you like.

If you have already worked with VMware on your PC or Mac, then just think of an AMI as a VMware virtual machine. If you are using Oracle VM for server virtualization, an AMI is pretty much like an Oracle VM template. Although technically-speaking, this is of course just a similar concept, since these virtual machines are incompatible.

Amazon recently announced plans to support Oracle VM on EC2. This is great news because EC2 is a fantastic environment in which to test-drive Oracle VM images with pre-installed Oracle software.

Setting Up an Account

Ok, let's cut to the chase: to create an account, simply go to the following URL:

http://aws.amazon.com/ec2

Creating an account is free. There is no fee for signing up to AWS and no long-term commitment. You only pay for the resources you use when you start an instance.

First, click on "Sign Up For Amazon EC2", then fill in your email and choose a password:

Figure 5: Registrations with AWS

Next, you need to provide personal data - such as your address - and accept the customer agreement. Be sure to read this agreement carefully.

USAGE TERMS OF THE AMAZON CLOUD

Among other things, Amazon's agreement prohibits the use of EC2 for spamming. You allow Amazon to "crawl or otherwise monitor the external interfaces of your application for the purpose of verifying your compliance with this Agreement. You may not seek to block or otherwise interfere with such crawling or monitoring".

Then, enter your credit card details and select your billing address. After the credit card details, there is another step to verify your identity. You must provide your phone number and then click on the "Call Me Now" button. Don't worry, there isn't a person calling you. It's just a computer generated voice.

You will receive a text message from Amazon when a PIN has been sent to your computer. Type the PIN into your phone to identity yourself.

Proof your ID

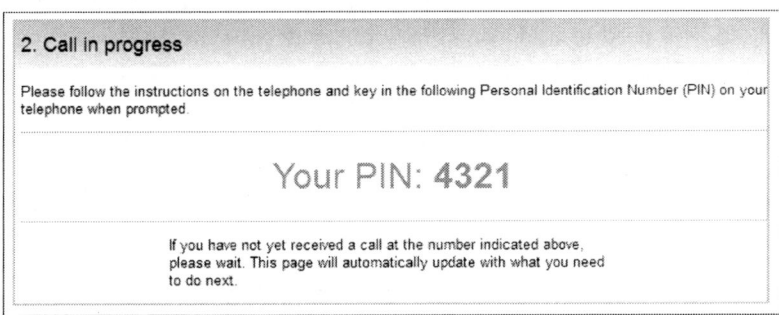

Figure 6: Sign Up For AWS

After completing this process you are almost done; all that is missing is a digital certificate. We will cover certificates and other credentials later on in this chapter.

A few seconds later, you will receive emails from Amazon stating that you have signed up for EC2, the Simple Storage Service and the Virtual Private Cloud. Every email contains a link to your credentials which are stored at Amazon. Don't worry about these identifiers for now; I will explain them in detail later.

Amazon Machine Images

When starting an instance, the most important choice is the AMI. There are a huge number of different Windows or Unix AMIs available e.g. OpenSolaris, SUSE, Ubuntu, Oracle Linux and the brand new Amazon Linux, and you can even build your own. Some of these AMIs are provided by Amazon, whereas others are provided by Oracle and contain pre-installed Oracle products. There are also public AMIs provided by people like you and me. Once you have chosen your AMI, you can use it to start any number of instances. Each AMI belongs to a certain region, so if for example, you later create your own AMI and store it in the European region, it will not be visible in the US region.

Most of the Oracle AMIs contain the standard or the enterprise edition of the Oracle database, although an AMI with WebLogic Server is also available (version 10.3.3 at the present time). Often an AMI with pre-installed software is all you need. However, the WebLogic AMI is only available in the US-East region and Oracle only provides the latest version. At the time of this writing there are some 45 AMIs posted by Oracle.

AMIs from Oracle

I recommend you check the list of the AMIs provided by Oracle for yourself at:

```
http://developer.amazonwebservices.com/connect/kbcategory.jspa
?categoryID=205
```

You should regard this list of AMIs as the first step to getting started. To run productive applications in the cloud, you need to understand how to create your own AMIs, in your region, with your custom software and configuration.

You will also need to think carefully about what happens when Oracle decides to remove one of the listed AMIs or to replace it with a newer version. But don't worry. We will cover all these issues later in the book.

QUESTION: IS IT SAFE TO START JUST ANY PUBLIC AMI?

Well, probably not. You never know what you are getting with the AMI, and as you know, these days it is better to be safe than sorry. I haven't actually heard any horror stories.

All AMIs show the ID of the owner who created them. Of course, the owner had been checked like you were when you set up the account. However, when running an *unknown* AMI, there is still a risk it contains viruses, backdoors, worms or whatever exists for a particular operating system.

My advice, therefore, is to use a reputable source for a base image and then build your own customized image.

Regions   To start an instance, you will also have to specify a geographical region. Amazon is running a separate cloud in each region. Four regions are currently available:

- US east
- US west
- Europe west
- Asia-Pacific

The Asia-Pacific region is new as of Spring 2010, so if your business is located in Bangkok or Sydney, there is now an AWS region closer to you. Usual practice is to simply pick the region closest to your business customers, in order to reduce network latency.

AWS AND YOUR WEB HOSTER

Compared to your Internet provider, which might be offering web space with a Linux, Apache, MySQL and PHP or Perl or Python (LAMP) stack in one location only, Amazon's offering is a more suitable foundation for a global enterprise due to the different regions it offers across the globe.

Another major difference between the AWS cloud and your web hoster, are the unique set of cloud services AWS offers, such as elastic load balancing, auto scaling and virtually unlimited cloud storage.

Every region consists of at least two availability zones. Amazon is running a separate data center in each availability zone. When you start an EC2 instance you can either select the availability zone yourself, or leave it to AWS to pick one. This way you can distribute a group of instances across two data centers. To increase their availability you only need to change *one* startup parameter.

Availability zones

Although availability zones are isolated from each other, they offer inexpensive, low latency network connectivity to other zones in the same region. Designing availability zones is no easy task for Amazon: to entirely insulate two data centers, they have to be designed totally differently: with different power suppliers, different Internet providers, independent cooling systems, etc.

AVAILABILITY ZONES

Availability zones help to overcome the biggest single point of failure in non-cloud architectures: your data center!

There are currently four availability zones in US/East and two each in US/West, Europe/West, and Asia-Pacific/SouthEast. So it is reasonable to conclude that Amazon is running at least 10 different data centers.

EC2 SLA Amazon guarantees the following service level agreement (SLA) for EC2 instances if you are using availability zones: Amazon will make reasonable efforts to make EC2 instances available with an annual uptime percentage of at least 99.95%. "Downtime" is defined as when more than one availability zone in which you are running an instance is unavailable to you. Meaning all of your running instances have no external connectivity during a five minute period and you are unable to launch replacement instances.

If the annual uptime percentage for a customer drops below 99.95% for the service year, that customer is eligible to receive a service credit equal to 10% of their bill.

Selecting an AMI

Ok, time to get some more hands-on experience. The good news is that you don't need an extra tool to access EC2. Although there are other tools available, we will start with the Amazon web console. So all you have to do is navigate to:

```
https://console.aws.amazon.com
```

Then click on "Sign in to the AWS Console" and log in with your user name (the email-address that you used to set up your account) and your password. Then, click on AMIs under Navigation:

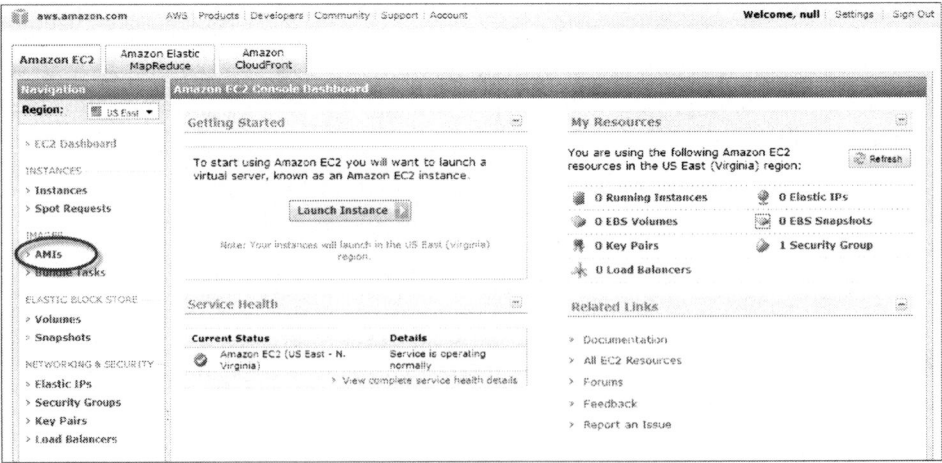

Figure 7: AWS Web Console

A list of AMIs relating to your selected region, image type, platform and search criteria will be displayed:

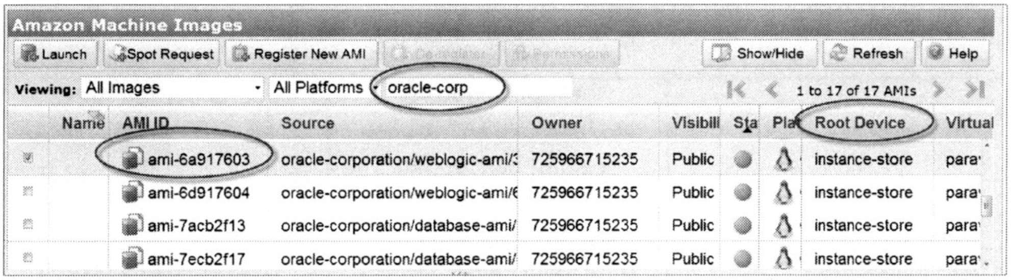

Figure 8: Available AMIs for EC2

Use the search criteria "oracle-corp" to check for the availability of Oracle AMIs in your region. For the purpose of this exercise, try to find an AMI provided by Oracle in the US East region containing the latest version of WebLogic, and right-click to launch an instance. At the time of this writing, the latest 32-bit WebLogic image is `ami-6a917603`.

Next comes the most tempting parameter of all: the number of instances. Leave it on one for now (seeing as this is just the first exercise to get you started). Later I will explain how to set up a Fusion Middleware Cluster running on three or more instances. Every AWS account has a built-in limit that restricts you from starting more than 20 instances at any one time. This limit can be increased by submitting a form containing your contact data and the reason for the change, at the following URL:

`http://aws.amazon.com/contact-us/ec2-request`

EBS- and S3-backed AMIs

You will see that two different kinds of AMIs are available: the older S3-backed AMIs and the newer EBS-backed AMIs. EBS and S3 offer alternative ways to store data in the Amazon cloud. We will cover cloud storage in the second part of this chapter (see section 3.2). A comparison of the two AMI types is shown in Table 1.

For now, remember that the Oracle WebLogic AMI is still one of the older S3-backed AMIs.

Once you select an AMI in the AWS management console, you can see if it is EBS- or S3-backed by looking at the column "Root Device". The root device can be EBS, which is a volume that *persists* the data (for both stopped and crashed instances). Alternatively, the root device can be set to "instance-store" for an S3-backed instance, which is a local instance store that is *not persisted* once the instance stops running.

Table 1: EBS-backed and S3-backed AMIs

	S3-backed AMI	EBS-backed AMI
Park instance?	No, because an instance cannot be stopped. An instance is either running or terminated.	Yes
Data persistence	Data on instance storage not persisted in case of failure or termination.	Data persisted on EBS volume when an instance is stopped or in case of failure. EBS volume deleted on termination is configurable.

For a more detailed discussion about the differences between AMIs please see section 6.3 about AMI design.

Selecting an Instance Type

The "Instance Type" setting determines how many CPU cores and how much RAM your first cloud instance will have. Currently, there is a choice of the following instances, with the micro instances and the cluster instance being the newest additions.

Amazon measures CPU power in compute units. One EC2 Compute Unit (ECU) is defined as follows: it provides the equivalent CPU capacity of a 1.0-1.2 GHz 2007 Opteron or of a 2007 Xeon processor, which is equivalent to an early-2006 1.7 GHz Xeon processor.

Usually, you select a suitable instance from the standard category. The high CPU instances will provide more CPU capacity. If you need more RAM in relation to the CPU capacity, then go for a high memory instance. I have already mentioned the cluster instances in the introduction of this book; they stand out because they offer a full bisectional 10 Gbps bandwidth between instances.

ECUs We will have a closer look at capacity, scalability and how to decide about the size and number of instances for a particular application in chapter 9.

Table 2: AWS Instance Types

Type	bit	GB RAM	Cores	ECU	ECU/Core	I/O perf	GB local Storage
Micro							
t1.micro	32/64	0.5	1	max 2	max 2	Low	1690
Standard							
m1.small	32	1.7	1	1	1	Mod	160
m1.large	64	7.5	2	4	2	High	850
m1.xlarge	64	15	4	8	2	High	1690
High Memory							
m2.xlarge	64	17.1	2	6.5	3.25	Mod	420
m2.2xlarge	64	34.2	4	13	3.25	High	850
m2.4xlarge	64	68.4	8	26	3.25	High	1690
High CPU							
c1.medium	32	1.7	2	5	2.5	Mod	350
c1.xlarge	64	7	8	20	2.5	High	1690
Cluster Instance							
cc1.4xlarge	64	23	8	33.5	4.2	very high	1690
cg1.4xlarge	64	22	8	33.5	4.2	very high	1690

Micro instances

The new micro instances are interesting because of their price; only $0.025 per hour (see Figure 19: EC2 Instance Pricing). The low price tag makes them ideal for experimenting, especially when you need to start up several instances simultaneously e.g. for elastic load balancing (covered in section 10.2) or auto scaling (covered in section 10.3).

Micro instances operate at two different CPU levels. They usually consume a consistent, low background level of CPU capacity. For short spikes they can consume up to 2 ECUs, which is approximately double the CPU capacity of a standard small instance. AWS throttles those micro instances that try to exploit the high level of CPU for longer than short spikes. For such load patterns, it is preferable to use another instance type which can consistently offer higher CPU capacity, or to start more of the micro instances using auto scaling in order to better distribute the load.

Cluster compute instance Cluster compute instances offer 23 GB of RAM and 33.5 ECUs based on two Intel Xeon X5570, quad-core "Nehalem" architecture with hyperthreading enabled and 10 Gbp/s Ethernet. These instances must be started from a special EBS-backed Amazon Machine Image (ami-7ea24a17) using Hardware Virtual Machine (HVM) virtualization.

HPC instances require a low latency and high bandwidth network connection, in order to reduce the communication overhead. To group these instances together, you can define placement groups in the AWS management console.

Cluster GPU instance Amazon's brand new cluster graphics processing units (GPU) are a compelling option for compute-intense applications. Nowadays GPUs are a supercomputer on a circuit board because they combine vector processing with massively parallel cores.

Cluster GPU instances provide two NVIDIA Tesla "Fermi" M2050 GPUs. Each GPU contains 448 cores, 3 GB of ECC RAM, and delivers up to 515 gigaflops of double-precision computations, so the peak GPU performance per instance is about 1 teraflops.

Currently, your database or application server won't be able to profit from the GPU processing. To take advantage of the GPU you have to use the low level CUDA API (CUDA is an acronym for Compute Unified Device Architecture), Java libraries for CUDA such as JCuda, or the vendor independent OpenCL language.

For details about JCuda check the following URL:

```
http://www.jcuda.org
```

There is a usage limit of maximum 8 HPC instances, which can be increased upon request. Cluster compute instances are currently only available in the US East region. No other regions, no spot images, no paid AMIs and no Windows operating systems are supported. In addition, auto scaling cannot launch cluster compute instances into placement groups, and within placement groups no reserved instances are available.

Shared/ dedicated resources CPU cores and memory are dedicated and guaranteed per instance, yet network and I/O subsystem are shared. So, even if more CPU is available on the physical machine, you will only be able to use what you pay for. This is in stark contrast to the model offered by Rackspace Cloud, where a minimum CPU allocation is guaranteed, yet bursting is possible if there is free capacity.

For shared resources, you can expect an equal share when demand is high, and an even higher share if the resource is not fully utilized. The minimum I/O performance depends on the instance types. Instances marked with I/O performance "high" in the table above can expect a higher minimum performance and a smaller variance.

Starting an EC2 Instance

To save money, let's focus on a small instance here (even if it is your company's credit card that you provided for billing). In any case, it isn't actually possible to select the new micro instance type with the S3-backed Oracle AMI, since micro instances only support the newer, EBS-backed AMIs.

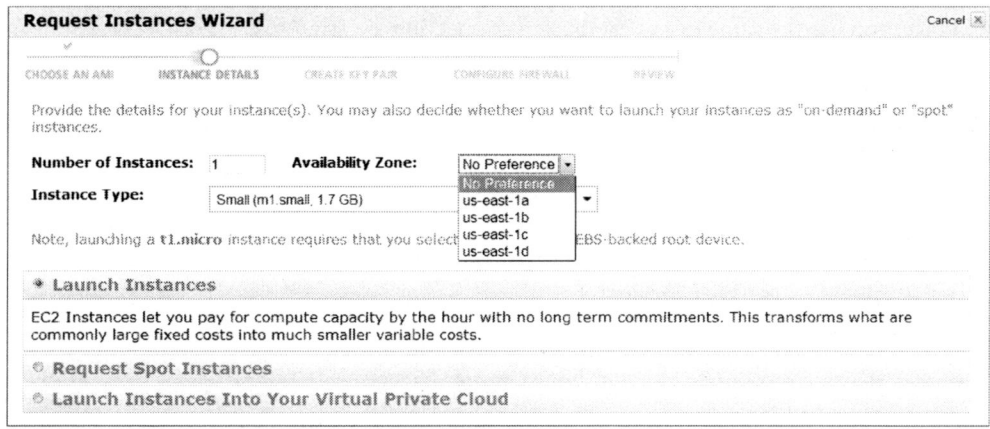

Figure 9: Request Instances Wizard

Also, leave all "Advanced Instance Options" such as kernel ID or RAM disk ID on the next screen with their default settings, before clicking continue to proceed.

Once you have selected an AMI, you can add up to 10 case-sensitive tags as name-value pairs. This is a great feature that helps to easily distinguish the individual instances. For example, if you have three instances running for a cluster test and another three instances for a load test, you could create a tag with key=Name and value=ClusterTestInstance or value=LoadTestInstance.

Key (127 characters maximum)	Value (255 characters maximum)	Remove
Name	ClusterTestInstance	✘
Run	1	✘
StartedBy	Frank	✘

Add another Tag. (Maximum of 10)

Figure 10: Instance Tags

The name key will be displayed in the AWS management console. The management console can also filter the displayed instances based on the tags. When you right-click on a particular instance you can edit or delete the tags.

Amazon Web Services 31

You can choose an availability zone within the selected region to increase the availability of the instances. Any availability zone will be okay – you do not have to set a particular availability zone.

The weakest of all authentication methods - user name and password - is disabled by default. Access to a running instance is granted based on a key pair. When starting the instance, you specify the key pair name as a parameter. Then, when you connect to the instance, you use the same key to establish a connection via ssh.

You must therefore create a key pair that can be re-used at a later stage. So don't forget the name you choose! I will name my key pair "access". Then click on "Generate & Download your Key Pair":

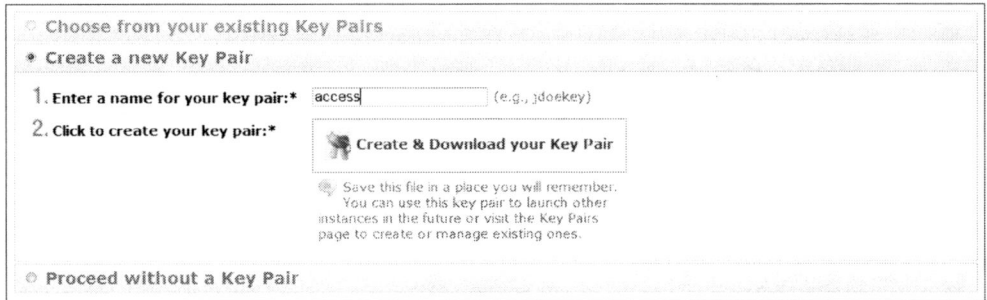

Figure 11: Create a new Key Pair

Next, save the key to your local computer.

In the following step, leave the security group at the default setting. We will modify it once the instance is started.

SECURITY GROUPS AND RUNNING INSTANCES

You cannot add a new security group to a running instance, but you can modify an existing security group. When you start an instance you can assign it as many security groups as you like. Usually you design security groups for a group of instances. For example, you can configure a security group for a software based load balancer, another security group for a set of web servers and a third group for a cluster of WebLogic server instances.

Then take a look at the overview and double check your launch settings:

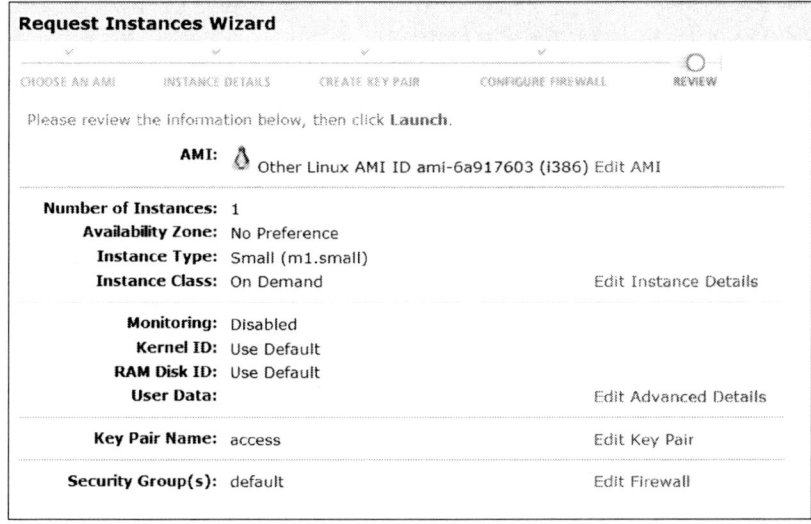

Figure 12: Overview Instance Configuration

Finally, hit the launch button. Your instance will first display the status "Pending", then it will change its status to "Running"; this means you are running your first cloud instance!

The name tag will be displayed automatically in the instance view. The management console allows for sorting and filtering of tags. Simply right-click on the little arrow displayed in the top left hand side in the Name column.

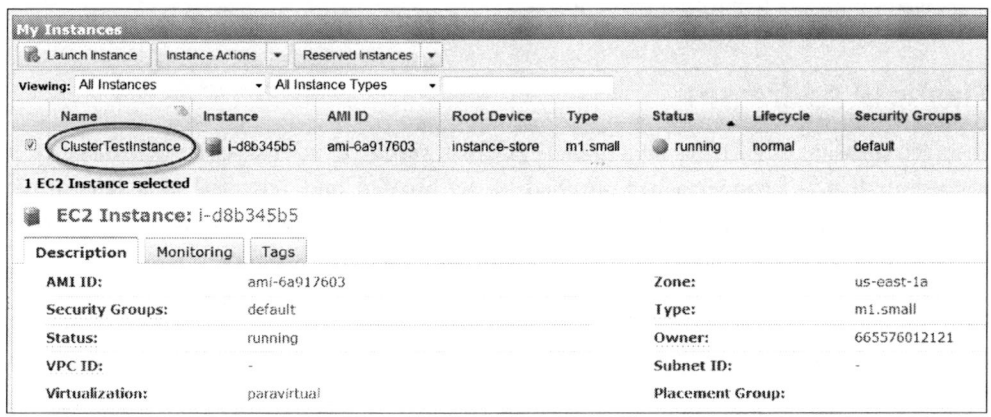

Figure 13: Running Instances

Here comes the last step: go to Networking & Security and modify the existing security group to include the secure shell (ssh) protocol, which uses TCP to connect to port 22. You must add the ssh port in order to access the new instance.

Group Name:	default				
Description:	default group				
Allowed Connections:					
Connection Method	Protocol	From Port	To Port	Source (IP or group)	Actions
All	icmp	-1	-1	default group	Remove
All	tcp	0	65535	default group	Remove
All	udp	0	65535	default group	Remove
SSH	TCP	22	22	0.0.0.0/0	Save

Figure 14: Security Group Settings for ssh

Instance Addressing

All Amazon EC2 instances come with two IP addresses: a private address, which is only reachable from within the Amazon EC2 network, and a public address, which is reachable from the Internet. The mapping between them is done via Network Address Translation (NAT).

Internal / external IP

A Domain Name Service (DNS) entry is provided for both IP addresses. The internal DNS can only be resolved within Amazon EC2. For every EC2 instance both addresses are displayed in the AWS management console.

Elastic IP Addresses

Installed software often relies on a fixed IP address, yet the IP address of an EC2 instance is unique in that it changes when stopped or terminated and restarted at a later time. Amazon provides elastic IP addresses, which are in fact more static than elastic. Elastic IP addresses map a fixed IP address to the dynamic address of the instance.

You can allocate an elastic IP using the AWS management console. Select Networking & Security / Elastic IP from the left column, then click on Allocate New Address. Once you have allocated the elastic IP, you can right-click on it and assign it to a running instance.

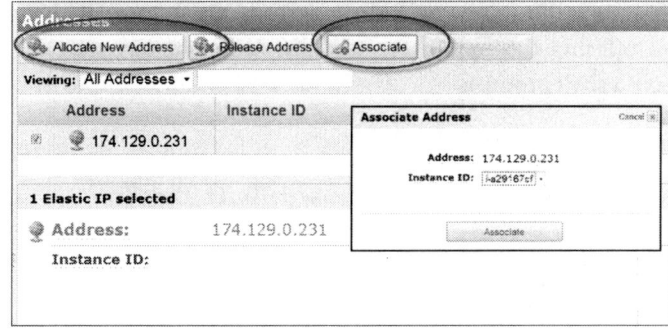

Figure 15: Allocate and Associate Elastic IP

Elastic IP addresses don't cost anything while you use them. This is one of the few things you get for free from AWS. However, when using elastic IPs you do have to pay for the running instance.

There is a fee of $0.01 per non-attached Elastic IP address per complete hour, which is $7.20 per month, so if you allocate an Elastic IP you'd better attach it to a running instance. The first 100 remaps per month are free, thereafter AWS will charge $0.10 per remap.

Getting Access to the Instance

Use the AWS console and right click on the instance to obtain the connection string containing the public DNS entry. Copy this string. This string conveniently shows how to connect to the instance using secure shell with the private key of the key pair you generated (your DNS name will be different).

Use the secure shell from the command-line to connect to your instance. Before the ssh command above will work, you must restrict the access rights of the local certificate to yourself only:

Certificate based authentication

```
chmod 400 access.pem
```

Then paste and submit the copied command string:

```
ssh -i access.pem root@ec2-184-73-33-167.compute-1.amazonaws.com
```

If you are running Windows, I suggest you get a Linux image for VMWare, Virtual Box or use a tool like cygwin or PuTTY for ssh. Always remember to specify the correct location of your private key.

When logging in, you have to accept the following license agreements - do read them carefully. You will see a menu offering the option to start the admin server, start the configuration wizard or to receive a shell prompt:

```
Choose a task that you want to perform
1)  Start the AdminServer in the Default Domain
    The Default Domain is installed at /mnt/domains/default_domain

2)  Launch the WebLogic Configuration Wizard
    This will start /opt/oracle/weblogic/common/bin/config.sh

3)  Use other WLS tools to deploy your domain and applications

Choose an option [1/2/3] or type 'q' to exit from tool :
```

Check for the type of CPU that Amazon provided you with in this virtual instance:

```
$ cat /proc/cpuinfo

model name : Intel(R) Xeon(R) CPU E5430  @ 2.66GHz
cpu MHz    : 2660.000
cache size : 6144 KB
bogomips : 6652.55
(output shortened)
```

While you are at it, verify the RAM as well:

```
$ cat /proc/meminfo

MemTotal:       1740976 kB
MemFree:        1518780 kB
(output shortened)
```

To retrieve the internal IP address of the instance, you can use a REST query. REST is a simple technology replacing the more complicated SOAP based web services. To retrieve some data all you need to do is submit a URL. You can use the command-line tool `curl` to submit a URL, or simply copy and paste the URL into your web browser.

We use it to get our own internal IP address. Remember that you can only issue these REST service calls from an EC2 instance.

For an overview of the available metadata run the command below. It will list all metadata available for an instance (the last "/" in the following command is required):

```
curl http://169.254.169.254/latest/meta-data/
```

To retrieve the local IP address:

curl http://169.254.169.254/latest/meta-data/local-ipv4

To obtain the public IP address, try the following:

curl http://169.254.169.254/latest/meta-data/public-ipv4

At the present time, unfortunately no support is available for IPv6.

The Oracle image comes as a so-called JeOS image. JeOS is short for "just enough operating system", which means you only have those packages installed which are absolutely necessary. As a result, there are neither X-windows nor a Gnome or KDE desktop installed.

Once you have finished looking around, make sure to terminate this instance using the AWS console. Double-check whether its status has changed to "terminated".

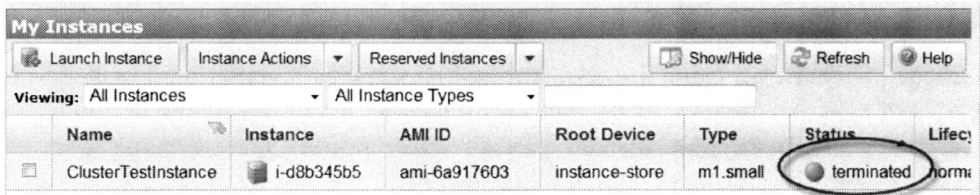

Figure 16: Terminated Instances in AWS

Remember that you can terminate an S3- and EBS-backed EC2 instance. However, once the instance is terminated it is lost, along with local storage and EBS volumes (for EBS volumes you can disable the behavior). Of course you then no longer have to pay for them.

EBS-backed instances can also be stopped. Stopping an instance is more like *temporarily* parking it, rather than terminating it forever. This is a great feature, because the instance won't delete the EBS-volumes (but the local instance storage). You don't pay for stopped instances and you can restart them again whenever you like. However, restarted instances don't run with the same IP address as before. Stopping is a unique feature of EBS backed instances; S3-backed instances can only be *permanently* terminated (not parked).

Amazon Web Services 37

STOP VS. TERMINATE

Stopped and terminated images perform a shutdown. You are not charged if the instances are not running.

A UNIX `halt` or `shutdown` will terminate your instance with an ephemeral, local file system and you will lose your data since the storage is volatile.

In contrast, an EBS based instance will perform a stop by default if you type in `shutdown` on a UNIX prompt. This means you won't be charged and the instance can be restarted with the same ID and the same EBS storage attached.

Amazon Linux

Amazon offers its own Linux distribution based on CentOS. It comes pre-installed with AWS API tools and libraries. At the time of this writing, AWS Linux is still in beta but is nevertheless already stable and usable.

The AWS team designed the Linux AMIs to have a low footprint, so they are another example of the JeOS. You can expect a reduced number of running processes that have to be secured and a minimum number of installed packages. This is also the reason why it comes without any desktop. The AMI includes Python and Perl, but not Apache HTTP server, PHP or MySQL.

AMIs are available as both 32-bit and 64-bit operating systems. The whole matrix of all regions in combination with EBS- or S3-backed images is available from the AWS management console.

Figure 17 lists the current AMIs. They will probably have been updated once you are holding this book in your hands, so check out the current AMIs at the following URL:

`http://aws.amazon.com/amazon-linux-ami`

Amazon Linux AMIs IDs				
AMI Name	US East (N. Virginia) AMI ID	US West (N. California) AMI ID	EU West (Ireland) AMI ID	AP Southeast (Singapore) AMI ID
Amazon EBS-Backed (32-bit)	ami-3ac33653	ami-b4ebbaf1	ami-827540f6	ami-da225c88
Amazon EBS-Backed (64-bit)	ami-38c33651	ami-aaebbaef	ami-807540f4	ami-d8225c8a
Amazon S3-Backed (32-bit)	ami-8ec035e7	ami-a2ebbae7	ami-9e7540ea	ami-d2225c80
Amazon S3-Backed (64-bit)	ami-8cc035e5	ami-acebbae9	ami-927540e6	ami-d0225c82

Figure 17: AWS Linux AMIs

Amazon regularly offers new AMIs with feature updates and security patches for the most recently released version. Major security alerts are published in the AWS Security Center. You can either switch to a new AMI (if you haven't done any major configurations on your AMIs), or use the AWS repositories to update your existing AMIs. AWS Linux uses yum as a packet manager because it's based on CentOS. By the way, the yum repositories are stored in S3, so updating or installing packages is a quick process. *CentOS based*

In AWS Linux remote login with the root user is not possible. The only user that can login remotely is "ec2-user". As usual, you have to set the security group and launch the instance with an ssh-key.

AWS Linux comes with the CloudInit package from Canonical (see the next section for more details about Canonical) in order to perform bootstrap operations such as the ec-2user configuration. The AMIs also support passing user-data-files, and these can be executed as startup scripts as described in section 6.3.

There are no additional costs for using the AWS Linux. For Amazon customers with paid premium support the AWS Linux is already included.

The biggest drawback is probably that AWS Linux is only available for the Amazon cloud and the EC2 virtual private cloud. You cannot obtain a copy of the AWS Linux to run on your PC - unlike when using Ubuntu, for example. *Cloud only*

Other AMI Offerings

The Cloud Market provides statistical data about available AMIs. As of mid 2010 there are over 5,000 AMIs listed for US-East, 2,000 for the EU-West, about 800 for the US-West and almost 500 for Asia-Pacific. You can check the near real-time data yourself under:

http://thecloudmarket.com

Older Ubuntu images from Alestic Eric Hammond from Alestic has built several Ubuntu AMIs. If what you are after is an older Ubuntu 9.10 AMI, it is still worth checking his site. He has now handed his work over to Canonical, yet continues to run a fabulous blog with excellent technical content that I highly recommend:

http://alestic.com

Canonical Canonical is a private company founded for the promotion of Ubuntu. It is the best source for Ubuntu AMIs. Take a look at their site:

http://www.canonical.com

NOTE: AMIs AND LOGIN USERS

You have to use different user names to log in to different AMIs. The default log in is always based on a certificate. You never specify a password (unless you enable password log in which is not recommended).

```
Most AWS AMIs:   root
Oracle AMIs:     root
Amazon Linux:ec2-user
Ubuntu Canonical: ubuntu
Ubuntu Alestic:   ubuntu (older Alestic AMIs use root)
```

Turnkey Turnkey Linux is an open source project involved in developing a free virtual appliance library for VMWare and EC2. The appliances are based on Ubuntu images where software packages such as Drupal, Joomla, Wordpress, or Tomcat are already installed and configured. All these images are ready to launch on EC2. Check their site at:

http://www.turnkeylinux.org/

Turnkey provides an Ubuntu image that includes EC2 AMI and API tools in a configured environment together with Ruby and Python support for Amazon Web Services. For convenience, this image also includes the Amazon Web Services documentation.

Here is the link to download this image:

http://www.turnkeylinux.org/ec2sdk

EC2 Tools

As you have seen, you can launch your instances using nothing but the AWS web console.

There are of course other GUI based tools around, one of which is ElasticFox. This comes as a plug-in for Firefox for running and managing Amazon EC2 instances. Have a look yourself and check out the guide for getting started under:

ElasticFox

http://developer.amazonwebservices.com/connect/entry.jspa?externalID=1797

EC2 Command-Line

AWS web console and ElasticFox are easy to use, but real administrators love the command-line. There is a set of command-line tools for EC2 and I recommend you install them right now. Although you can go a long way only using the AWS web console, eventually you will need more control. Are you feeling tempted to script the steps we walked through in the current chapter?

This is how it works: conduct a simple wget to download the tools from Amazon to your local client computer. You will in fact retrieve the zip file from Amazon's cloud storage S3 (which is covered in the following section), then unzip the tools and create a logical link:

```
wget http://s3.amazonaws.com/ec2-downloads/ec2-api-tools.zip
unzip ec2-api-tools.zip
ln -s ec2-api-tools-1.3-46266 ec2-api-tools
```

You also need a JDK to run the tools. So if you haven't got one yet, do so:

```
sudo apt-get install sun-java6-jre
```

Now, security for EC2 is not that easy to understand, but to use the EC2 command-line tools, you do need to get an X.509 certificate along with its private key. The good news is that you can easily create the certificate and the key using the AWS web console.

To get the credentials needed for the command-line tools, go to your AWS account site under:

http://aws.amazon.com/account/

Then click on "Security Credentials" and create a new certificate:

Figure 18: AWS Security Credentials

Create an X.509 certificate

Download the certificate and the private key. Both files are related to each other in a unique way; that's why the main part of their file name is identical. In my case their names are:

cert-RMF56SFPQ7TOI3JYCSANMAJ563I6RWJ2.pem
pk-RMF56SFPQ7TOI3JYCSANMAJ563I6RWJ2.pem

To keep things tidy, it might be a nice idea to have all EC2 files under an ec2 subdirectory, which is where I store all my EC2 credentials.

API CERTFIFICATE AND ACCESS KEYS

Make sure you specify the correct files for the certificate and the private key. Do not use the access key that was previously generated.

Setting environment variables

Last but not least, you have to set some environment variables in order for the commands to work in your shell. As a bash user, you can put the following under ~/.bashrc (modify these values and use your settings):

```
export EC2_HOME=$HOME/ec2-api-tools
export PATH=$PATH:$EC2_HOME/bin
export EC2_PRIVATE_KEY=$HOME/ec2/pkRMF56SFPQ7TOI3JYCANMAJ563I6RWJ2.pem
export EC2_CERT=$HOME/ec2/cert-RMF56SFPQ7TOI3JYCANMAJ563I6RWJ2.pem
export JAVA_HOME=/usr/lib/jvm/java-6-sun
```

Source the .bashrc or open a new bash to make all your settings work and try your first commands. To retrieve all images with Amazon Owner, use the ec2-describe-images or the abbreviated ec2dim command:

```
ec2-describe-images -o amazon
```

Usage scenario: Windows 2008

I have to admit that I am not really a Windows guy when it comes to running server software. Still, EC2 can be extremely useful if you need a Windows system every now and then. Yesterday, a customer of mine called and asked if I could offer consultation on setting up clustering for high availability for a critical security system running on 64-bit Windows Server 2008. While still on the phone, I ran the following command:

```
frank@ubuntu:~/ec2$ ec2-describe-images -o amazon | grep 64 | grep 2008 |
cut -f2-3

ami-cdc22ea4  amazon/Windows-Server2008-x86_64-Base-v102
ami-63c32f0a  amazon/Windows-Server2008-x86_64-SqlExpress-v102
ami-2bc32f42  amazon/Windows-Server2008-x86_64-SqlStandard-v102
```

This told me that there is a public Windows Server 2008 available that I can just fire up and use for as long as I need. Needless to say, I accepted the consulting engagement and used the Windows instances to prepare a solution demo. Solving real problems while writing a book is much better than just writing it.

Let's take the command-line a bit further and check for the previously mentioned regions:

```
frank@ubuntu:~/ec2$ ec2-describe-regions


REGION  eu-west-1       ec2.eu-west-1.amazonaws.com
REGION  us-east-1       ec2.us-east-1.amazonaws.com
REGION  us-west-1       ec2.us-west-1.amazonaws.com
REGION  ap-southeast-1  ec2.ap-southeast-1.amazonaws.com
```

To find out about all availability zones for eu-west-1 you would issue the following command:

```
frank@ubuntu:~/ec2$ ec2-describe-availability-zones --region eu-west-1

AVAILABILITYZONE  eu-west-1a available  eu-west-1
AVAILABILITYZONE  eu-west-1b available  eu-west-1
```

AMIs and Regions

Note: if you are interested in AMIs for the European region, you need to add a --region eu-west-1 switch to the command-line above, as the default setting uses the US region.

You can override this behavior by setting the environment variable EC2_URL to https://eu-west-1.ec2.amazonaws.com

EC2 Instance Pricing

My major concern is usually money: how much will it set me back? Well, the good news is you can get started for free!

Free usage tier Amazon offers a free usage tier to every new customer. This covers the cost of running an EC2 micro instance with a load balancer, 10 GB of EBS storage, 5 GB of S3 storage, and 30 GB of Internet data transfer. You can use this free micro instance for whatever you like. It doesn't matter if you run it continuously, or just start it when you feel like exploring the cloud. After 12 months, or if your usage exceeds the free tier, you start paying. (Unfortunately, this offer doesn't apply to those with an existing AWS account).

Figure 19 presents an overview of the pricing for on-demand instances, taken from Amazon's documentation.

Amazon's fees depend on their own cost. Billing is per instance-hour consumed for each instance. A partial instance-hour e.g. if you run an instance for only 25 minutes, will be billed as a full hour. As you can see, using an instance with Windows is slightly more expensive because the license is included; also, the prices differ by region. We will have a closer look at using a Windows AMI later on.

Reserved Instances Reserved instances are an alternative option if you are willing to pay a one-time fee for a lower per-hour instance price. See Figure 20 to check if this would be a suitable option for you.

| US – N. Virginia | US – N. California | EU – Ireland | APAC – Singapore |

Standard On-Demand Instances	Linux/UNIX Usage	Windows Usage
Small (Default)	$0.095 per hour	$0.12 per hour
Large	$0.38 per hour	$0.48 per hour
Extra Large	$0.76 per hour	$0.96 per hour
Micro On-Demand Instances	**Linux/UNIX Usage**	**Windows Usage**
Micro	$0.025 per hour	$0.035 per hour
High-Memory On-Demand Instances		
Extra Large	$0.57 per hour	$0.62 per hour
Double Extra Large	$1.14 per hour	$1.24 per hour
Quadruple Extra Large	$2.28 per hour	$2.48 per hour
High-CPU On-Demand Instances		
Medium	$0.19 per hour	$0.29 per hour
Extra Large	$0.76 per hour	$1.16 per hour
Cluster Compute Instances		
Quadruple Extra Large	N/A	N/A

* Cluster Compute Instances are currently only available in the US – N. Virginia Region.

Figure 19: EC2 Instance Pricing

| US – N. Virginia | US – N. California | EU – Ireland | APAC – Singapore |

	One-time Fee			
Standard Reserved Instances	1 yr Term	3 yr Term	Linux/UNIX Usage	Windows Usage
Small (Default)	$227.50	$350	$0.04 per hour	$0.06 per hour
Large	$910	$1400	$0.16 per hour	$0.24 per hour
Extra Large	$1820	$2800	$0.32 per hour	$0.48 per hour
Micro Reserved Instances				
Micro	$54	$82	$0.01 per hour	$0.016 per hour
High-Memory Reserved Instances				
Extra Large	$1325	$2000	$0.24 per hour	$0.32 per hour
Double Extra Large	$2650	$4000	$0.48 per hour	$0.64 per hour
Quadruple Extra Large	$5300	$8000	$0.96 per hour	$1.28 per hour
High-CPU Reserved Instances				
Medium	$455	$700	$0.08 per hour	$0.145 per hour
Extra Large	$1820	$2800	$0.32 per hour	$0.58 per hour
Cluster Compute Reserved Instances				
Quadruple Extra Large	N/A	N/A	N/A	N/A

* Cluster Compute Instances are currently only available in the US – N. Virginia Region.

Figure 20: Reserved Instances Pricing

Spot Instances Spot instances offer a third pricing model; you bid for unused capacity on a fluctuating spot price. Amazon provides an API that allows you to retrieve historic data. Your instances only run when the spot price is lower than your bid. When the spot price becomes higher than your bid, your instances will be stopped.

This model makes spot instances well suited for batch processing that is not time-critical.

Your bill will continue to increase for as long as you have an instance running, and data transfer is an additional cost. The following rules apply for data transfer:

- There is no charge for data transfer between an EC2 instance and other AWS services in the same region.
- For data transfer in the same availability zone using the private IP, there is also no charge.
- Data transfer across different availability zones, yet within one region, is charged as regional data transfer at a rate of $0.01 per GB in/out.
- For data transfer between different regions, the Internet data transfer is charged on both sides (see Figure 21).

Internet data transfer is billed as per Figure 21.

Data Transfer In	US & EU Regions	APAC Region
All Data Transfer	$0.10 per GB	$0.10 per GB

Data Transfer Out ***	US & EU Regions	APAC Region
First 1 GB per Month	$0.00 per GB	$0.00 per GB
Up to 10 TB per Month	$0.15 per GB	$0.19 per GB
Next 40 TB per Month	$0.11 per GB	$0.15 per GB
Next 100 TB per Month	$0.09 per GB	$0.13 per GB
Over 150 TB per Month	$0.08 per GB	$0.12 per GB

Figure 21: AWS Internet Data Transfer Pricing

EBS INSTANCE PRICING

Pricing for EBS instances can be a bit misleading if you look solely at the table for the instance prices provided by Amazon.

EBS instances are based on an EBS volume. Once an EBS-backed instance is started, this volume can be seen in the AWS management console under Elastic Block Store / Volumes.

You have to pay for this EBS volume. There is a fixed fee for every GB per month, plus a small fee for every 1 million I/O requests. The fee for the size of the volume is calculated on an hourly basis. For more details see section 3.2 about AWS Cloud Storage.

Reducing Costs

I'd love to add some more thoughts about costs. Amazon usually publishes the cost per hour e.g. a standard large instance costs you $0.38 per hour. At first this doesn't sound like a lot, and compared to the costs of running a data center, it is certainly negligible.

However, human beings tend not to be very good with extremely small or extremely large numbers. I therefore recommend you do the math and calculate the monthly costs very carefully. The large instance adds $273.60 to your monthly bill, which equals $2383.20 a year, and this doesn't include the Internet traffic, nor the elastic load balancing, nor extra storage costs for private images or data volumes. So remember to always calculate the total for *all* services. Throughout this book I will include information about costs for other services such as storage, load balancing, and content distribution networks in the relevant sections. *Cost Warning*

Amazon provides a calculator to help you calculate the total for all AWS services. It's browser based and can be accessed at the following location:

http://calculator.s3.amazonaws.com/calc5.html

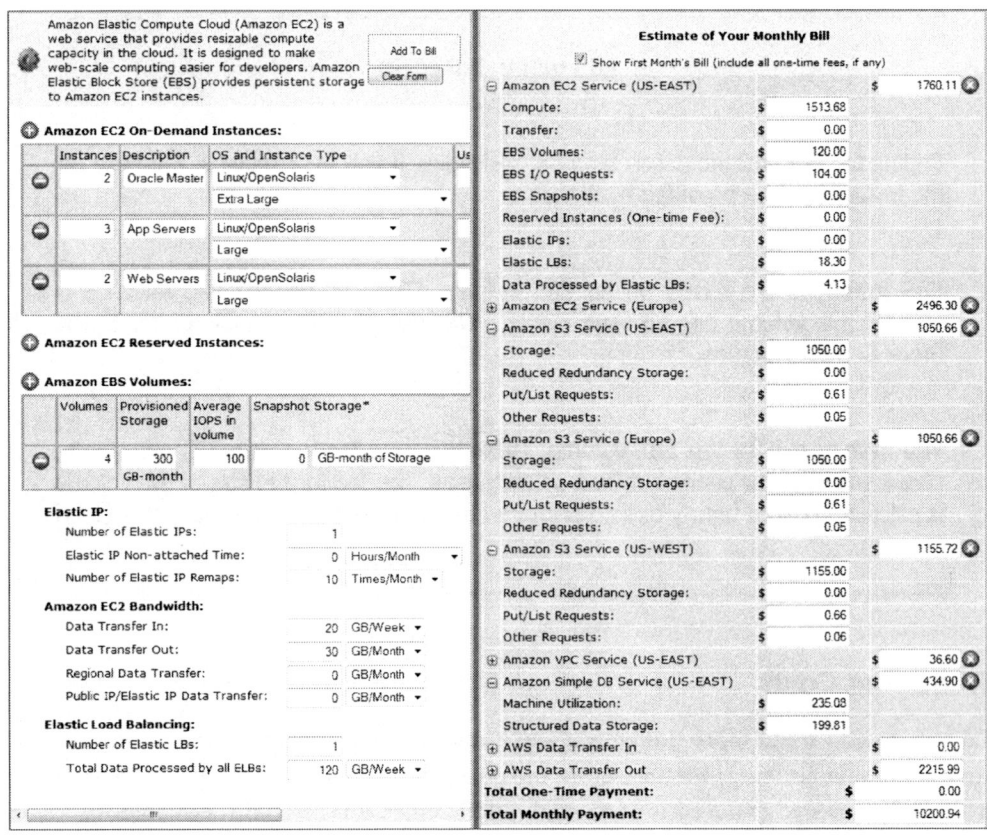

Figure 22: AWS Calculator Example Web Application

Anybody working regularly with AWS can recount a personal story of a forgotten instance (and the most dramatic stories are not about a cheap micro instance). I've got a number of suggestions that might save you some money.

- Above all, you want to avoid paying for unused resources. Using auto scaling is a great mechanism for running only the required instances, and for example, to scale down at night when fewer EC2 instances are required.
- Often the monthly bill tells you that there something is still running somewhere. Make sure you stop unused resources as quickly as possible. If you know in advance that you want them to be stopped at the end of the day, then use the Unix at command to schedule the termination of the instances.

- Although AWS management console provides dashboards, there is no super-dashboard. Instead, you have to flip through all tabs yourself (starting from from the "S3" tab to "EC2" and all the tabs up until "RDS"). Only after checking all tabs can you be sure you have an accurate overview of the current resources for the selected region.
- Remind yourself that the AWS management console is always displaying resources per region. Once you switch to another region, e.g. from Asia/Pacific to Europe, you will no longer be able to see instances running in Asia/ Pacific (see a snapshot in Figure 23).
- The console is sometimes out of sync. When this happens, remember to click on the refresh button so as to avoid only seeing outdated information (see snapshot in Figure 23).
- The command-line tools I introduce later will work with resources for the default region in the US (unless you specify otherwise). Remain vigilant at all times e.g. when working in Europe do not start and then forget an instance in the US.
- Always double check for running instances before leaving for a sabbatical or a trip around the world.

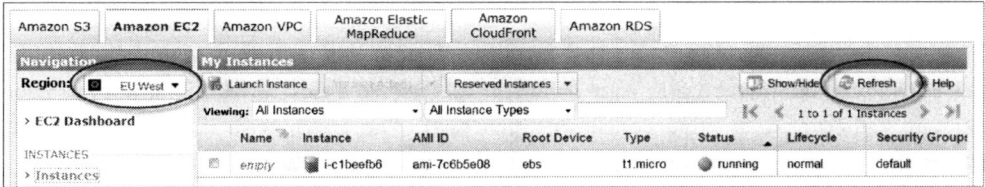

Figure 23: AWS Console Region Setting and Refresh

3.2 Amazon Cloud Storage

Disk storage comes in various forms in an AWS environment:

- Local Storage or instance storage
- Amazon Elastic Block Store (EBS)
- Amazon Simple Storage Service (S3)

Instance Storage

The S3-backed EC2 instance which you started in the previous chapter already had ephemeral, local storage attached to it. Depending on the instance type, the amount of local storage varies from 160 GB to 1.6 TB, which is often this more than sufficient. This storage is overwritten with zeros when you terminate your instance, or if it crashes, but not if you reboot or stop it. In terms of security this is a useful feature, because it guarantees that I wouldn't be able to look at anything that you had worked on in a previous instance. Of course this also means that this local storage is not really persisted, which sounds like an oxymoron, and was the source of many debates for a long time.

Actually, the situation with S3-backed instances is only half as bad as it initially sounds, since it is possible to rebundle your instances and create a new AMI containing all your changes (albeit a fairly time consuming process!). The good news is that AMI's with persistent storage are also available, and we will cover these on the next page.

Amazon itself notes, "*the first write to any location on an instance's drives performs slower than subsequent writes. For most applications, amortizing this cost over the lifetime of the instance is acceptable. However, if you require high disk performance, we recommend initializing drives by writing once to every drive location before production use.*"

You can initialize a filesystem with the UNIX command dd. The command below copies zeroes from the input file /dev/zero to the the output file (the /dev/sdb device):

```
dd if=/dev/zero of=/dev/sdb bs=1M
```

Depending on your security requirements, you should consider encrypting your file system. Encryption gives you privacy; even if a hacker could somehow access your disk, the data wouldn't make any sense to him. The main concern surrounding encryption is performance, since encrypting and decrypting the data requires rather resource intensive algorithms.

> **ENCRYPTION OF FILE SYSTEMS**
>
> Amazon encourages you to use encryption for your file system. There is no general rule about how much this will slow you down, but there is no easier place than the cloud to give it a try and compare performance data.

The performance of the local storage depends on the performance of the instance itself. The instance stores of large and extra large instances have a higher and more consistent performance when compared to those of small instances, since fewer instances share the same physical machine. The exposed spindles of large and extra large instances can be combined and used to configure a RAID. *I/O performance*

Elastic Block Storage

An Amazon Elastic Block Store (EBS) volume is a persisted, off-instance volume, with high availability and reliability, that can be mounted as a block device. When you create an EBS volume, it behaves like a raw, unformatted block device, yet you can of course create a file system on it. A particular volume can be attached to one AMI only. However, one AMI can have several volumes.

Since EBS is off-instance and persistent storage, you can use it to overcome an instance failure. If an instance with an EBS volume attached to it fails, the volume detaches. You can then fire up a new instance and attach the volume to this new one instead.

EBS uses a storage area network (SAN) and can be organized as a redundant array of independent disks (RAID). You can create a snapshot from a volume and later create a new volume based on this snapshot.

> **UNMOUNT VOLUMES**
>
> Don't forget to unmount an EBS volume from the instance before detaching. Otherwise the file system will be damaged.

Performance   Amazon EBS volumes perform consistently for all instance types, whereas the performance of local storage depends on the instance size.

Root Device   It is now also possible to use EBS volumes as a root device for Windows and Unix. For AMIs using local storage as root devices, there is a limit for the root file system of 10 GB. EBS allows larger root devices of up to 1 TByte, which can be resized anytime and remounted to another instance in the event of an instance failure.

Whenever you create volumes you will be charged for the storage (we will cover the costs later).

Here is the EBS command-line to create a volume of 10GByte in the eu-west-1 region:

```
frank@ubuntu:~/ec2$ ec2-create-volume -s 10  --region eu-west-1 --z eu-west-1a

VOLUME vol-78658611  10  eu-west-1a   creating 2010-03-02T09:20:55+0000
```

The creation of such a small volume should only take a couple of seconds. Check here if the volume is available yet:

```
frank@ubuntu:~/ec2$ ec2-describe-volumes --region eu-west-1 vol-78658611

VOLUME vol-78658611  10  eu-west-1a   available 2010-03-02T09:20:55+0000
```

You can of course also use the AWS web console to create your own volume or to check for existing volumes. If you are based in Europe, don't forget to switch to the correct region setting, otherwise the volume will not be displayed. Remember that AMIs and volumes are per region and the default setting is US.

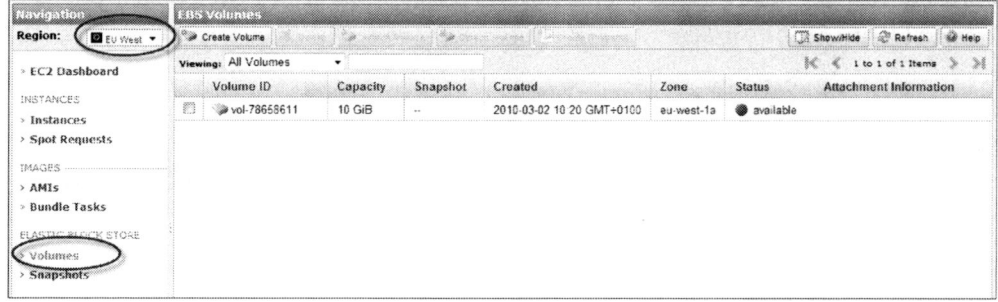

Figure 24: Volumes per Region

Starting an EBS-backed Windows Instance

To start an EBS based instance running Windows 2008, first select a suitable image:

```
frank@ubuntu:~/ec2$ ec2-describe-images -o amazon --region
eu-west-1 | grep 64 | grep 2008 | cut -f2-3

ami-eba78c9f  amazon/Windows-Server2008-x86_64-BaseMultiLang-v102
```

Then launch a large instance type from the command-line (assuming you have a key pair xess already created, as described in section "Starting an EC2 Instance" on page 31):

```
frank@ubuntu:~/ec2$ ec2-run-instances --region eu-west-1 -m
-k xess -t m1.large ami-eba78c9f

RESERVATION r-c6be69b1676573782306  default
INSTANCE i-c67bdeb1    ami-eba78c9f    pending    xess   0    m1.large   2010-
03-02T10:49:38+0000    eu-west-1a    windows    monitoring-pending    ebs
```

Since the AMI uses an EBS volume as a root disk, you are able to see the two volumes attached:

Volume ID	Capacity	Snapshot	Created	Zone	Status	Attachment Information
vol-78658611	10 GiB	--	2010-03-02 10:20 GMT+0100	eu-west-1a	available	
vol-886487e1	30 GiB	snap-a221d1cb	2010-03-02 11:49 GMT+0100	eu-west-1a	in-use	i-c67bdeb1:/dev/sda1 (attached)

Figure 25: EBS Volumes in AWS Console

Have you ever tried to use the ping command to check if the instance is really up and running? As ping uses the ICMP protocol and ICMP is blocked by default, first you have to add it to the security group:

```
ec2-authorize default -P icmp -t -1:-1 -s 0.0.0.0/0
```

Before you are able to connect to the instance, you have to retrieve the Windows password. Simply right-click on the running instance in the AWS console, select "Get Windows Password" and paste your private key into the window to decrypt it, as shown in Figure 26:

Figure 26: Retrieve Windows Password

Here is the alternative way to obtain the password (using the command-line interface):

```
frank@ubuntu:~/ec2$ ec2-get-password -k xess.pem -region
eu-west-1 i-c67bdeb1
```

Ensure that the RDP protocol is added to the security group setting. Then right-click on the AWS web console to connect to the instance. You will be offered a shortcut file to download and a short description about how to connect to the running instance using Windows Remote Desktop Connection.

If you cannot connect to the remote desktop verify that RDP (or ssh, if you are trying to connect to a UNIX machine) is not blocked by your enterprise firewall. Talk to your network admin or try it from your Internet service provider at home.

You will see a security exception because the certificate being used is not issued by a trusted authority. Confirm this exception to proceed.

Getting back to the topic of EC2 storage and EBS, I recommend you download a free copy of HDTune from `http://www.hdtune.com/download.html` and test the performance of your EBS based hard disk. The download should only take a minute as the EC2 instances have a high bandwidth Internet connection.

Simple Storage Service

The third, and certainly the most cloud-like type of storage, is Amazon's Simple Storage Service (S3). S3 provides virtually endless amounts of relatively cheap storage. S3 is different from what you typically see in a UNIX or Windows environment: it stores an unlimited number of objects ranging from 1 byte to 5 Gigabytes. However, S3 is neither a block device nor a file system.

You cannot see any disks behind S3, yet data is of course at some point written to a number of disks. The data is replicated across different availability zones, but stays within its region. So whenever Amazon adds new disks, S3 will deliver even more availability, speed and throughput.

S3 is designed to be highly reliable. A broken disk doesn't matter, as it will be replaced by another inexpensive commodity disk, without any downtime. You can expect this to happen frequently due to the type of disks being used, but the design of the distributed storage will easily cope with it. Checksums are used for integrity and an SLA of 99.9% availability for any monthly billing cycle is guaranteed.

Amazon also provides an SLA for durability. Durability is defined as the probability that an object will remain intact and accessible after a period of one year.

Standard S3 storage has a durability of 99.999999999% and will survive the loss of two AWS regions. Amazon claims that from 10,000 stored objects, on average only one could be lost every 10 million years.

You can also opt for reduced redundancy storage (RRS). Amazon claims RSS still has a durability of 99.99, which is 400 times the durability of a normal disk drive. RSS sustains the failure of one AWS region, and storage costs only $0.10 per GB, compared to $0.15 per GB for regular S3 storage.

There was one reported outage of S3 in 2008. One out of three S3 locations was down for about 2 hours. Amazon handled this event in a professional manner. For further information see:

`http://techcrunch.com/2008/02/15/amazon-web-services-goes-down-takes-many-startup-sites-with-it/`

Just remember that S3 stores objects, not files. Later, we will examine a number of tools that allow you to treat files as objects and store them within S3, but I can assure you that it helps to look at S3 as an object store rather than as a file system.

Buckets full of objects All objects are stored in so-called "buckets", which are used to separate objects from each other in namespaces. Since these namespaces have to be unique, it is a good idea to choose a bucket name that represents you and your business. For the name use between 3 and 63 lower-case letters only including "." and "-". For the keys representing the object names you can use any UTF-8 encoded character.

Versioning S3 supports versioning. If you never enable versioning for a bucket, then your objects in that bucket are in an unversioned state with a version ID of null. Storing an object in a version enabled bucket S3 adds a version ID to each object, which is returned by the REST request in the `x-amz-versionid` header. An HTTP get operation without the version parameter retrieves the latest version of the object. To list, retrieve or delete a particular version of an object, you need to specify the version ID with the operation. It is also possible to suspend versioning.

Another interesting feature supported by S3 is the ability to add key-value pairs as metadata.

S3 Tools

There are plenty of tools available for convenient access to S3. A rather lengthy compilation can be found under `http://www.aboutonlinetips.com/amazon-s3-tools`.

On a Windows platform, I like to use the following S3 Browser: `http://s3browser.com`.

Supply your credentials when starting up the S3 Browser for the first time. You will be asked for the access key ID and the secret key. Both values can be found under your AWS account if you navigate to "Security Credentials", as shown in Figure 28:

Figure 27: S3 Brower Credentials

Please note that the labels are a bit misleading. For "Access Key" in the S3 Browser, copy the Access ID from your account. For "Secret Key", click on "Show Secret Key" on your account settings and copy it as shown in Figure 27:

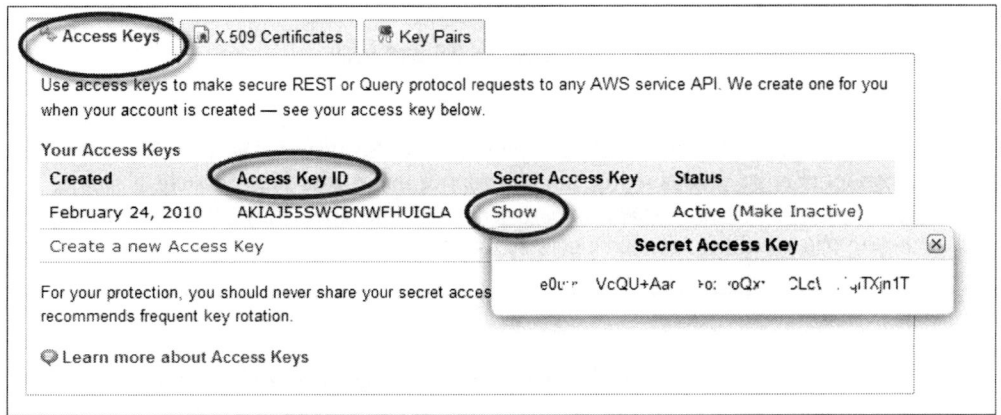

Figure 28: Retrieving Your Access Key ID and the Secret Key

Once you have passed security, the rest is a piece a of cake: creating a new bucket name and uploading files to that bucket can easily be done with the S3 browser GUI as seen in Figure 29:

Amazon Web Services 57

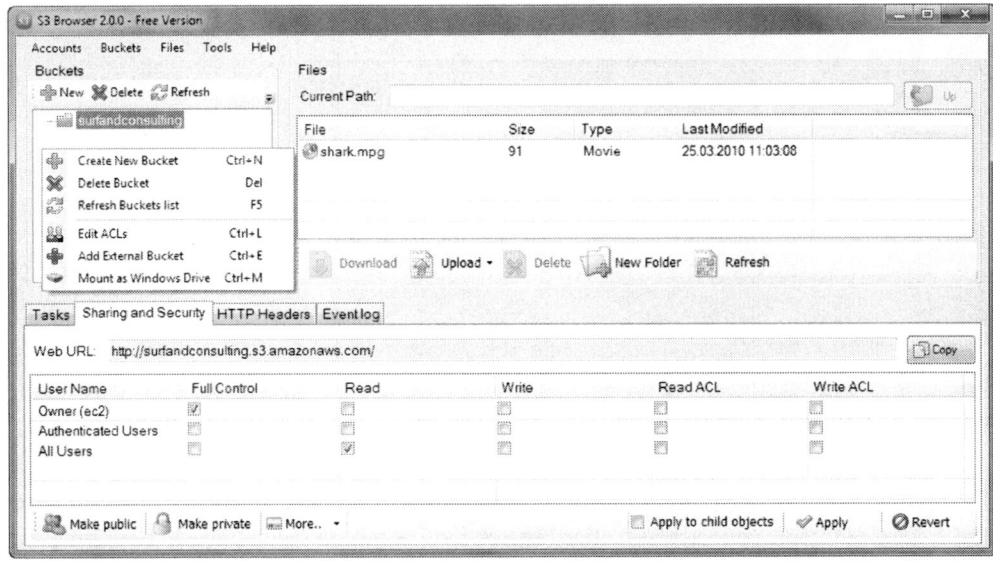

Figure 29: S3 Browser GUI

LIMITATIONS OF THE S3 BROWSER

One of the biggest drawbacks of the free edition of S3 Browser version 2.0 is that you cannot change access rights, i.e. you cannot make your files publicly available. However, S3 Browser's sales department told me that they are considering changing this in a future version - so stay tuned.

CloudBerry S3 Explorer is another browser for S3 storage with a useful free edition that supports changing access rights for files. It is available at the following URL:

`http://cloudberrylab.com`

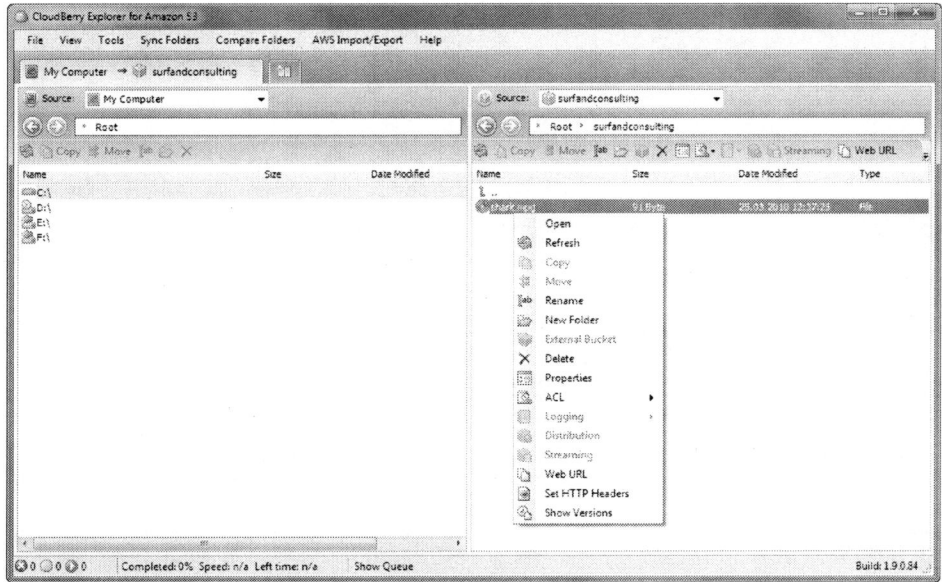

Figure 30: CloudBerry S3 Explorer

To access Amazon S3 buckets and objects you must use the virtual hosted-style request. For example, if you choose to retrieve a video MPEG file named shark.mpg that I have stored under the bucket name surfandconsulting, you could use the following URL to download the file (if it is publicly-accessible):

http access for S3

http://surfandconsulting.s3.amazonaws.com/shark.mpg

Now, this means you can retrieve your S3 data via HTTP. Or, to put it another way: you get a web server as a service!

The example above is just for illustrative purposes. Most likely there is no shark video, but do give it a try! If you try this REST request, you could end up with a NoSuchBucket error if no one is using this bucket name.

The actual reason why there is no such file is that I would not only be paying for the storage required, but also for the I/O requests generated every time someone tried to retrieve the file. Speaking of costs, check Figure 31 for the EU pricing table posted at the time of this writing.

Amazon Web Services 59

| US – Standard | US – N. California | **EU – Ireland** | APAC – Singapore |

Storage (Designed for 99.999999999% Durability)		Reduced Redundancy Storage (Designed for 99.99% Durability)		Data Transfer*		Requests	
Tier	Pricing	Tier	Pricing	Tier	Pricing	Type	Pricing
First 50 TB / Month of Storage Used	$0.150 per GB	First 50 TB / Month of Storage Used	$0.100 per GB	All Data Transfer In	Free until June 30th, 2010**	PUT, COPY, POST, or LIST	$0.01 per 1,000 Requests
Next 50 TB / Month of Storage Used	$0.140 per GB	Next 50 TB / Month of Storage Used	$0.093 per GB	First 1 GB / month data transfer out	$0.000 per GB	GET and All Other Requests***	$0.01 per 10,000 Requests
Next 400 TB / Month of Storage Used	$0.130 per GB	Next 400 TB / Month of Storage Used	$0.087 per GB	Up to 10 TB / month data transfer out	$0.150 per GB		
Next 500 TB / Month of Storage Used	$0.105 per GB	Next 500 TB / Month of Storage Used	$0.070 per GB	Next 40 TB / month data transfer out	$0.110 per GB		
Next 4000 TB / Month of Storage Used	$0.080 per GB	Next 4000 TB / Month of Storage Used	$0.053 per GB	Next 100 TB / month data transfer out	$0.090 per GB		
Storage Used / Month Over 5000 TB	$0.055 per GB	Storage Used / Month Over 5000 TB	$0.037 per GB	Greater than 150 TB / month data transfer out	$0.080 per GB		

Figure 31: S3 Pricing in Europe

You are paying for storage, for requests to access your objects in S3, for the data transfer out, and to remove your objects.

If the complicated S3 price structure reminds you of mobile phone contracts in the early days, then you are not wide off the mark. At the start of a project, it can be particularly hard to predict the total S3 storage costs. Therefore, it's best to first get started and then carefully observe how much space and bandwidth and how many I/O operations are required. Then you can extrapolate your experience to future loads.

Once you know the basic parameters, you can use Amazon's cost calculator to estimate your total monthly bill. Or, as a bucket owner, I could reverse the situation and make *you* pay for my bucket. Have a look at the following note from Amazon:

> ### WHO IS PAYING BIG BUCKS FOR THE BUCKET?
>
> "In general, bucket owners pay for all Amazon S3 storage and data transfer costs associated with their bucket. A bucket owner, however, can configure a bucket to be a Requester Pays bucket. With Requester Pays buckets, the requester instead of the bucket owner pays the cost of the request and the data download from the bucket. (The bucket owner always pays the cost of storing data)".

Now let's extend the example above to another dimension. Imagine you are back from the once in a lifetime trip to Cocos Island with a DVD full of HD video footage and your buddies can't wait to have a look at it! Typically, your personal web space at your hosting company is less than the size of a Blue Ray DVD (which has a capacity of up to 50 GByte). My web space, for example, allows for only 3 GByte. So most likely there isn't enough space on your web space for the content of a DVD.

S3 with BitTorrent

Well, all you need to do is upload it to S3. Storage will cost you less than five Dollars for 30 GBytes of video (plus Amazon will charge you 1 cent per 10,000 I/O requests). But how can your dive buddies get hold of the video? For sure, HTTP isn't the best protocol for the distribution of 30 GByte of data. Fortunately, Amazon S3 supports the BitTorrent protocol, which replaces the point-to-point client-server download with a peer group model. The peer-to-peer model will save you both money and bandwidth, since the peers will simultaneously upload chunks of the downloaded data to other peers. And this will of course be useful not only for your diving videos, but also for huge database dumps, software distributions or complete backup images of a computer.

Here is what you need to access your content on S3 via the BitTorrent protocol: simply add another parameter ?torrent to the URL. Remember the shark example? It becomes:

http://surfandconsulting.s3-external-3.amazonaws.com/shark.mpg?torrent

The torrent file will be generated the first time you access it, and the time to generate it will be linear to the file size.

In addition to the REST API, there are bindings for programming languages such as Ruby, PHP and Python. For insightful examples take a look at the AWS documentation under the following URL:

Language bindings

http://docs.amazonwebservices.com/AmazonS3/latest/gsg/index.html?WorkingWithS3.html

There is also a Java toolkit called JetS3t (pronounced "jet set") available from the Maven central repository or via the following URL:

http://jets3t.s3.amazonaws.com/index.html.

FedEx your hard disk to the cloud Using the AWS Import/Export beta-feature, you can prepare a set of eSATA, USB 2.0 or 2.5 / 3.5 inch internal SATA hard drives and mail them to Amazon. The idea is simple: you bypass the Internet. Amazon will connect them directly to one of their machines at the higher speed of your hard disk interface. Assuming you bundle up enough disks, even a mailed parcel will provide a higher throughput than the Internet.

The whole idea behind the AWS Import/Export offering reminds me of one of Andrew S. Tanenbaum's famous quotes: "*Never underestimate the bandwidth of a station wagon full of tapes hurtling down the highway.*" (Tanenbaum, 1996)

3.3 Creating Your Amazon Machine Image

After reading through this chapter you might draw the conclusion that this is all you need for your project - if only you could install your middleware software and projects and create your own EBS based, persistent AMI yourself.

Now, the good news is that creating your own AMI is easy and it will get you a long way - even without spending too much time thinking about availability, scalability or how to efficiently deploy Oracle middleware in the cloud (all these topics will be covered in the following chapters).

By far the easiest way to create an AMI with your software on it is to start with a reputable EBS based AMI, let's say one of those provided by Amazon itself or Canonical, and then to install all the software you need and create a new image. These images are stored as Amazon EBS snapshots and you pay the standard storage rates to Amazon for storing them. These images also show up in the Amazon web console under "AMI", where you can de-register them if you don't need them anymore and want to get rid of them.

So basically, all you need to do after running an AMI and configuring the instance with all the software that you need, is to create a new EBS-backed AMI. You can do this from the AWS management console by right-clicking on the running instance as shown in the screenshot below:

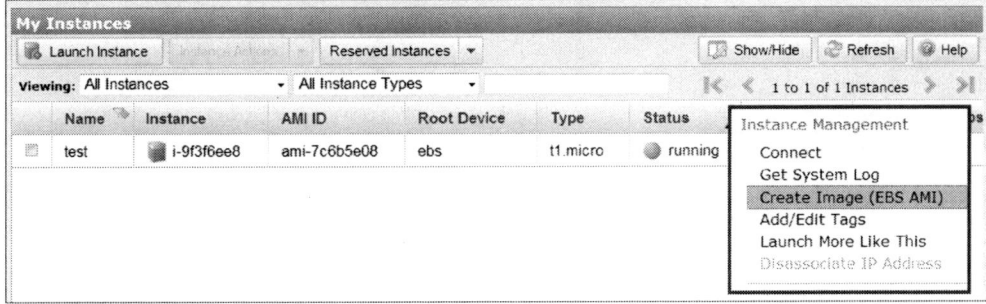

Figure 32: Create New EBS AMI

Then select the name of the new image and add a meaningful description:

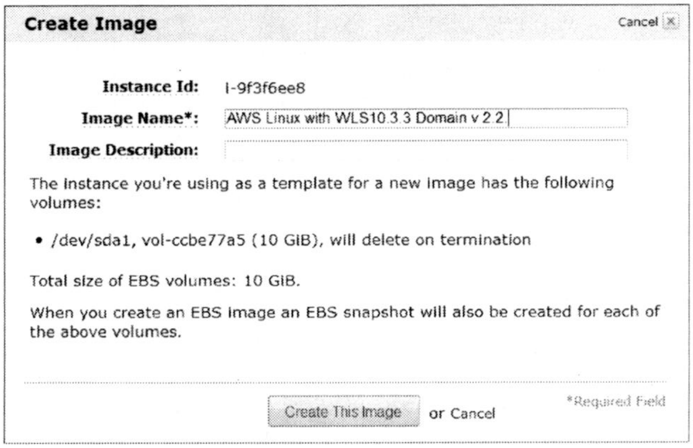

Figure 33: Create New Image

During the process of creating an image, first a snapshot is created, and then a new AMI based on the original template image.

Using the command-line, you can create a new EBS-backed image with the following syntax:

```
ec2-create-image instance_id
```

While your customized AMI is registered with EBS, you will see the corresponding snapshot listed in the AWS management console under Elastic Block Store / Snapshots, as shown in the screenshot below:

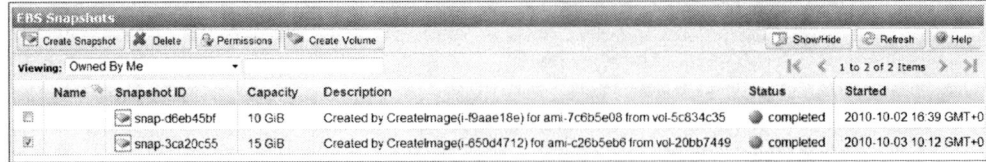

Figure 34: Snapshots Corresponding to AMI

This snapshot can only be deleted once the AMI is deregistered. Deregistering an AMI deletes the image. To deregister, switch to the Amazon Machine Image and right-click on the AMI:

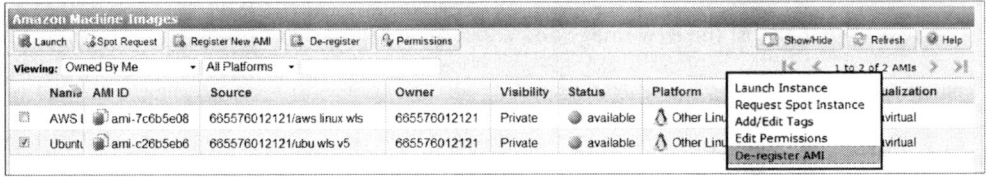

Figure 35: Deregister AMI

CREATING AMIS FROM SCRATCH

It's pretty straightforward to start with a preconfigured AMI and create an image of it. Starting from scratch is a totally different kettle of fish. Currently only Amazon itself can create EBS-backed Windows AMIs from scratch, most probably due to license restrictions.

You should definitely consider starting with one of the available AMIs. However, if you are not afraid of multi-line shell script commands, then see Eric Hammond's blog entry for a detailed description about how to create an Ubuntu AMI from scratch:

http://alestic.com/2010/01/vmbuilder-ebs-boot-ami

3.4 EC2 Command-Line Example

Let's have a look at the most common EC2 commands. In this example we use a daily build of Ubuntu Lucid 10.04. Ubuntu Lucid comes with long-term support, security fixes and updates. For the desktop version there is a three-year guarantee, and for the server version a five year guarantee.

Starting an Ubuntu Desktop EBS Image

You can use the `ec2-describe-images` command to list all available images and then grep for a 64-bit Ubuntu Lucid desktop version with EBS. Make sure you specify the correct region or set the `EC2_URL` as described in the EC2 command-line module:

```
frank@ubuntu:~$ ec2-describe-images -a | grep lucid | grep 64 | grep desk | grep ebs
```

I picked the latest release from the list, so your response should look similar to the following:

```
IMAGE ami-195e746d  099720109477/ebs/ubuntu-images-testing/ubuntu-lucid-daily-amd64-desktop-20100505  099720109477  available  public  x86_64  machine  aki-bf7c56cb  ebs
```

Then, to start a large EC2 instance in the desired region use the command `ec2-run-instances` with your access key. Since we did not specify a security group, it will be running in the default security group:

Run EBS based instance

```
frank@ubuntu:~$ ec2-run-instances ami-195e746d --region eu-west-1 -t m1.large -k xess
```

It is a common mistake to specify the access key file such as xess.pem, however `ec2-run-instances` only expects the name of the key.

The command will return the parameters of the starting instance:

```
INSTANCE i-d8bc3eaf ami-195e746d  pending  xess 0 m1.large 2010-05-19T12:33:09+0000  eu-west-1b  aki-bf7c56cb  monitoring-disabled
```

Right after the command returns, the instance is still pending and not yet running. Check back a few minutes later with the `ec2-describe-instances` command and the instance ID to find out whether it has started to run:

```
frank@ubuntu:~$ ec2-describe-instances --region eu-west-1
i-d8bc3eaf
```

Get Public IP   If the instance is in state running already, the output will contain the public IP and DNS entry. The command will return something similar to the output here:

```
INSTANCE  i-d8bc3eaf  ami-195e746d
ec2-79-125-48-67.eu-west-1.compute.amazonaws.com
ip-10-229-123-80.eu-west-1.compute.internal running  xess  0
m1.large  2010-05-19T12:33:09+0000  eu-west-1b  aki-bf7c56cb monitoring-
disabled 79.125.48.67  10.229.123.80
ebs BLOCKDEVICE /dev/sda1  vol-382adc51
2010-05 19T12:33:11.000Z
```

ssh   Now change to your local machine and try to connect to the cloud instance running on EC2:

```
frank@ubuntu:~$ ssh -i ec2/xess.pem ubuntu@79.125.48.67

The authenticity of host '79.125.48.67 (79.125.48.67)' can't be
established.
RSA key fingerprint is 3a:f6:82:2f:fe:26:7f:d5:f9:2b:06:82:5a:87:03:5b.
Are you sure you want to continue connecting (yes/no)? yes
Warning: Permanently added '79.125.48.67' (RSA) to the list of known
hosts.
Linux ip-10-229-123-80 2.6.32-305-ec2 #9-Ubuntu SMP Thu Apr 15 08:05:38
UTC 2010 x86_64 GNU/Linux
Ubuntu 10.04 LTS
```

NX Client   There are various ways to access the desktop, which I will describe in more detail in the Rackspace chapter on page 78. NX is a particularly effective way to gain access to a remote Unix desktop, because it efficiently compresses the X protocol. Here we will use an NX client which is available for Windows and can be downloaded for free.

To enable the NX client to connect, you need to set a password for the Ubuntu user on the cloud instance:

```
ubuntu@ip-10-229-123-80:~$ sudo passwd ubuntu
```

Then download NX client to your local machine from the following location:

```
http://www.nomachine.com/download-client-windows.php
```

Install and run the client, then connect to the Ubuntu desktop using the public IP address of the instance. Once you are connected, this is the perfect time to download and install Oracle WebLogic Server. It is best to download it directly from the cloud instance because it provides a great bandwidth.

As you picked an AMI with an EBS root device, you can check for the EBS volume with the command `ec2-describe-volumes`:

```
frank@ubuntu:~$ ec2-describe-volumes
VOLUME  vol-382adc51   15  snap-1eea2c77  eu-west-1b in-use  2010-05-19T12:33:10+0000
ATTACHMENT vol-382adc51   i-d8bc3eaf /dev/sda1  attached 2010-05-19T12:33:13+0000 dd
```

If you change to the AWS web console and check which actions are possible for the instance, you will see that you can terminate, reboot or stop the instance.

You could reboot the instance with the `ec2-reboot-instances` command and the instance id.

If you are finished for the day, then stop your instance with:

```
frank@ubuntu:~$ ec2-stop-instances i-d8bc3eaf
```

You can check that the instance is actually stopped with the `ec2-describe-instances` command. Once stopped, you no longer pay for the instance. The EBS root device remains available (and you keep being charged for it), but this does mean that you can re-start the instance with all your preconfigured software at anytime. To re-start previously stopped instances use the command `ec2-start-instances`.

Resizing an Instance

Instead of simply starting it as it was before, we upgrade the instance to a bigger one using the `ec2-modify-instance-attributes` command: *Type attribute*

```
frank@ubuntu:~$ ec2-modify-instance-attribute i-d8bc3eaf -t m1.xlarge
```

You can only modify an instance while it is stopped. The command will return something similar to the following output:

```
instanceType  i-d8bc3eaf m1.xlarge
```

Amazon Web Services 67

After a short while it should be running again. Please note that it will start with a new public IP address:

```
frank@ubuntu:~$ ec2-describe-instances

INSTANCE  i-d8bc3eaf  ami-195e746d
ec2-79-125-73-87.eu-west-1.compute.amazonaws.com
ip-10-229-131-47.eu-west-1.compute.internal running xess 0 m1.xlarge
  2010-05-19T19:53:11+0000  eu-west-1b aki-bf7c56cb monitoring-disabled
79.125.73.87   10.229.131.47   ebs BLOCKDEVICE /dev/sda1 vol-382adc51
  2010-05-19T12:33:11.000Z
```

Creating Images, Snapshots and Volumes

Create new AMI

It is easy to create a new image from a running instance using the command `ec2-create-image`. You can give a name to the image with the –n option:

```
frank@ubuntu:~$ ec2-create-image i-d8bc3eaf -n wls1032bin
IMAGE ami-ef22089b
```

You can create an incremental snapshot of an EBS volume that will be stored in S3 with the command `ec2-create-snapshot`. It will take a while for the snapshot to be created. You can check on the status with the command `ec2-describe-snapshots`:

```
frank@ubuntu:~$ ec2-describe-snapshots

SNAPSHOT snap-42cc0f2b vol-382adc51  pending 2010-05-19T20:21:32+0000  75%
  676573782306  15 Backup after OFM installation
```

Create Volume from Snapshot

Based on the snapshot you can create a new volume. The command requires that you pass an availability zone as a parameter:

```
frank@ubuntu:~$ ec2-create-volume --snapshot snap-42cc0f2b
-z eu-west-1b

VOLUME vol-661fe90f  15  snap-42cc0f2b  eu-west-1b  creating 2010-05-
19T20:32:31+0000
```

It is also possible to start a new instance and expose an Amazon EBS volume as a device created from a snapshot. However, this device cannot be the root device:

```
frank@ubuntu:~$ ec2-run-instances ami-195e746d --region eu-west-1 -b
'/dev/sdb=snap-42cc0f2b' -t m1.large -k xess
```

```
INSTANCE  i-e06ae897  ami-195e746d  pending  xess   0  m1.large   2010-05-
19T20:55:31+0000  eu-west-1baki-bf7c56cb  monitoring-disabled
```

When using the ec2-run-instances command, you can add the –b command-line switch to override the AMI's block device mapping with the following syntax:

`-b device = blockdevice` where `blockdevice` can be one of the following:

- none, to suppress the mapping, e.g.
  `/dev/sdb = none`
- ephemeral[0-3] to map instance storage, e.g.
  `/dev/sdc=ephemeral0`
- `[snapshot-id][:size[:delete-on-termination]]`' to expose an EBS volume created from the specified snapshot. The parameter `size` can be used to provide a volume which is larger than the original e.g.
  `/dev/sdb=snap-42cc0f2b:100:false`

3.5 AWS Cloud Services

That isn't all. There is much more to discover in the Amazon cloud. I will explain more AWS cloud services in later chapters of this book where topics such as databases in the cloud, availability, scalability, etc. will be covered. Here is an overview of these services, listed together with the section of the book explaining them:

- AWS SimpleDB, see section 7.2.
- AWS Relational Database, see section 7.3.
- AWS Simple Queue Service, see section 9.7.
- AWS Elastic Load Balancing, see section 10.2.
- AWS CloudFront, see section 10.4.
- AWS CloudWatch, see section 11.5.
- AWS Simple Notification Service, see section 11.6.

4 Rackspace Cloud

Amazon is certainly the "top dog" among IaaS providers - sometimes it almost seems as if Amazon Web Services is used as a synonym for pay on demand computing resources. However, there are other players who are challenging the dominance of Amazon in the cloud computing market. One of the most notable is Rackspace Cloud; a cloud hosting division wholly owned by the popular American hosting provider Rackspace. Rackspace Cloud was formerly known as Mosso, prior to being rebranded in 2009. Rackspace bought the Mosso virtualization technology when it acquired a company called Slicehost in 2008.

This chapter introduces the key features of Rackspace Cloud. To help you select a provider, section 6.2 contains a comparison between the Rackspace Cloud and Amazon Web Services.

4.1 Rackspace Cloud Servers

Signing up for Rackspace Cloud and Files

To sign up for the Rackspace Cloud, navigate in your browser to:

`http://www.RackspaceCloud.com`

Click on "Order Now" and provide personal details, including your billing address and credit card details. You are then kindly asked to accept the usage terms - all 23 pages of them!

Rackspace promises to call you back within 15 minutes to verify your ID. In my case, and on a Saturday afternoon to boot, I waited only 5 minutes to receive a call from the US on my mobile phone. And yes, surprisingly, it was a real person on the other end of the line.

The Cloud will give you a ring

After confirming all details, including the bizarre letter "ü" in my street name (when dealing with US companies I am always tempted to check their support for internationalization), they activated my account.

RACKSPACCLOUD USAGE TERMS

I am a Techie. A detailed analysis of the usage terms or a comparison to those from Amazon Web Services is something I prefer to leave to the lawyers.

Even though I enjoy the hubris of not making a detailed comparison, I'd like to point you towards some of the more interesting sections of the agreement:

The usage terms require you to "agree that you will maintain at least one additional current copy of your programs and data stored on the Rackspace Cloud system somewhere other than on the Rackspace Cloud system."

"You may not use the Services for the development, design, manufacture, production, stockpiling, or use of nuclear, chemical or biological weapons, weapons of mass destruction, or missiles..."

"We collect and store information related to your use of the Services, such as use of SMTP, POP3, IMAP, and filtering choices and usage. You agree that we may use this information for our general business purposes and may disclose the information to third parties in aggregate statistical form, provided that we do not include any information that could be used to identify you."

Create an API key To get started, and create the user account, click on "Customer Login". Then, using the Rackspace Cloud web console select "Hosting" from the left hand side of the menu and click on "Cloud Files". The first time you select "Cloud Files" you will be asked to create an API key for the programmatic usage of Cloud Files. This key will be added to your account as shown in Figure 36.

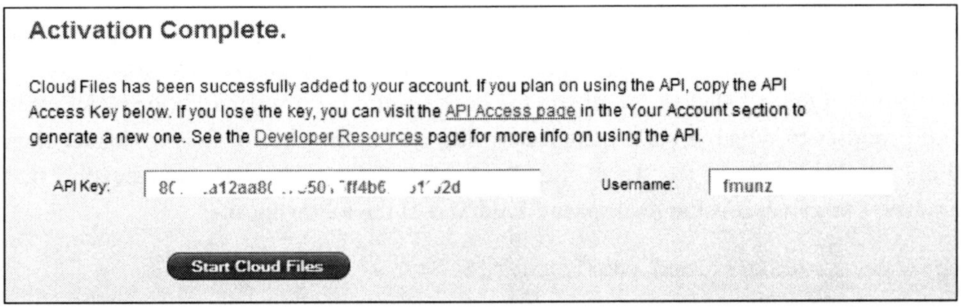

Figure 36: Create API Key

Cloud Support and Service

The level of support that you receive from Rackspace Cloud is absolutely fabulous. Try as I might, I can't recall a similar experience. Its objective is to provide infrastructure hand-in-hand with a high level of customer service. Its approach is simple: you can chat to them 24/7. In order to check some facts, I tried the chat application several times myself, and was amazed by the high quality of the answers provided (and I was chatting to different people, mostly on a Saturday or Sunday). And all this even though at the time I was only running the smallest possible machine for 1.5 cents per hour. Do you know any other company that offers this level of customer service free of charge?

Excellent customer service

Locations

Rackspace Cloud is currently running two data centers in the US: one in Dallas and one in Chicago. A further Center is located in the UK (cloud hosting is currently unavailable there, but scheduled for late 2010). There are no other locations closer to South-East Asia or Australia, but Rackspace does have plans in the pipeline to offer cloud services in Hong Kong from 2011. In any case, the good news is that Rackspace Cloud partners with a content delivery network, so your static content can in fact be located much closer to your customers whether they be in Paris, Perth or Phnom Penh.

There is a service level agreement for cloud servers. Rackspace Cloud guarantees 100% availability for the data center network and power supply for any given billing cycle - excluding scheduled maintenance. For a failed cloud server, an estimated timeframe of one hour, measured from the identification of the problem, is given until the problem will be resolved.

SLA

According to Rackspace Cloud, when two instances are started in the cloud they will run on two different physical hosts.

Now, of course, the interesting question is what will happen if Rackspace fails to meet the SLA? Well, they operate a credit scheme e.g. for every 30 minutes of network or power downtime, you are entitled to 5% of the fee of the cloud service. In addition, Rackspace Cloud promises to repair broken instances within one hour, but if it fails to deliver then you are entitled to 5% of the fee of the cloud services for each extra hour beyond that guarantee. You can access the Rackspace Cloud SLA at the following site:

```
http://www.rackspacecloud.com/legal/sla
```

Machines and Pricing

Month-to-month billing is the only option available, so you cannot get a discount even if you prepay for a year. The actual charges are handled on an hourly billing schedule.

The cheapest Linux instances come with 256 MB RAM, 10 GB of disk space and start from US$ 0.015. The maximum RAM size available is 15.9 GB. Windows instance pricing is higher than that of Linux because it includes the cost of the Windows license.

Bandwidth costs an extra 22 cents / GB outbound and 8 cents/ GB inbound.

Server Size		Linux®		Windows®	
RAM	Disk	Hourly	Estimated Monthly	Hourly	Estimated Monthly
256 MB	10 GB	$0.015	$10.95	—	—
512 MB	20 GB	$0.03	$21.90	—	—
1,024 MB	40 GB	$0.06	$43.80	$0.08	$58.40
2,048 MB	80 GB	$0.12	$87.60	$0.16	$116.80
4,096 MB	160 GB	$0.24	$175.20	$0.32	$233.60
8,192 MB	320 GB	$0.48	$350.40	$0.58	$423.40
15,872 MB	620 GB	$0.96	$700.80	$1.08	$788.40

Figure 37: Rackspace Cloud Pricing

100% Availability?

Rackspace Cloud offers an SLA for its servers stating that a problem with a running instance will be fixed within one hour. This statement comes with a guaranteed 100% availability of network and power supply. An availability of 100% sounds fantastic, but does that mean you can be complacent?

I don't think so. Think about super critical systems on which human lives depend i.e. the kind of systems for which everyone would do the utmost possible to prevent a failure, regardless of cost. Electricity grids, spaceships, nuclear power plants, and airports are good examples. Most of us have always understood that 100% availability is impossible to achieve, even before the 2003 North East Blackout in the US, the explosion of the Challenger, the Chernobyl disaster or the closure of all major airports in Europe when the Eyjafjallajoekull volcano errupted in far away Iceland.

So even if Rackspace Cloud is doing its utmost, you shouldn't assume everything will definitely be okay. Have monitoring in place, use stateless instances that can be re-launched quickly and have a good contingency plan waiting in your top drawer (we will cover all these topics later).

Rackspace simply did the math and calculated the risk of paying out 5% of their cloud hosting revenues in case of a failure: for a medium sized server that costs $44 / month, you will receive a reimbursement of $2 for an unplanned 30-minute outage. However, I reckon this $2 is nothing compared to the business that you potentially missed out on.

To conclude: to my mind 100% is a pretty good SLA-backed promise. Just make sure you understand the implications for *your* business.

You can select between Linux (RedHat, Gentoo, Debian, CentOS, Ubuntu, ArchLinux, Fedora and Oracle Enterprise Linux) and Windows (Windows Server 2003 and Windows Server 2008 R2).

Rackspace Cloud instances can be resized with the Rackspace management console. Resizing takes just a couple of minutes and the instance is automatically restarted during the process.

No sharing! Currently, it is not possible to share your images with other users, which would help explain why the list of possible images is rather short.

All servers have access to a local RAID 10; a high-performance RAID level with a stripe of mirrored disks.

There is no external firewall shielding the Rackspace Cloud from the Internet. Instead, Linux servers run preconfigured iptables and Windows servers use their internal firewall to protect themselves.

Network bandwidth cap A bandwidth cap applies to all Cloud Servers. The cap depends on the size of the server. For the smallest server, the cap is 10 Mbs/20 Mbs for the public/private network. Rackspace's largest instance with 15.5 GB RAM has a cap of 70 Mbs/140 MBs for the public / private network.

Addressing Cloud Servers

Rackspace Cloud servers come with a dedicated public IP address as well as a separate private IP address. All IP addresses are static and no NAT is used. It is however possible to share IP addresses and you may also request additional IP addresses. The cost is $2.00 per month per additional IP.

Network traffic between cloud instances is free if you use the private network.

Starting a Rackspace Cloud Instance

Okay, the time has come to launch your first instance in the Rackspace Cloud. Starting an image is really straightforward and can be done from Rackspace's web based console. Navigate to "Hosting", select "Cloud Servers" and then click on "Add Server" as shown in Figure 38.

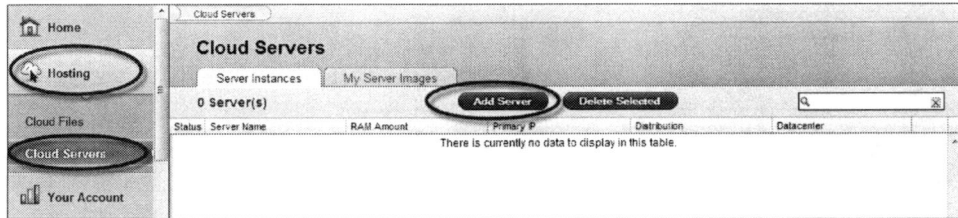

Figure 38: Add Cloud Server

A list of supported operating systems will be displayed.

So we can draw comparisons with the Amazon experience, let's go for an Ubuntu 9.10 image. Add a name for the server, select its size and then click on "Create Server", as shown in Figure 39. Soon after, a message with the root/administrator password will appear – and then disappear again a few seconds later. But don't worry, the same data will be sent to you via email.

Try and see if you can ping the instance and then connect to your new instance with ssh:

```
frank@ubuntu:~/ec2$ ssh -l root 173.203.119.28
```

```
root@173.203.119.28's password:
Linux firstRackspaceTest 2.6.32.9-rscloud #6 SMP Thu Mar 11 14:32:05 UTC
2010 x86_64
```

This is a good time to remind you that you were never asked where you wanted to place the server. This was because a new customer's cloud server will automatically be placed in Chicago. Customers can override this default by contacting the support team and requesting a different datacenter.

Location

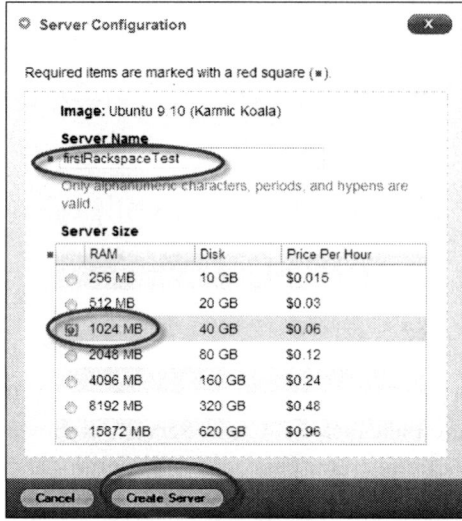

Figure 39: Server Configuration

Since March 2010, Rackspace Cloud has offered the options of Oracle Enterprise Linux 5.4 and Oracle Enterprise Linux JeOS 5.3. Since the images are provided by Oracle, this may sound like a good basis for installing Oracle Fusion Middleware or other Oracle products on top of these images. However, the Rackspace' hypervisor is not approved by Oracle and Oracle only offers limited support, as shown in Figure 40:

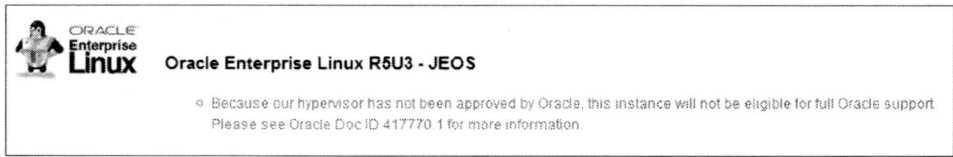

Figure 40: Oracle Enterprise Linux with Limited Support

Connecting to a UNIX Desktop

All Rackspace Linux images come as server images per default. This means that neither X11, nor Gnome, or KDE, or indeed any other desktop (such as fvwm, should anyone remember it!) is installed. This is fine for server images running production applications where no graphic is needed. However, to get things started it is often more convenient to have a desktop running, as this enables you to obtain all your graphical tools.

Ubuntu images on EC2, built by Alestic, came as server *and* desktop images, which I really appreciated. Don't get me wrong, it's not absolutely necessary, because most tools, such as the WebLogic domain wizard, can either run in a text-mode or can easily be replaced by the command-line. What a desktop does do, is speed things up if you are exploring something in the cloud – which is something you will often do.

You can add an -X switch with the ssh command to enable X-forwarding. If you connect from let's say a Linux computer (or in my case, a virtualized Ubuntu running in a VMWare) with X11 running, then you will be able to display an X-based graphical application on your local computer. For a UNIX based client this is usually all that you need on the client's end.
UNIX client

Assuming your client is running Windows, but that you've got an image with an X-server and a desktop running in the cloud, then there are a few different ways to connect to it - even from a Windows environment.
Windows client

VNC is a very popular tool used to connect to the desktop of a remote machine, be it Windows or Linux. To use it, you have to run a client on the local side and install a VNC server on the server side. The commercially supported version from RealVNC is also offered as a free version under `http://www.realvnc.com`.
VNC

For Rackspace, there is a detailed description in the Wiki explaining how to set up VNC:

`http://cloudservers.RackspaceCloud.com/index.php/VNC_Install`

TightVNC is a completely free version of VNC for both private and commercial use. See their web site at `http://www.tightvnc.com`.
TightVNC

NX is a desktop virtualization solution provided by a company called NoMachine. They designed the NX libraries to provide a self-tuning protocol with compression and reduced round-trips for X11, even over slow connections. Take a look at their homepage: `http://www.nomachine.com`. They provide a free version (limited to two connections).
NX

FreeNX was created in 2004 as the first completely free and GPLed server implementation of NX: `http://freenx.berlios.de`.
FreeNX

Cygwin is another solution: `http://www.cygwin.com`. It provides a UNIX environment for Windows and comes with an X-server that can display your X based applications on your UNIX host. The software was written by Cygnus Solutions, which now belongs to Red Hat.
Cygwin

If you are okay with the server images, that's fine. If you prefer the desktop, then go for it - it can always be removed at a later stage. If you look into hardening your images, then it is of course preferable to start with a minimal operating system and to only add what is absolutely essential.

Adding a Desktop with NX to a Linux Server Image

Probably you sometimes find yourself wishing that a Linux desktop image existed - but it doesn't. As explained above, not only are all Rackspace images server images without a desktop, but most Linux images on Amazon's EC2 don't have a desktop installed either. Alestic used to build server and desktop AMIs for EC2, but Canonical only builds server images.

However, it is still possible to install a desktop with the NX server on a server image. The following section explains the necessary steps.

When I started, I found a problem with the locale setting in Ubuntu 9.10 from Rackspace. Should this happen to you, to resolve it, you need to install the language pack and then reconfigure the locale:

```
sudo apt-get install language-pack-en-base
sudo dpkg-reconfigure locales
```

You should test it e.g. with `perl -v`, which should no longer be complaining about any locale settings.

Next, create a new "ubuntu" user and set a password. The Ubuntu user will be used to connect to the remote desktop once everything is correctly set up:

```
sudo useradd -d /home/ubuntu -m ubuntu
passwd ubuntu new_password
```

Installing NX involves three packages. A script is available from Alestic that will install all of them, which you can even run remotely with a little utility called `runurl`. I will explain this utility in more detail in section 6.3. For now, get the `runurl` utility and make it executable:

```
sudo wget -qO /usr/bin/runurl run.alestic.com/runurl
chmod 755 /usr/bin/runurl
```

To see details of the script you are going to execute, copy and paste the following URL into your browser: run.alestic.com/install/desktop. If you feel uncomfortable executing a script which is hosted on a remote site, then either copy the script or simply cut and paste the commands.

Then run the script by executing the following command:

```
runurl run.alestic.com/install/desktop
```

The script will need a couple of minutes (even on a fast machine), to download and install the gnome desktop with the NX environment for the server.

Once complete, double check that the file `/etc/ssh/sshd_config` contains the following two lines (if it doesn't, correct it):

```
# Change to no to disable tunnelled clear text
passwordsPasswordAuthentication yes
AllowUsers ubuntu
```

For the Rackspace Ubuntu image, I also had to add the following entry to the `hosts.allow` file:

```
sudo echo 'SSHD: ALL' >> /etc/hosts.allow
```

Next, restart ssh with: `sudo /etc/init.d/ssh restart`

Then start and configure the Gnome desktop and the X-server:

```
sudo /etc/init.d/gdm start
sudo dpkg-reconfigure xserver-xorg
```

To tell you the truth, depending on the Linux distribution, the way the distribution was built, and the particular cloud environment, you can easily spend hours debugging desktop connections problems, whereas using ssh with X-forwarding is typically easier and faster.

Troubleshooting connection problems

In case you encounter problems when using NX to connect to a remote desktop, and assuming you are trying to connect from a Windows machine to an Ubuntu desktop, I recommend you check the log files in the following directory for problems:

```
%USERPROFILE%\.nx
```

Then switch to the remote site. Uncomment the following line (which ensures that the shutdown procedure doesn't remove the temporary NX directory at the end of the session):

SESSION_LOG_CLEAN = "0" in the file /usr/NX/etc/node.cfg

Next, increase the log level in the node.cfg file and in the /usr/NX/etc/server.cfg file:

SESSION_LOG_LEVEL = "7"

Once the session is terminated, you will find session directories containing logs with the following naming scheme:

~/.nx/C-(Server Name)-(Display ID)-(Session ID)

Creating a Rackspace Server Image

You can create a Rackspace server image from your running instance. This image will be located with the server. If you locate your image with the server it will be deleted when you delete the server. Only images on Cloud Files can survive the lifetime of a server.

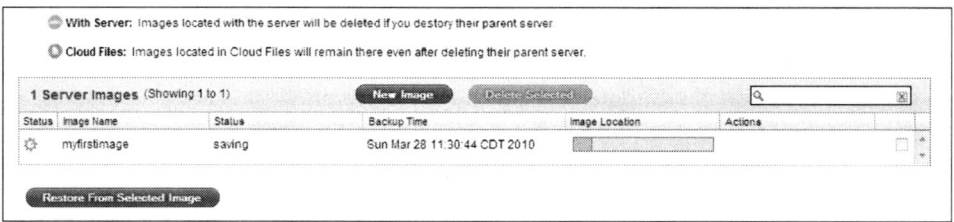

Figure 41: Create Rackspace Server Image

REST Access to Cloud Servers

REST is an acronym for Representational State. Assuming that you have a BEA/Oracle background, which is pretty much a dead cert if you are reading this book, it is likely that you are used to SOAP based web services, as support for REST in the Oracle world is somewhat limited. Given that REST-full applications are increasing in popularity and all cloud platforms come with a REST interface, it is well worth taking some time to look into the details, useful tools, and exploring REST using some examples.

If you already consider yourself to be an expert in REST, then skip this introduction and read William Vambenepe's blog entry which compares Amazon's and Rackspace Cloud's API, and analyzes the practical benefits provided by REST:

http://stage.vambenepe.com/archives/863

So what exactly are the key principles? Well, firstly, you should use the HTTP methods (PUT, GET, POST and DELETE) the way they were intended, together with stateless communication. Secondly, you should use links wherever possible. And thirdly, you should identify all relevant resources with IDs.

Is there really more than GET and POST used in HTTP?

Let's look at an example. To retrieve the details of a running server under an account with {accountID} you will use HTTP GET with the following URL:

servers.api.Rackspace Cloud.com/v1.0/{accountID}/servers/detail

That's it. Similarly, you could use HTTP POST to create a new resource with a unique ID, PUT to update it, and DELETE to remove it. It should by now be apparent why using URLs together with IDs is essential for this style of web application development, commonly referred to as "REST-full".

One of the promises made by REST based web services is that they are conceptually easier (after reading this chapter you will be able to decide for yourself if this is the case), and they also come with less overhead.

From WSDL to WADL

REST-full web services use a Web Application Description File (WADL) instead of the Web Service Description File (WSDL) that is used with SOAP based web services.

This WADL file serves the same purpose as the WSDL: it describes the interface of the service, lists all the operations, possible return codes and faults, together with their parameters. Nowadays, we also have the new WSDL 2.0 (with its expanded scope) which, in addition to SOAP based web services, can also be used to describe web services based on REST.

I recommend typing the following URL into your web browser so you can examine the Rackspace Cloud WADL:

http://docs.Rackspace Cloud.com/servers/api/v1.0/application.wadl

To use the REST API, you must get an API key from the Rackspace Cloud web console under "Your Account / API Access". You have to use this API to send a REST request: put that API key into an X-Auth-Key HTTP header, and your user name into the X-Auth-User HTTP header.

It is also possible to use `curl` to create such a request. Use the -D - switch to see the returned headers, since they will contain the authorization token in which we are interested:

```
curl -D - \
-H "X-Auth-Key: a8681231231231231231231231231231231231231231231231231231231231231231231231231231231231231231231231231231231231231231231231231231231231231" \
-H "X-Auth-User: fmunz" \
https://auth.api.Rackspace Cloud.com/v1.0
```

The output will be similar to the following:

```
HTTP/1.1 204 No Content
Date: Tue, 06 Apr 2010 16:02:45 GMT
Server: Apache/2.2.3 (Mosso Engineering)
X-Storage-Token: 521af9e4-8251-479c-8315-f0a0b77d0507
X-Storage-Url: https://storage5.clouddrive.com/v1/MossoCloudFS_3ee25dab-6f60-4a56-866e-1f98c39d4ff0
X-Server-Management-Url: https://servers.api.Rackspace Cloud.com/v1.0/481588
X-CDN-Management-Url: https://cdn.clouddrive.com/v1/MossoCloudFS_3ee25dab-6f60-4a56-866e-1f98c39d4ff0
X-Auth-Token: 521af9e4-8251-479c-8315-f0a0b77d0507
Content-Length: 0
Connection: close
Content-Type: application/octet-stream
```

The response returns the authentication token, which must be added as an HTTP header to every request:

```
X-Auth-Token: 521af9e4-8251-479c-8315-f0a0b77d0507
```

Within the response there is a second line named X-Server-Management-Url that contains information needed for a REST request. This URL contains the account, which is the last part of the URL. Information about the account is a bit vague in the Rackspace Cloud documentation, but this is where it can be found:

```
X-Server-Management-Url: https://servers.api.Rackspace Cloud.com/v1.0/481588
```

In this case, the account ID is 481588. Again, this demonstrates two of the REST principles: the usage of IDs and the usage of links as return values.

An easy way to continue exploring the Rackspace Cloud REST API is to download the open source version of SOAPUI from `http://www.soapui.org`. SOAPUI is a commonly used, free, graphical tool for testing SOAP and REST based web services.

SOAPUI

So, let's assume you have already retrieved the authentication token, are well-aware of your account id and now want to use the REST API to obtain information about your running servers in Rackspace Cloud using SOAPUI.

Get running servers via REST

After starting SOAPUI, create a new project by copying the WADL from above as shown in Figure 42.

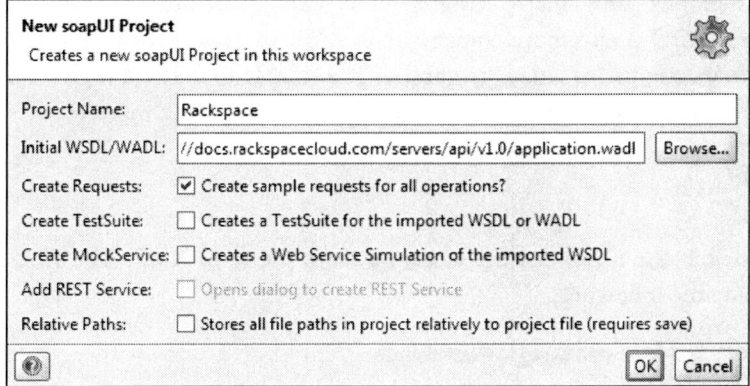

Figure 42: WADL Based SOAPUI Project

Once the project with the methods is created, select the example request of the following method:

`servers [v1.0/{accountId}/servers]`

Fill in the X-Auth-Token and accountId parameter, then click on the green triangle to run the request. The response value in JSON format is shown in Figure 43.

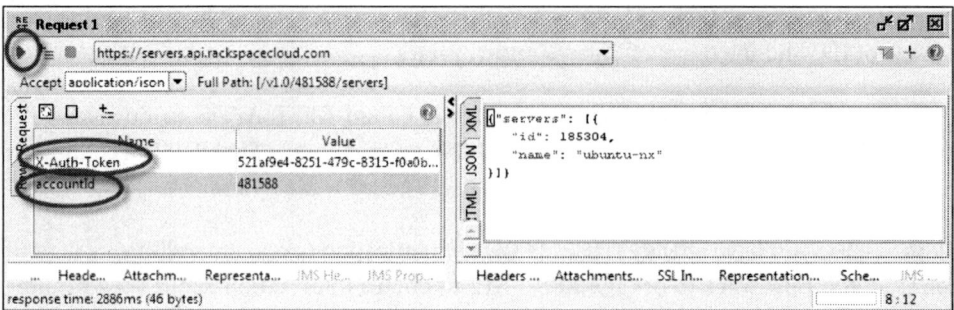

Figure 43: SOAPUI REST Request

JSON JSON, which is short for JavaScript Object Notation, is often used for REST-full web service because it is simpler and maps directly onto data structures of modern programming languages. JSON is also more compact than XML and easier for humans to read. In addition, a rather long list of language libraries is available to convert high level language objects into their JSON representation. Have a look at the following web site:

http://www.json.org/

In SOAPUI you can switch the format of the response from JSON to XML. The XML response will be similar to the following:

```
<Response xmlns="https://servers.api.Rackspace
Cloud.com/v1.0/481588/servers">
    <servers>
        <e>
            <id>185304</id>
            <name>ubuntu-nx</name>
        </e>
    </servers>
</Response>
```

Now, for the hard-core command-line interface user amongst you, let's see, how we can achieve this with curl. To retrieve slightly more detailed data, construct the following shell command which asks for the server details:

```
frank@ubuntu:~/ec2$ curl -D - -H "X-Auth-Token: 521af9e4-8251-479c-8315-
f0a0b77d0507" https://servers.api.RackspaceCloud.com/
v1.0/481588/servers/detail
```

The -D option tells the `curl` command to dump header information to `stdout` (so the single "-" is not a typo). To also include the X-Auth-Token header to the request the -H option is used.

If a server is running, the result will be similar to the following:

```
HTTP/1.1 203 OK
Server: Apache-Coyote/1.1
vary:  Accept, Accept-Encoding
Last-Modified: Wed, 31 Mar 2010 05:01:10 GMT
Cache-Control: s-maxage=1800
Content-Type: application/json
Content-Length: 236
Date: Tue, 06 Apr 2010 17:38:25 GMT
X-Varnish: 752369634 752369589
Age: 17
Via: 1.1 varnish
Connection: keep-alive

{"servers":[{"progress":100,"id":185304,"imageId":14362,"flavorId":3,"sta
tus":"ACTIVE","name":"ubuntu-
nx","hostId":"5a269814ea997a10c6d1ac98673ca5b3","addresses":{"public":["1
73.203.119.51"],"private":["10.179.55.115"]},"metadata":{}}]}
```

Have a look at the last line, which is the interesting part of the HTTP response. It is a JSON representation containing server ID, state, name and a public/private IP address.

4.2 Rackspace Cloud Files

In addition to the local storage that comes with your instances, you can create objects in Rackspace's cloud storage which are called Cloud Files.

Features

As with S3 from Amazon, Cloud Files store objects rather than files. Objects are put into containers, so you therefore need to create at least one container if want to store an object. You can create as many containers as you like, but you cannot nest them. The container names must not contain a forward slash and must be less than 256 bytes long (excluding URL encoding).

The size of the objects stored in Cloud Files can range from 1 byte to 5 Gbyte. Objects can also store metadata with them, which is handy for organizing them. Versioning is not available for objects supported by cloud files.

Metadata but no versioning

Remember that once in a lifetime trip to Cocos Island that you took in your imagination while looking at the S3 example? Well, if you decide to store your diving footage using Cloud Files, you could use its metadata and key-value pairs to sort your underwater videos. Keep it at less than 90 key-value pairs, with a total length of less than 4,096 bytes for all key-value pairs in total.

If you intend to distribute a database backup or the content of a DVD, then you can use the Rackspace Cloud web console to create or remove containers and upload or delete files as shown in Figure 44:

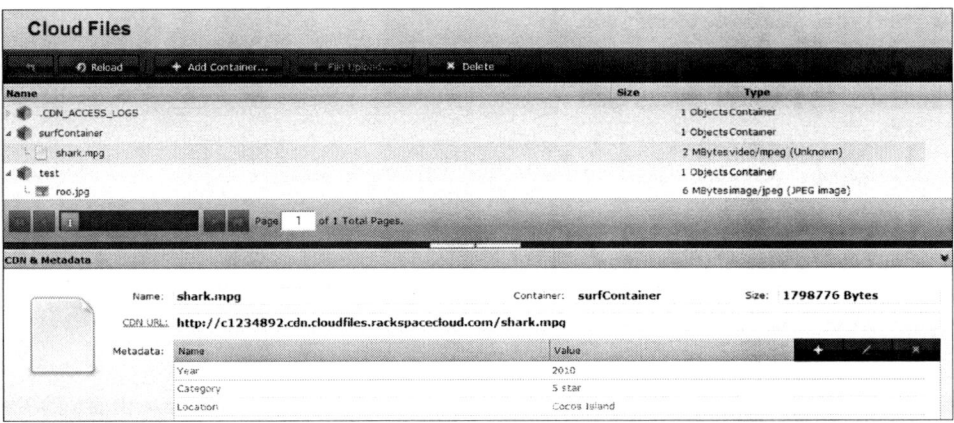

Figure 44: Cloud Files Web Console

Limelight

Content at the edges

Rackspace has a partnership with Limelight Networks, a company that operates a Content Distribution Network (CDN). Limelight's objective is for customers to bypass the Internet in favor of its own private high speed network, which claims to directly connect to 70 connection points with a bandwidth of over 2 Terabits/s. Limelight also operates local caches where content is stored close to the client.

To enable a container to be distributed via Limelight, simply right click on the container in the web console and select "Publish to CDN". Files within a CDN-enabled container are accessible to anyone using the CDN in the File / CDN & Metadata section of the console.

The costs for using the CDN are derived from the basic cost for Cloud Files plus a fee for downloading ($0.22 / GB) and uploading ($0.08 / GB).

There is one URL per container. To access the content, simply add the name of the object to the container URL. In our video example the URL becomes:

http://c1234892.cdn.cloudfiles.Rackspace Cloud.com/shark.mpg

Now, by using this URL the video is retrieved once from Cloud Files, and thereafter the CDN of Limelight is used to deliver it to all requestors. Now let's assume the original video has changed after you have spent a night editing it. In that case, you can specify a time to live (TTL) period which will determine when an object expires and how often the cache needs to be refreshed.

Cloud Files APIs

Assuming you are developing an application, you use the Cloud Files API to create a container and upload a file. All these operations have to include a valid authorization token. To do so, the following language bindings are supported by Cloud Files (according to Rackspace Cloud's documentation):

- PHP (requires 5.x and the modules: cURL, FileInfo, mbstring)
- Python (requires version 2.4 or newer)
- Java (requires JRE 1.5 or newer)
- C#/.NET (requires .NET Framework v3.5)
- Ruby (requires 1.8 or newer and mime-tools module)

REST Access to Cloud Files

Instead of using a high level programming language with one of the Cloud Files APIs listed above, you can use the simple REST web service interface.

As with the Rackspace Cloud servers, first you have to get hold of the authentication token. Section 4.1 explains how to retrieve this token using your account data. After retrieving your authentication token, also please take note of the X-Storage-Url.

You will use this URL to interact with Cloud Files via REST, as shown in the example below, which is retrieving the content of your Cloud Files account:

List content

```
frank@ubuntu:~/ec2$ curl  -H "X-Auth-Token: 521af9e4-8251-479c-8315-f0a0b77d0507"  https://storage5.clouddrive.com/v1/MossoCloudFS_3ee25dab-6f60-4a56-866e-1f98c39d4ff0
```

This request will list your Cloud Files content. In my case, there are three containers:

```
.CDN_ACCESS_LOGS
surfContainer
test
```

Create a new container

To create a new container, send a REST request using the HTTP PUT verb and add the name of the container to the URL:

```
frank@ubuntu:~/ec2$ curl -X PUT -D -  -H "X-Auth-Token: 1d6faec9-d6e4-43d2-a735-faed1145167f"
https://storage5.clouddrive.com/v1/MossoCloudFS_3ee25dab-6f60-4a56-866e-1f98c39d4ff0/underwater
```

A new container with the name "underwater" is created and a status "Created" is returned with HTTP 201:

```
HTTP/1.1 201 Created
Date: Wed, 07 Apr 2010 09:21:43 GMT
Server: Apache
Content-Length: 0
Content-Type: text/plain
```

The command above lists the content of your Cloud Files account. Use this to check that the container really exists.

REFRESH RACKSPACE CLOUD BROWSER

When using the web browser console to check for the newly created container, and to avoid seeing old data, remember to hit the refresh button first.

To upload a new image into the container you just created, send an HTTP PUT which is specified by the –X option; request additional headers be sent to `stdout` with the option "-D -", and use the -T switch to specify the file to upload:

```
frank@ubuntu:~/ec2$ curl -X PUT -T mantaray.jpg -D -  -H "Content-Type: image/jpeg" -H "X-Auth-Token: 1d6faec9-d6e4-43d2-a735-faed1145167f"
https://storage5.clouddrive.com/v1/MossoCloudFS_3ee25dab-6f60-4a56-866e-1f98c39d4ff0/underwater/mantaray1.jpg
```

The HTTP return will contain the status code 201 for "Created" and an Etag which is the HTTP header containing the MD5 checksum:

```
HTTP/1.1 100 Continue
HTTP/1.1 201 Created
Date: Wed, 07 Apr 2010 09:50:52 GMT
Server: Apache
Etag: a53ac43d01bcbee66b01ea47be5bf9f4
Content-Length: 0
Content-Type: text/plain
```

To ensure that your file is created correctly, it is advisable to calculate the Etag first and add it to the PUT request. Alternatively, you should manually verify the returned Etag against the MD5 checksum.

A well-designed system is typically one in which solutions are available for the common problems you may encounter. There is no need to have a Masters in cryptography or to implement the MD5 algorithm in some fancy dynamic language. To verify the checksum returned by Cloud Files, a simple md5sum from your UNIX shell is good enough:

```
frank@ubuntu:~/ec2$ md5sum mantaray.jpg
a53ac43d01bcbee66b01ea47be5bf9f4  mantaray.jpg
```

You can add the name of the container "underwater" and the parameter ?format=json to the URL, so the URL will look as follows (use your own storage URL):

```
https://storage5.clouddrive.com/v1/MossoCloudFS_3ee25dab-6f60-4a56-866e-1f98c39d4ff0/underwater?format=json
```

Adding ?format=json instructs the service to return additional information in a JSON representation of the underwater container. So the output will be as shown below:

```
[{"name": "mantaray2.jpg", "hash": "a53ac43d01bcbee66b01ea47be5bf9f4",
"bytes": 23152, "content_type": "image\u002fjpeg",
"last_modified": "2010-04-07T09:50:52.891042"},

{"name": "mantaray.jpg", "hash": "a53ac43d01bcbee66b01ea47be5bf9f4",
"bytes": 33252, "content_type": "image\u002fjpeg",
"last_modified": "2010-04-07T09:50:19.099588"}]
```

As you can see from the output, I uploaded another image.

More ?parameter=x tricks

You can achieve even more by simply adding parameters. Replace the `format=json` by `format=xml` and the return type will be serialized to an XML representation.

You should expect long lists to be returned sometimes. Imagine a whale fanatic back from a trip to Antarctica with thousands of whale pictures shot and stored in one Cloud Files container. If you expect a lot of objects to be returned, you can limit the number by adding a parameter `?limit=n` where n is an integer less than 10,000.

For example, if you add `?limit=100` and the last file returned was antarctica_00201.jpg (assuming that some pictures were already deleted and the numbering is no longer consecutive), then you can re-issue the same request to retrieve the next 100 pictures, using the following two parameters:

`?limit=100&marker=antartica_00201.jpg`

Tools for Cloud Files

And yes, graphical tools are also available (you don't even have to use `curl` and the RESTfull API).

Cloud Files Manager

One of them is called Cloud Files Manager. A free version (which expires after 7 days) is available under the following URL:

`http://www.cloudfilesmanager.com/`

This tool is useful and the GUI is tidy and nicely arranged. It is somehow more convenient to navigate with a GUI than with the Rackspace Cloud web console. Take a look for yourself in Figure 45 and compare it to Figure 44.

Fireuploader

Also take a look at the fast Fireuploader plugin for Firefox (also free), which supports queued uploads and downloads. You can enable the distribution of containers via the CDN and edit the key-value metadata of files. In addition to Cloud Files, you can also use it to upload content to Flickr, Picasa, YouTube, Facebook, and various other Web 2.0 offsprings. The plugin can be downloaded from the following site:

`http://www.fireuploader.com`

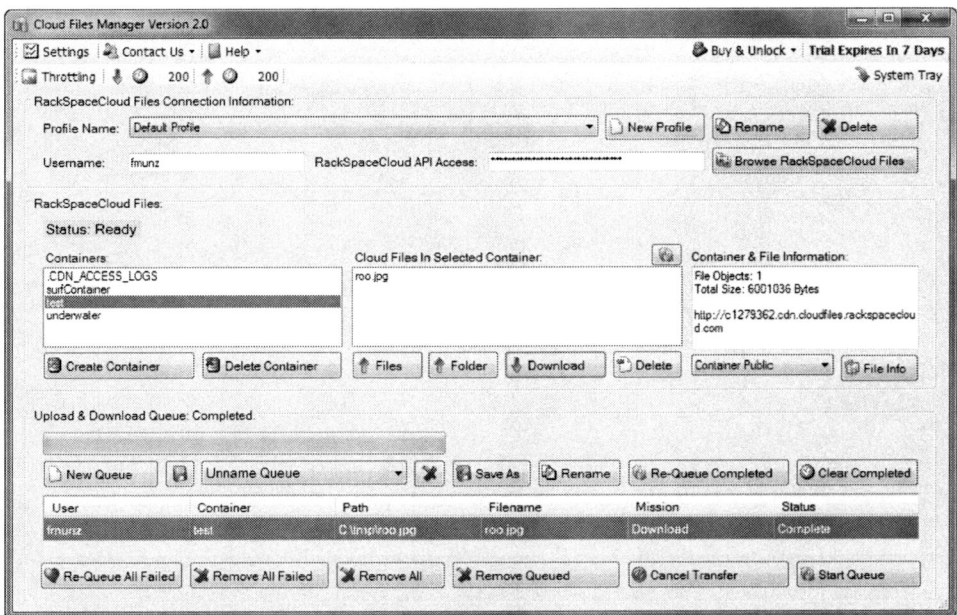

Figure 45: Cloud Files Manager

You are better off (at least in this particular situation) if you are a Mac user, as you will have at your disposition the free Cyberduck tool which supports Rackspace Cloud Files as well as Amazon S3 and ftp, sftp and WebDAV.

Cyberduck

5 SOA and Oracle Fusion Middleware

This chapter briefly introduces the concept of service-oriented architecture and the most relevant Oracle Fusion Middleware products. This chapter is not about the cloud at all. Instead, my objective here is to provide a concise and easy to understand introduction to the world of Oracle SOA; I appreciate that if you are not a middleware and SOA expert, the sheer number of products and vast array of marketing materials can make Oracle Fusion Middleware seem intimidating and confusing at first.

Subsequent chapters build on the principles and products in this chapter and demonstrate how to run middleware solutions in the cloud.

5.1 Service Oriented Architecture

Service Oriented Architecture (SOA) is an IT strategy that aims to narrow the gap between business requirements and IT solutions. SOA promises more agile business processes, faster implementation of IT solutions, and reduced long-term costs due to service reuse.

The key idea behind an SOA is to organize the discrete functions of enterprise applications into reusable and interoperable services. Services are first class citizens in an SOA representing the solution logic.

Workflow engines orchestrate the services, contain the business process steps, and the sequence in which they are executed. These steps are graphically modeled by an executable workflow that can be quickly changed as well as easily monitored.

The Big Picture in Layers

I would like to provide a deliberately simple picture of an SOA here i.e. a viewpoint about SOA from a system architecture perspective. First, we will take a 'product independent' look at the different layers that constitute an SOA.

If you are interested in a more academic view of SOA, then I would recommend the OASIS model. However, please note: the OASIS model is an abstract model which can be used for a range of service oriented architectures and their analysis. It is difficult to understand and surprisingly, it doesn't contain a single diagram showing the layers of an SOA:

http://docs.oasis-open.org/soa-rm/soa-ra/v1.0/soa-ra-cd-02.pdf

Full-blown service oriented architecture (which is more often seen on presentation slides than in real projects), is often based on a surprisingly high number of middleware infrastructure components, which generally map to vendor products. In real projects, you will usually only find a subset of these products.

In the following paragraphs, the more general components will be mapped to concrete products, starting in section 5.2.

Let's take a more detailed view at these layers, starting with the bottom of the stack in Figure 46. A simple SOA stack consists of a service implementation layer, a service virtualization layer and a service orchestration layer, as shown in the following diagram:

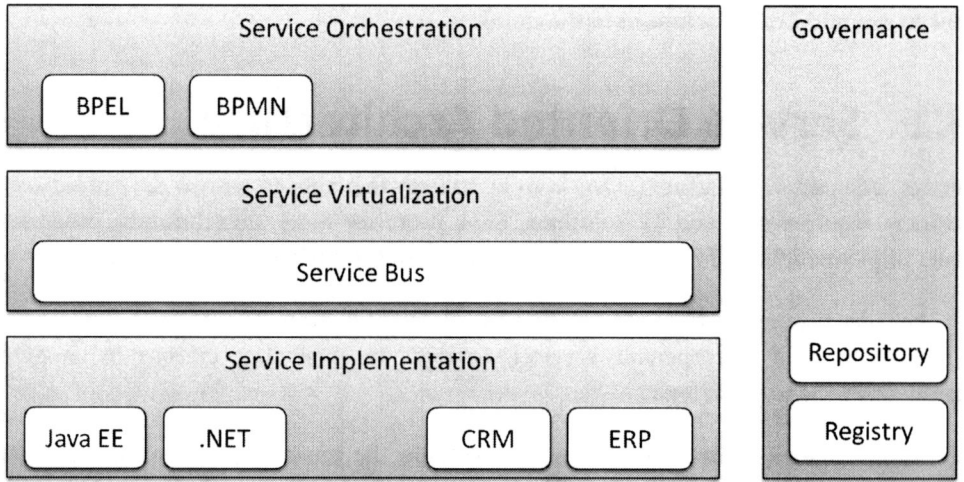

Figure 46: SOA Stack

Service Implementation

The service implementation layer contains all services. At the start of a new project, services are often implemented using either a Java EE application server or a .NET framework.

It sometimes seems as if all services in an SOA world have to be web services using SOAP over HTTP. However, the service implementation's technical interface can be *any* transport protocol e.g. RMI for Enterprise Java Beans (EJB), JMS, email, or even FTP for legacy systems.

Also, the service implementation itself is not limited to Java EE and .NET. The service can be implemented using any language and protocol: starting from REST based web service implemented in Ruby or Groovy, to a legacy billing system written in C++ with an ftp interface expecting a flat file - anything is possible.

Service Virtualization

In the world of SOA, the service virtualization layer often replaces the traditional enterprise application integration (EAIs) system. A service bus is the principal performer here. Its tasks are to reduce the complexity of service integration i.e. to bridge transport protocols and perform the message routing and message transformation. A service bus can also aggregate messages or callout to other services - but will never orchestrate services (service orchestration occurs in the orchestration layer).

Now, the key feature of a service bus is that it is *configuration driven* and optimized for stateless routing with high throughput. Looking at the tasks listed above, you will realize that they can be achieved using an EAI broker. But in that case, you would have to build and deploy your changes. Whereas with a service bus, only a configuration change is required and that can be done online (with a running bus).

Configuration Driven

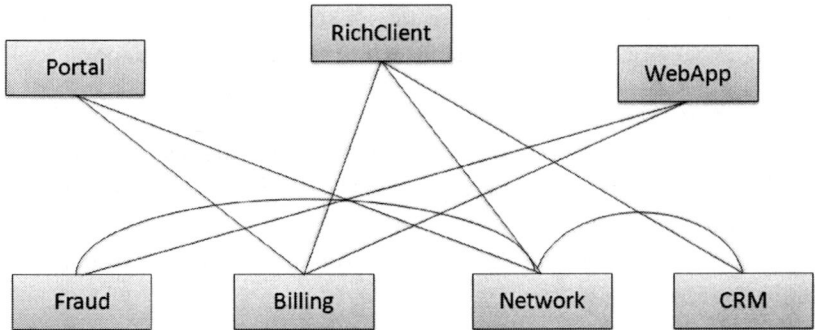

Figure 47: Point to Point Integration with Square Number of Interfaces

Since all clients talk to the service bus and the service bus forwards incoming service invocations to the services, the overall complexity of the distributed system is reduced. The

Reduced Complexity

service bus reduces a square number of interfaces between n instances (clients and services) to a linear number of interfaces.

See Figure 47 and Figure 48 for an illustration of this point using a telecommunications scenario.

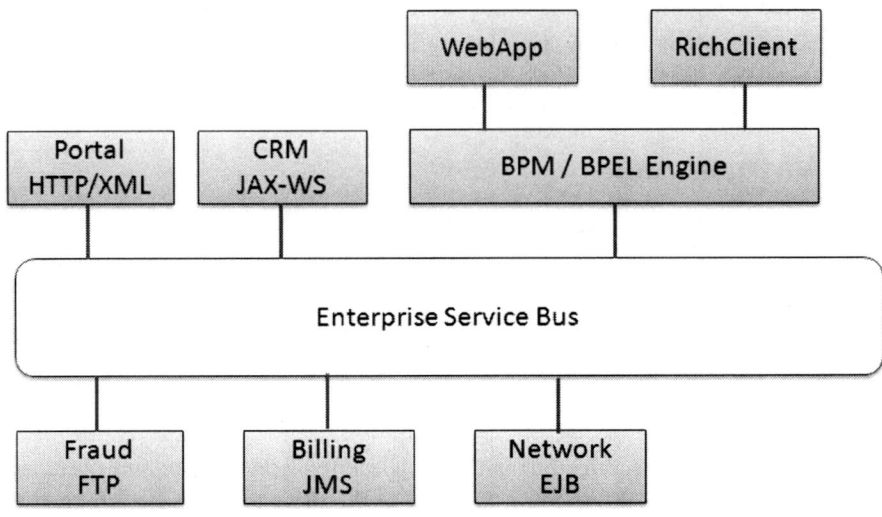

Figure 48: Service Bus with Linear Number of Interfaces

Decoupling   The service bus decouples the caller on the client side (which could be a BPEL or a BPMN engine), from the physical location and the data format of service implementation.

Canonical Data Model   Larger companies, in particular, should consider putting a canonical data model (CDN) in place; this is also referred to as common data model (CDM). For example, every major car company probably has a unique data type representation of a car's tire throughout the company. As another example, a large telecommunications company would benefit from a unique data type representation of a SIM card or a customer address record that can be used in all subsidiaries across the globe.

The canonical data model is implemented in the virtualization layer. Only non-conforming client data formats (e.g. a proprietary client, which cannot be changed and has to be integrated after an acquisition) have to be transformed to the canonical data format of the service virtualization layer. In addition, the CDN of the service bus is transformed to the proprietary format of the service implementation, if necessary.

Service Orchestration

Service orchestration occurs in the top of the three layers. In this layer, multi-step business logic is executed by a Business Process Modeling (BPM) engine or a Business Process Execution Language (BPEL) engine. Service orchestration is never performed by the service bus.

Instead of invoking the service implementation directly, the BPM system always invokes services which are exposed on the service bus and it is the service bus that decides where to route these calls.

A BPM engine, sometimes referred to as a workflow system, is well suited to long running processes (stretching over many years), human interactions (including web based forms) and the versioning of services.

A key benefit of using a BPM tool is that the business architect can model the workflow (usually with the support of a technical architect). The modeled workflow is then executed in the workflow engine.

This means the workflow is a visually easy to understand contract of the business model, which at the same time is executable. The workflow also serves as documentation for business processes – so the documentation is never out of synchronization with the business process.

When only orchestration is required on a technical level for web services, a BPEL engine is perhaps preferable to a BPM system. With BPEL, there is no human interaction (and no state is persisted between the individual steps of a workflow).

BPEL4People is an extension of BPEL that includes asynchronous communication with humans and supports four eye scenarios and escalations.

By orchestrating and reusing existing services in BPM or BPEL engines or other clients, we expect to reduce the gap between business requirements and IT solutions. This is because changes in the business logic do not require the service implementation to be rebuilt, tested and deployed.

Governance

Governance is the process that ensures your SOA project is carried out according to best practices, architectural principles, legal and industry regulations etc.

OASIS definition   I'd like to give you a taste of the official OASIS definition, which is a touch more formal: "*Governance is the prescribing of conditions and constraints consistent with satisfying common goals and the structures and processes needed to define and respond to actions taken towards realizing those goals.*"

These days, the importance of governance for SOA is widely understood. An SOA strategy can only be successful if governance is defined and enforced.

Governance is about service lifecycle management and service portfolio management. One governance issue pertains to determining what production ready service means: what metadata does a production ready service need? Who decides when it is in production? Where can you find the service? Whose number will be called if the service is not functioning properly?

Anne Thomas Manes has written an article about governance "The Elephant Has Left the Building", which I recommend you read (my informal definition of governance is derived from this article):

```
http://intelligententerprise.informationweek.com/showArticle?articleID=16
4301126
```

Governance certainly involves a lot of documents, a lot of processes and a lot of communication. Registries and repositories are the middleware components that enforce governance.

Registry   A registry is an electronic listing with metadata of your services. The key idea is that you somehow have to be able to browse and lookup your services, since you can only reuse a service if you know that it exists.

The standard that defines how to talk to a registry is called Universal Description, Discovery and Integration, or UDDI. UDDI uses SOAP messages to lookup and submit service listings to a registry.

There is an ongoing discussion about the usefulness of registries and where to position them. The idea of having a global UDDI registry failed to materialize when IBM, SAP and Microsoft announced their discontinued support.

In a classical SOA world with SOAP based web services, registries are often positioned as a runtime mechanism. I personally don't share this viewpoint, since too many unanswered questions remain: what if the registry cannot resolve a service at runtime? Can you afford to change your infrastructure so that every client does a service lookup in the registry at first and all available service implementations automatically register to the registry? What if your services are JMS, file or ftp based and haven't got a WSDL?

Best practice is to leave the runtime resolution of a service request as a task for the service bus. The service bus in turn uses a registry to import the service interfaces of the service implementations and to export its proxy services for the service bus clients.

Repository

A repository is used at design time. It either stores files directly, or else cross references back to a document management system. Repositories become handy when resources, such as XSD files, are required at different locations, and in order to ensure that everything is consistent, you want to guarantee that only one copy of a file exists.

The repository is responsible for all SOA assets and their relationships. It supports the lifecycle management and versioning, dependency management and impact analysis for change processes, as well as enforcing service reuse.

5.2 Oracle Fusion Middleware

Oracle Fusion Middleware (OFM) is one of the most important and expansive middleware offerings currently available. Quite a few of the core Oracle SOA products (such as the Oracle BPM, Oracle Service Bus and Oracle WebLogic server), came into being with the acquisition of BEA. Take a look at Oracle's Fusion Middleware offerings under the following URL:

http://www.oracle.com/technetwork/middleware/fusion-middleware/overview/index.html

At the time of writing, Oracle Fusion Middleware comprises more than 70 individual products and bundles, some of which are beyond the scope of this introduction. Also, let's not forget that the focus of this book is cloud computing. Based on these factors, I decided to narrow down the list of products I will cover. We will therefore be dealing purely with those products that you would most likely use in your own environment, and the ones that you would encounter working as a consultant across industries.

The following list shows the Oracle products covered in detail in this book:

- WebLogic
- Oracle Service Bus
- Oracle BPM
- Oracle Repository
- Oracle Registry

Figure 49 provides a summary overview of the core Oracle Fusion Middleware products: shaded products are those which are most extensively covered in this book, whereas products with a dashed frame are just examples of the integration of non-Oracle products:

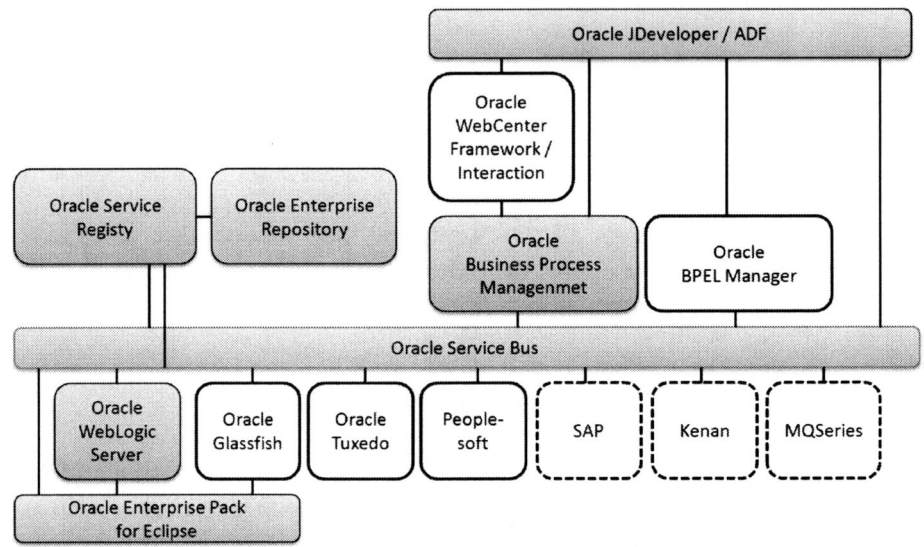

Figure 49: Oracle Fusion Middleware Core Products. Dashed lines are examples of non-Oracle products.

SOA Suite

Oracle SOA Suite is a subset of Oracle Fusion Middleware, that contains Oracle Service Bus and some additional products such as Oracle BPEL Process Manager, Business Activity Monitoring and Complex Event Processing.

Service Component Architecture

With the release of Oracle SOA Suite 11g, the Service Component Architecture (SCA) was introduced. SCA contains a language independent *assembly model* that deals with the aggregation of *components* and the linking of components through wiring to build *composites* (a standardized deployment model). A composite can contain a mix of components such as BPEL, human workflow and the Oracle Mediator.

Components are accessed via service interfaces, and gain access to other components by referencing their service interface. Wires are used for interconnections as shown in Figure 50.

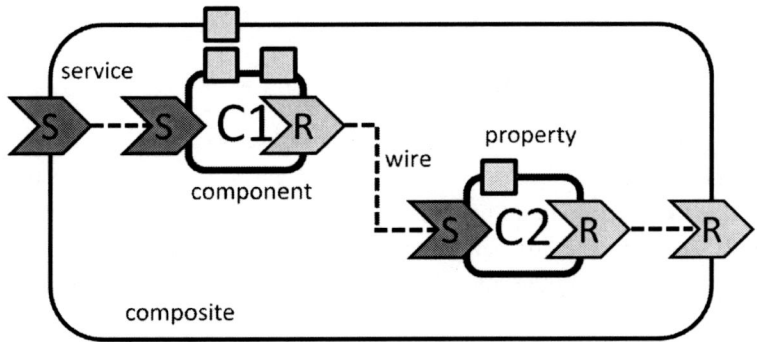

Figure 50: SCA Composite

Examples of components include an Oracle BPEL process, an Oracle Mediator, Oracle Business Rule, human workflow task, or other implementation technology. Designers use graphical tools to create composites.

For business data such as service parameters and returns values, SCA suggests the use of Service Data Objects (SDO).

Oracle Application Development Framework (ADF) simplifies the Java EE development and is directly supported by JDeveloper. ADF implements the model-view-controller (MVC) pattern. The model abstracts the business service layer and allows the view and controller to work with different business service implementations.   *ADF*

Development Environments

There is a long history of integrated development environments (IDEs) for OFM. Starting with WebLogic 9, in which an Eclipsed based version of Workshop was bundled with WLS, which became increasingly useful and popular. And before WebLogic 9 there was a Workshop, which wasn't Eclipse based, and to put it politely, was no fun to work with at all.

With WebLogic 10.3, which was the first version of WebLogic released by Oracle, things changed. Oracle now offers an Oracle Enterprise Pack for Eclipse (OEPE) that contains the necessary WebLogic plugins that you can add on top of a bare Eclipse installation. The newest version of OEPE also supports the Glassfish application server.   *OEPE*

JDeveloper However, the main IDE regarding Oracle Fusion Middleware is Oracle's JDeveloper. Oracle Enterprise Pack for Eclipse will be offered for Oracle Service Bus and for the Java development with WebLogic and Glassfish, whereas JDeveloper will cover everything from Java to Oracle Service Bus and to BPM.

5.3 Oracle WebLogic Server

I would like to use the following paragraphs to provide a quick overview of the most important aspects of WebLogic. My intention is to explain the overall system architecture in conjunction with the underlying building blocks of WebLogic. It is important to understand these details since, on the one hand, most other Oracle middleware products are based on WebLogic server and, on the other hand, details such as clustering JMS and JDBC aren't easy to understand - even in a classical, non-cloud architecture.

There is no way that this short introduction can replace some thorough training. A couple of days of professional training is money and time well invested if you are new to WebLogic or Oracle Fusion Middleware, since the alternative is to read through thousands of manual pages. The complexity is not due to the Java EE standards, but rather to all of the WLS specific details of which you have to be aware.

Even if you consider yourself a WebLogic expert, I recommend skimming over the following text just to make sure you grasp everything we will need later when we explore ways to efficiently run WLS in the cloud.

Basics and Terminology

Installation Let's have a quick look at the installation of WebLogic. The product installation creates a directory that was historically named BEA_HOME directory, but is nowadays commonly referred to as ORACLE_MIDDLEWARE directory (albeit not yet consistently). This directory contains all necessary jar files and scripts - the most important of which is the weblogic.jar containing the weblogic.Server class. If you haven't already done so, I encourage you to download the installer and to install the product on your local machine in order to gain your own experience. The installer comes with a GUI (even on Unix) and the installation only takes a couple of minutes.

Domain The base which contains all other WebLogic resources for a particular project is called a domain. A domain is defined as a logically related group of WebLogic servers. Looking at the file system, it is correct to say that a domain is simply a folder that contains all necessary files for a project, except the installation of the product itself.

You should expect to find the following files (amongst others) in a domain directory:

- Start and stop scripts for the servers under DOMAIN_DIR/bin
- The core configuration file in DOMAIN_DIR/config/config.xml
- Log files for each server in DOMAIN_DIR/servers/SERVER_NAME/logs

It's best practice to keep the domains in a directory which is not a subdirectory of ORACLE_MIDDLEWARE. There are a number of reasons for this:

- Firstly, domain upgrades are easier and more obvious if a domain is not located in a subdirectory of a certain version of the WebLogic installation.
- Secondly, you want to have different file owners and permissions for the WebLogic installation and the domain directories anyway, so a domain owner cannot change or accidentally corrupt the content of the WebLogic installation directory on a multi project machine.

Server

Within a domain, one or many servers are configured. Here, the term "server" is not used as synonym for a machine, a computer or a hardware server, because a server in the WebLogic world is a running JVM. Actually, I am tempted to say it is a JVM running on your favorite operating system, which is still the easiest way to visualize it.

Nowadays, it could also be a JVM running directly on a hypervisor (a virtualization platform) such as Oracle VM. Virtualization is covered in chapter 12.

Admin Server

On a laptop or a development machine with limited RAM and CPU cores, you will only have one WebLogic server in your domain. Since it is the only server, there will be a web based administration console deployed on it and the server will be called an admin server.

Managed Server

Certainly, for large production deployments, you want to have more than one server within a domain. These additional servers are called managed servers because they are managed by the admin server. Once you have your application ready, you will deploy it on the managed servers, and not on the admin server.

The admin server is a full-blown WLS, but it doesn't process requests. Actually, it is even more than a normal managed server, as it hosts the admin web console, it collects JMX based runtime data from all managed servers, and it writes a domain-wide log file.

The managed servers share the load and do all the work, and the admin server is used for monitoring and configuration. In fact, you should design your domains in a way that you can even shut down the admin server if it will not be needed for a while.

No single point of failure

When shutting down the admin server, you will lose the domain-wide logging (if enabled), together with the possibility of using the admin console. Still, the managed servers in a domain will continue to do their work and process client requests.

When starting up, a managed server will try to contact the admin server to retrieve its configuration data, which is then cached locally.

Managed Server Independence

It's important to understand that there is only ever one admin server. Still, the admin server is not a single point of failure since the managed servers will happily continue doing their work without the admin server. Once they have their local copy of the configuration data, you can start them without the admin server. This feature is called managed server independence (MSI) and is enabled by default.

You can have as many managed servers as required within a single domain. Quite a few people have doubts about the scalability of a domain, yet I have met customers who run up to 40 managed servers within a single domain. However, a more typical domain will consist of an admin server with just two or three managed servers.

Nodemanager

There is another process which is not a part of a WebLogic domain: the nodemanager is installed and configured once per machine and enables starting and stopping of WebLogic server processes from the web based admin console.

Without the nodemanager, there is no way the admin server could start a managed server, not even on the same machine. Of course you could always use ssh to open a shell on a remote machine and run the WebLogic start script, but if you like the comfort of using the admin console, then you must also configure the nodemanager.

To be able to access the nodemanager, it has to be running. The nodemanager process is started when booting a Unix machine (you have to add it to the boot sequence). On Windows, the nodemanager is installed as a service and runs in the background (Oracle provides a script with the WebLogic installation to install the nodemanager as a Windows service).

The nodemanager keeps track of the managed servers that it has started. With the default configuration, it acts as a watchdog and restarts a managed server that fails.

NODEMANAGER AUTO-RESTART AND MEMORY LEAKS

Quite often the nodemanager's auto-restart feature is the last remedy for unstable and buggy applications with memory leaks i.e. in situations where the development team has long since left the office, leaving the operations team to figure out for themselves how to operate the application.

In any case, the nodemanager is certainly a useful mechanism to improve the availability of an important application.

Finally, the nodemanager is a prerequisite for whole-server migration, which is explained in the following section.

When you configure a machine, you link a WebLogic server instance to the physical hardware where it's running. This relationship is helpful when starting a WebLogic server with the admin console via the nodemanager: you only specify the WebLogic server instance and the admin server will then contact the corresponding machine in order to start the server.

Machine

WebLogic Cluster

A set of managed servers can be configured as a cluster. The admin server itself is never part of the cluster. A cluster is a feature of WebLogic Server for which you pay extra money (clustering is only available in the WebLogic Enterprise Edition and not in the WebLogic Standard Edition). Don't confuse the WebLogic cluster with external cluster software such as Veritas, Sun or with the DRBD block device (the foundation for a Linux cluster).

A WebLogic cluster provides failover capability because it replicates the state of HTTP sessions and stateful session beans. To enable in-memory session replication, set the `<persistent-store-type>` in the `weblogic-webapp.xml` descriptor file as follows:

Session replication

```
<session-descriptor>
        <timeout-secs>300</timeout-secs>
        <persistent-store-type>replicated_if_clustered
        </persistent-store-type>
</session-descriptor>
```

If enabled and configured correctly, the primary session context is replicated to a second WebLogic server and a secondary session is created. Should the primary session (P) fail for t=t1, the requests will be directed to the secondary session (S). Once the cluster detects the failed server, a new primary session is created as shown in Figure 51.

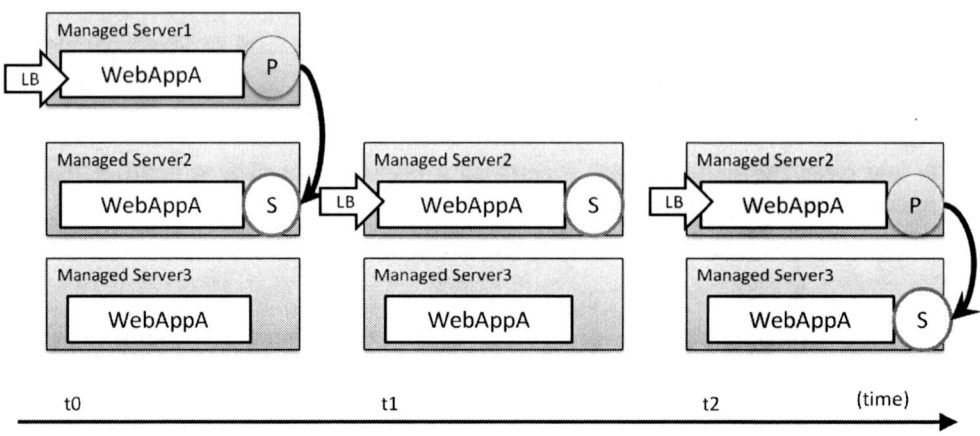

Figure 51: HTTP Session Replication

There is no load balancer required for EJBs: Replica-aware client stubs contain the load balancing and the fail-over functionality for clustered EJBs.

Load balancing Load balancing for HTTP is frequently misunderstood: it is never, ever provided by a WebLogic cluster. Instead, HTTP load balancing for a cluster is always achieved with an external load balancer. The WebLogic installation includes plugins for the most common web servers (Apache, SunOne and Microsoft). These plugins need to be installed and configured on the web server. The web server plugin then acts as a load balancer for HTTP and also includes failover capabilities. See section 10.2 for a more detailed discussion of load balancers.

Deployment In addition, you can deploy your applications to a cluster as one, single unit. Later, if you expand the cluster by adding more servers to it, the deployment will be automatically available on the added members since they are part of the same cluster.

Whole-server migration A WebLogic cluster has an almost Terminator-like self-healing feature which is called whole-server migration; if one of the managed servers in a cluster dies and cannot be restarted, it will automatically be restarted on another machine. Actually, one of the cluster members, the elected cluster-master, will orchestrate this migration from the failed machine to the candidate machine. When using whole-server migration the cluster will migrate a whole server to another machine, including all its configurations and all its deployments.

CLUSTER, MIGRATION AND FILE SYSTEMS

It is much easier to work with a shared file system such as NFS or ZFS. However, a distributed WebLogic cluster with local file systems on every machine is also possible.

In a WebLogic cluster, there is no mechanism that will automatically transfer a file from one machine to another machine. Server migration on the other hand, requires that all necessary files for configuration and deployment exist on the target machine and in the same location. So, at least for server migration, it is beneficial to either have a shared file system or avoid using any local files.

Service migration is another WebLogic option which provides availability for pinned services. The term 'service' is used here generically to cover services such as Java Messaging Service (JMS) or Java Transaction API (JTA). *Service migration*

These services can be migrated from one managed server to another using service migration. In the past, service migration was a purely manual process, yet since the release of WebLogic 11g it is an automatic service (yet can still be done manually if so desired).

Oracle Coherence

Oracle Coherence was originally developed by Tangosol; a company acquired by Oracle in April 2007. Coherence is an in-memory data replication mechanism for the JVM that works as a transactional cache.

Oracle SOA Suite uses Coherence for replication, and a WebLogic cluster for the transaction logs only. It is expected that the next release will only require Coherence. *SOA cluster*

5.4 Oracle Service Bus

OSB versus OESB/Mediator

Oracle Service Bus is the former BEA service bus (known as AquaLogic Service Bus or ALSB during BEA times). When Oracle acquired BEA, Oracle already had its own service bus, so renamed it Oracle Enterprise Service Bus (OESB). Since the release of Oracle SOA Suite 11g, the Oracle Enterprise Service Bus is called Mediator (because it is used to mediate between the SOA Suite components). In OFM 11g, Mediator is a component in an SCA assembly and is only used for routing and transformations between SCA-components within a composite, but not for wiring SCA components externally.

Oracle Service Bus is independent of the Oracle SOA Suite. Therefore, it is the better choice if you are looking at external service virtualization. Oracle integrated its JCA framework into the Oracle Service Bus, which means that JCA adapters of the BPEL product can be now be correctly deployed with OSB.

The remainder of this chapter deals with the Oracle Service Bus (OSB), the former BEA product.

Oracle Service Bus

Oracle Service Bus implements the layer that separates service implementation from service orchestration. Service Bus itself acts as a service virtualization layer. To better understand service virtualization and the kind of problems it solves, let's take a look at the following usage scenario.

Imagine you are running a successful business chartering dive boats off the coast of Australia, Fiji, the Philippines and South Africa. Every boat in your fleet has a little device that allows guests to transmit their underwater pictures and videos. These pictures will be displayed seconds later in all your booking offices world-wide (as a PR exercise to attract even more customers). Let's also assume, that the boat's device is using SOAP based web services via mobile internet to contact the server at your headquarters and to transmit the images (with some additional metadata such as location and visibility) underwater.

To improve the system's performance, one day you will have to migrate the server to a new hosting provider. Simultaneously, you'd like to update a particular service from version v1.0 to v2.0 with new functionality and apply some changes in the interface.

However, installing new software for the devices onto all of the boats requires a staggered approach, which takes time, and can only be completed when the boats come back to the harbor. The installation could take up to three weeks for the most expensive and remote trips (those trips that we all dream of). At no time will all the boats be accessible simultaneously. This is why both versions of the software will overlap and be live for a while.

With the SOAP based web services, the location of the service is in the <port> section of the WSDL. The <types> section defines the data types of the interface using XML schema tags. So, most of its clients will be pointing to the former location of the server using an old interface version.

Now, you probably wish you had some "logical switch" that could detect the requests for version v1.0 and send them to the still active implementation, and direct the requests for v2.0 to the new implementation.

With Oracle Service Bus you can easily adapt things to accommodate such changes. With an SOA in place, the clients will talk to the service bus instead of directly talking to the service implementation.

The following section explains proxy and business services, which are essential for functionality of Oracle Service Bus. Thereafter, I will continue to use this example to clarify how a service bus helps to solve the aforementioned problems.

Proxy and Business Services

The service bus uses a proxy service as an endpoint for incoming requests. A transport layer abstracts the proxy from the transport protocol. So, the functionality of the proxy service is independent of the incoming transport protocol:

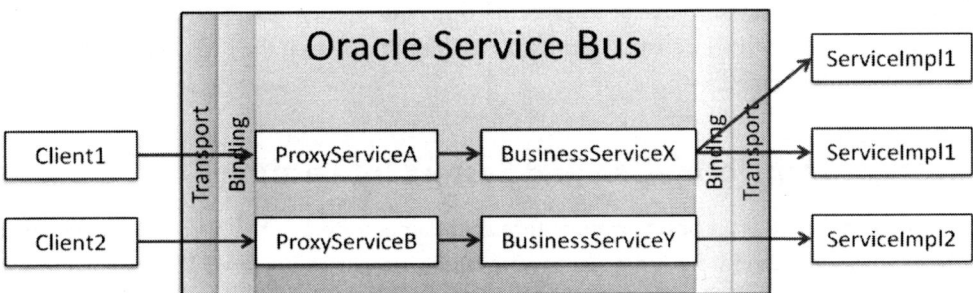

Figure 52: Oracle Service Bus Design

After the transport layer, the message passes through a binding layer, which transforms the message into a canonical, logical representation. The message parts, such as payload or header, will be accessible via variables such as $body or $header.

The outgoing endpoint in Oracle Service Bus is called business service. The naming is unfortunately a bit misleading since the business service is not actually the service implementation itself: the business service is just a piece of configuration within Oracle Service Bus (but separate from a proxy service), which defines the interface and location of the service implementation.

Location Transparency

The proxy service defines to whichever business service the message is routed. When you change the routing to another business service, another service implementation will be called. This is an easy and elegant way to deal with the issue of location transparency, as per our example when the address or the port of the server changes.

Content Based Routing

Actually, there is much more that can be done in a proxy service. Inside a proxy service, you can define a message flow to include if-then decisions, loops, alerts, Java call-outs and message transformations. Referring back to our example, you can check a message for the content of a version element in the header or an XML <version> in the message itself. Based on this expression you can decide to route the business service representing the implementation v1.0 or v2.0.

This is how you configure the "logical switch" for our example. The technical name for it is 'content-based routing'.

Compared to let's say a message selector in JMS, the beauty here is that content based routing will work with all transport protocols: it doesn't matter if the proxy service is SOAP based, file, JMS or email.

Message Transformation and System Integration

Now, imagine there is an online photo store that comes with a SOAP web service API that you want to integrate into your system - something similar to Flickr or Picasa. This photo store accepts SOAP messages, yet the format, when compared to your own application, will be different.

You therefore have to change the incoming SOAP requests using an XQuery or XSLT transformation in the proxy service of the service bus, to match the format of the new system.

Protocols

Oracle Service Bus supports a number different transport protocols. Apart from the list of standard protocol like HTTP, email, file, ftp, JMS, EJB 3 etc, there are a number of Oracle product-specific protocols supported:

- Local transport for proxy services calling other proxy services directly.
- SB transports to invoke another service bus proxy using RMI.
- SOA-DIRECT protocol for SOA Suite interaction.
- BPEL transport to interact with Orcale BPEL Process Manager.
- DSP to interact with Oracle Data Services Platform.
- JPD for calling Oracle WebLogic Integration Java Process Definition.
- MQ transport to interact with IBM WebSphere MQ.
- Tuxedo transport with transactional integrity.

Architecture

Oracle Service Bus consists of a number of deployments running on WebLogic server. You can see these deployments if you open the WebLogic admin console and look under deployments.

The newest version, OSB 11g, is packaged without WebLogic application server and uses the Oracle Unified Installer. OSB 11g comes with a Coherence based result cache, support for EJB 3 and the integration of the SOA Suite with SOA-DIRECT protocol. This is also the first version to come with the Java Derby database instead of the Pointbase database (which was bundled with the previous versions for non-commercial usage).

OSB 11g

During the installation, a database is required. However, there no state is stored. The sole purpose of the database is for the reporting feature of OSB.

You can connect Oracle Service Bus to the Oracle Service Registry. To do so, specify the URL of the registry in the service bus admin console.

Most things written about WebLogic also hold true for Oracle Service Bus. There are however a number of restrictions that apply to OSB, but not to WLS:

- If there is more than one managed server, you have to put the managed servers into a cluster. OSB uses uniformly distributed destinations, which only work in a cluster. We will cover implications and restrictions of distributed destination in the cloud later on in section 9.3.
- You can only have one OSB cluster within a domain. This limitation does not exist for a WebLogic only domain.
- When expanding the OSB cluster, you have to manually add JMS server, JMS system modules and a number of distributed destinations to the newly added server.

5.5 Oracle BPM / WebCenter

Oracle BPM provides the ability to model, simulate and deploy business processes. Oracle BPM is based on the former BEA Aqualogic BPM product (ALBPM). BEA bought a small company with the name Fuego in order to include ALBPM in their middleware suite.

The new Oracle BPM is fully based on SCA and the ADF frontend WebCenter Framework Integration. It consists of the Studio and Composer to model and implement the business processes, and the BPM Run Time with the BPM engine for the execution of the processes.

WebCenter Framework — Oracle's portal framework, WebCenter Framework, extends the classical enterprise portal functionality with advanced personalization, a look and feel based on themes and skins, mashups, and the Common Enterprise Meta Data Service (MDS) for the storage of these settings.

WebCenter Spaces brings in the functionality to create social communities and networking. Private dashboards and team sites for global teams can be created dynamically and integrated with other information sources.

Portals — Oracle owns at least four different portal products already but there are more portals that have to be integrated due to the Sun acquisition:

- WebCenter is Oracle's key portal product.
- Oracle Portal
- WebLogic Portal (WLP).
- WebCenter Interaction (which is different from WebCenter) is the former BEA Aqualogic User Interface (ALUI), which in turn was the former Plumtree portal. WebCenter interaction can be used to create more sophisticated user interactions based on portals, collaborative communities and composite applications.

ESB OR EAI?

A great deal of confusion surrounds enterprise service buses (ESB) in general, and enterprise application integration (EAI) brokers.

OSB is Oracle's new version of BEA's Aqualogic Service Bus (ALSB). However, BEA also used to offer a classical EAI system called WebLogic Integration (WLI), which is still on Oracle's price list but will be discontinued.

Comparing OSB and WLI side by side in a table will show you that both list the same transport protocols such as SOAP based web services, file, (s)ftp, JMS, RMI, etc.

Both systems also come with the ability to model an executable graphical flow, which is called message flow for OSB and Java Process Definition (JPD) for WLI.

The two key aspects that distinguish OSB from a WLI are as follows:

- OSB is configuration driven. You can apply all changes on-line. You don't have to build an ear file. You change the routing, activate and it's done. If so desired, you could also build and test them with an IDE.

- OSB is stateless (it does use a database, but only for reporting).

- OSB provides transactional integrity and delivery guarantees for message flows, but it is stateless.

BPA Suite and ARIS

Oracle's Business Process Analysis Suite (BPA) is integrated with the Oracle BPM. The key feature of the BPA suite is the support for the round-trip engineering of the ARIS models. The acronym ARIS is so commonly used that the real name (Architecture of Integrated Information Systems) is often forgotten.

These ARIS models can be converted to the executable BPEL/BPMN language, enriched by the SOA developer using JDeveloper, executed in the process engine and synchronized back to the ARIS format.

Design Time

The Studio modeling environment used to be Eclipse based, but is now based on JDeveloper (see section 5.2 for a detailed discussion of IDEs for OFM). BPM Studio supports the Business Process Management Notation (BPMN) 2.0 standard.

BPM Composer is a web-based, user-friendly collaboration tool that enables process analysts to collaborate with process developers. Using Composer, a process analyst can create new projects based on a catalogue of preconfigured components created by a process developer, such as services, tasks and rules.

Runtime

Oracle BPM Run Time is the process engine that controls the workflows. The BPM process engine interprets BPEL and BPMN. The BPM runtime provides the functionality for user interaction, process management, and monitoring and system administration.

Architecture

The process engine for Oracle BPM runs on WebLogic server and supporting transactions. Oracle BPM needs an enterprise engine database to store the state of the process instances running on this instance.

5.6 Oracle Service Registry

The Oracle Service Registry is a UDDI version 3 compliant registry. The registry is the former BEA Aqualogic Service Registry (ALSR). Please note that WebLogic itself comes with an internal UDDI registry which only supports UDDI version 2.

Systinet The registry was built by a company named Systinet, founded by Roman Stanek. Roman also founded Netbeans and GoodData (the latter being a company that offers on-demand business intelligence running as SaaS and hosted on Amazon AWS). Systinet was bought by Mercury Interactive, which in turn was bought by HP.

Interestingly enough, other companies such as Oracle and TIBCO also licensed Systinet's registry technology. This is the reason why almost all of the big companies' registry products are technically rather similar.

A common usage scenario for the registry demonstrates how registries enable governance:

Often two registries are set up. There is a publishing registry, which points to a production registry; both share an encrypted connection. Developers publish their services to the publishing registry. A mini-workflow informs a person to check if the service is working correctly, to verify if all metadata is supplied and so on. When the person in charge approves the service, the service is promoted from the publishing to the production registry.

Publish / production registries

On the other hand, clients such as BPM or BPEL tools can only consume services from the production registry.

Architecture

During Systinet times, the registry used to be a single jar file that could be run standalone in a JVM. Nowadays, Oracle Service Registry is running on top of WebLogic Server.

Publishing and production registries use SSL for encrypted communication. X.509 certificates are used to establish trust between the registries.

5.7 Oracle Enterprise Repository

Oracle Enterprise Repository is the former BEA product AquaLogic Enterprise Repository (ALER). Governance is a hot SOA topic and that's why in February 2010 Oracle bought Amberpoint, another top governance platform provider.

Oracle Enterprise repository has a built-in workflow engine. This workflow engine comes with preconfigured standard processes that can be modified to meet your own governance requirements. The repository can bi-directionally synchronize information with Oracle Service Registry and track the usage of resources.

The Oracle Enterprise repository can retrieve runtime information from the service bus to improve the usage and dependency analysis for the items stored in the repository.

Interaction with service bus

Architecture

Oracle Enterprise Repository is running on top of WebLogic server. During installation a database is needed. After installing the repository software, you have to use the domain wizard to create a WebLogic domain to support the repository.

6 Designing for the Cloud

This chapter explores how to use Oracle Fusion Middleware in the cloud. It is the base for the subsequent chapters about databases, scalability, availability and monitoring.

We will start with design principles for the computing cloud. Then follow with a detailed comparison of the main IaaS providers. After that we'll cover different strategies for building cloud images, and how to introduce a design blueprint for distributed WebLogic applications in the cloud.

6.1 Design Principles

You may wonder if a certain design is required or if you have to follow certain principles to build applications for the cloud. Often you read, no, just go ahead and build scalable applications as you would do in a classical, non-cloud environment.

This is only half of the truth. Of course any scalable and distributed application will perform well in the cloud. But then, if your application is based on complex middleware, such as WebLogic Server or Service Bus, you need to understand how to provision these environments in the cloud, and how to benefit from (or when to avoid) built-in middleware features that support availability and scalability.

Designing for Availability

Consider that you can suddenly lose an instance in the cloud. Sometimes this is called "plan for failure". Losing one part of your distributed application shouldn't stop your whole business. This is an important principle; to achieve this, decouple the building blocks of your application and use asynchronous communication.

I will cover the aspects that are vital for understanding availability in chapter 9.

If you lose an instance, you want to be informed about it, so you require a monitoring system. Monitoring is covered in chapter 11.

Designing for Scalability

Sometimes this is simply called "elasticity". I prefer the term scalability here, because it encompasses more; it includes topics such as load balancing, content distribution networks, and auto scaling.

Load balancing is offered as an AWS cloud service to distribute incoming requests. Amazon's Content Distribution Network, CloudFront, provides scalability for static content.

Rapid elasticity is a unique feature of the cloud, based on AWS auto scaling. To provide true elasticity, you have to design a system architecture where new instances can be started quickly and running instances are resilient to restarts.

All these aspects of scalability are covered in chapter 9.

6.2 IaaS Platform Choice

Searching the web reveals dozens of postings from people evaluating Amazon Web Service and Rackspace Cloud, and also includes some Amazon vs. Rackspace comparisons. I encourage you to do your own Google search to get an overview of these stories. I am trying to keep it neutral and stick to an analysis of the different features of the platforms. Few users have explored both platform options. Sometimes, the initial decision to go with one or the other IaaS platform is based on a particular killer feature (or its absence), but in general you should compare the entire offerings including all provided services and non-functional aspects -such as costs and SLAs.

I have summarized the differences in Table 3 and marked the better option in bold letters, wherever this was possible.

Comparing the performance of both platforms in an objective way would be an interesting and challenging task, but it's also walking on thin ice. The actual performance difference that you could observe for a particular application depends on many factors and cannot be quantified easily and in general terms. We analyze some of these factors in more detail later on in the chapter about scalability. In general, nobody will be able to easily predict the performance for an arbitrary application running on a cloud platform.

If you try to conduct such a comparison yourself, then don't forget that application performance per dollar spent is more important than raw system performance (measured by a more or less synthetic benchmark). So, first of all, you have to understand your application. Also, consider the non-functional requirements such as availability, which again depend on whether you start a number of small and low performing instances or one big instance. All these factors are difficult to isolate since they depend on each other.

EC2 and Rackspace Cloud Server

Looking at the features of both platforms, there is an interesting difference for applications with a small footprint. RSC offers smaller instances where the smallest instance costs less than the smallest AWS instance. If you are on a budget or you are not running a full-blown WebLogic installation, with lots of heap assigned to the JVM, this can be the better choice because RSC instances guarantee a floor limit, but allow CPU bursting. Also, an increased number of small instances results in increased overall availability.

On the high end, AWS is unbeatable with 68.4 GB of RAM -that is four times the maximum RAM you could squeeze out of the biggest RSC instance. Although using that much heap for a single JVM is only possible if you are running a 64-bit JVM.

Whereas RSC claims it wants to earn your business every month, you can get cheaper pre-paid or spot instances from AWS.

Location could be the killer criteria: There is no RSC location in Europe, but more often than not, European companies cannot use IT infrastructure in the US. Often this is due to legal issues, since it is not possible to send data out of the country of origin or region of some countries. Sometimes it is because of the risk of espionage: the more important your data is, the more likely it is that some other person, company, or even country is trying hard to get a copy of it. Latencies are another reason. Brokers try to minimize the distance to the stock exchange, because for real-time trading, fractions of a millisecond can decide millions.

The worldwide availability of cached information on a content delivery network is provided by AWS and RSC as well. Remember, that CDNs only help with reducing the latencies for the delivery of static content. Concerning presence at different geographic locations, Amazon is the clear winner, managing to cover three different cultural regions.

AWS supports a number of other cloud services, e.g. for message passing, notifications, databases, load balancing and auto scaling. All these services are off-instance and don't require any installation.

Table 3: Comparison Cloud Instances and Machines

Cloud Instances and Machines		
	Amazon Web Services EC2	**Rackspace Cloud Server**
ID Verification	Text message based	A person is calling you
Invoice based billing	Yes	
One-on-one Support	400$	**Excellent, free and 24/7**
Default access	Certificate based	Root login
CPU	Upper limit	Floor limit (with bursting)
Minimum cost in US for on demand Linux server	0.02 $ / hour (0.613 GB)	**0.015$ / hour** (256 MB RAM)
GB / $ at min RAM in US	30,6	17,1
Max RAM	68.4 GB (at 2,4$ / h)	15.8 GB (at 0,96$ /h)
GB /$ at max RAM in US	28,5	16,5
Cheaper prepaid instances	Yes	No
Locations North America	2 regions = 6 availability zones	2 data centers
Locations Europe	1 region = 2 availability zones	Planned for 2010
Locations Asia	1 region = 2 availability zones	-
Choice of geographically distributed machines	Yes	No
Resizable instances	Yes (but not via GUI)	Yes
Max emails / day	Limit for new accounts (can be raised upon request)	5000/day 250 per 20 mins
Instance bandwidth limit	No	Yes
Additional IP addresses	No	Yes $2.00 per month per IP
Floating IPs for WebLogic	No	No
NAT used	Yes	No
Reverse DNS	No	Yes
Support for IP Multicast	No	No
External Cloud Firewall	Yes: Security Groups	No (iptables, Windows FW)
Cloud Loadbalancer	Yes	No

Table 4: Cloud Images

	Cloud Images	
	AWS EC2	**RS Cloud Server**
Images with WebLogic pre-installed	Yes, WLS 10.3.3 but only in US	No
Images with custom OS	Yes	No
Support for Linux	Yes	Yes
Support for Windows	Yes	Yes
Available server images	Many	Few
Sharable server images	Yes	No

At RSC you cannot create share your images or create your own image with your particular operating system installed. I recommend that you first check if a RSC machine image exists with the operating system that suits your needs. There are a huge number of different images for AWS but a rather limited list for RSC.

RSC has a clear advantage over AWS because RSC lets you configure reverse DNS, so your email sender contains the correct DNS name, which will pass SPAM filters more likely than the AWS DNS entry. RSC also publishes a clear statement about the number of emails that can be sent per day.

Instance Storage

The approach that both platforms take regarding instance storage is quite different. Local storage at RSC is a RAID 10 and therefore it's persistent and highly available.

AWS has ephemeral local storage but offers SAN-based EBS as persistent storage which can also be used to boot the instances. EBS continues to be available when an instance is stopped and can be mounted to another instance, but only to one at a time.

At RSC you can configure an instance, create a snapshot and stop the instance. Snapshots belonging to an instance will be removed when the instance itself is removed, but they can be persisted to Cloud Files.

Cloud Storage

At first glance, the cloud storage offering of both platforms is rather similar in concept. Both platforms offer a content distribution network. Both can store metadata with objects, but only Amazon's S3 provides versioning for objects.

Maybe the most important difference, and a major drawback for the RSC offering, is that you cannot share your RSC, whereas you can store and share your EC2 AMIs on S3.

There are a few other differences, such as the shorter length of bucket- or object names, which are not practically relevant in most cases.

Table 5: Cloud Storage

	Cloud Storage	
	S3	**Cloud Files**
Grouping element	Bucket	Container
Grouping element length	63	256
Identifier length	1024	4096
Max size	5 GB	5 GB
Metadata	Yes	Yes
SLA availability	99.95 for each region	99.9
SLA durability	99.999999999% 99.99% with reduced redundancy	
Versioning	Yes	No
CDN	**CloudFront**	**Limelight**
CDN edges	8 in US 4 in Europe 3 Asia	**70 worldwide**
Server images on cloud storage	Yes	Yes

Conclusion

To conclude this summary, AWS is the more versatile and more powerful platform with more data centers at different locations.

RSC is a great choice if you prefer an easier approach combined with excellent and free support service, in contrast, the possibilities offered by AWS come with a certain level of complexity. At the moment, RSC is a compelling choice if a cloud platform located exclusively in the US, with a limited number of non-sharable machine images and a worldwide CDN, suits your needs.

On the other hand, AWS provides a fast growing, unparalleled set of cloud services such as auto scaling, elastic load balancing, monitoring, relational database server, as well as queuing and notification services. We will examine these services in the remainder of the book.

Since AWS is the more complex and expansive platform, I will focus mainly on AWS for the remaining chapters. Whenever it eems interesting enough we will have a look at RSC, too.

6.3 AMI Design

When moving to the cloud you have to think about the right AMIs for your installation. The type of AMIs you are using, how you build them, and what to include with them are the core decisions. It is definitely worth thinking about a strategy that suits you best, since changing it later comes at a high cost.

It is important to understand the shared responsibility model of the AMIs. Amazon doesn't care what kind of operating system you are running in an AMI. They don't mind if you install security patches. AWS will run any of your AMIs. So you have to make sure that they are secure and up to date.

S3 vs. EBS AMIs

This is a good opportunity to revisit EBS- and S3-backed AMIs again. See Table 6 for an overview of the differences.

As already explained in the chapter about AWS, the EBS-based AMIs are newer and nowadays they are used more frequently. They support a root image of up to 1 TByte. Even if your instance crashed, you could remount the EBS volume and save the data.

When you use the AWS management console to start an EBS-backed instance, it will only show the EBS volume. Local storage is available for EBS-backed images, too. With the command-line it is possible to attach the local storage when the instance is started. However, you cannot assign local storage to EBS-backed instances when they are already running. On the other hand, S3-backed instances start with the local instance storage already attached. There is one exception though; micro instances don't support local storage at all.

Table 6: S3 vs. EBS AMIs

	S3-backed AMI	EBS-backed AMI
Available since	Start of AWS	December 2009
Park instance?	No. Instance is running or terminated.	Yes. Instance can be stopped.
Data persistence	Data on instance storage not persisted in case of failure or termination.	Data persisted on EBS when instance is stopped or in case of failure. EBS persistence after termination can be set.
Instance storage mounted per default	Yes	No
Max size of root device	10 GByte	1 TByte
Boot time	Few seconds up to one minute	Less than 5 minutes
Create new AMI	Requires AMI tools installation and a script of several commands to rebundle AMI.	One command
AWS management based creation of new AMI	No	Yes
Charges	Instance +S3 for AMI storage	Instance usage + EBS volume usage + EBS snapshot for AMI
Upgrading	Instance attributes fixed for the life of an instance	Instance type, kernel, RAM disk, and user data can be changed while the instance is stopped.
Paid AMIs	Yes	No

EBS-backed AMIs boot quickly - a really convenient advantage. In my case, the AWS management console shows a customized EBS-backed AWS Linux image as running only a few seconds after this instance was started.

Only EBS-backed instances allow you to change the instance type, kernel and RAM disk while the instance is stopped (see the example in section **3.4** titled "Resize an Instance").

Designing for the Cloud

I guess it is obvious that EBS-backed images have a lot of advantages, but is there any room left for S3-backed AMIs? When should you still consider them? Here are some examples when to consider S3-backed images.

- Instances which are stateless and don't need any EBS file system. E.g. a full-baked or scripted AMI containing an application server that uses a remote database.
- AWS DevPay is an online billing and account management service that enables S3-backed AMIs that the client has to pay for. DevPay isn't supported by EBS-backed images.

KIBIS AND GIBIS

Don't be surprised to encounter kibis and gibis in the AWS documentation. AWS laudably uses the new binary prefixes, such as GiByte instead of the old GByte or GB when indicating a power of 2 (according to the IEC 60027-2 Amendment 2 and ISO/IEC 80000 standards - in case you are interested).

The second syllable is derived from the word "binary" -shortened to "bi", so gibi is short for "gigabinary" or 2^{30} which is in the ballpark of 1.05×10^{6}.

For a detailed discussion, take a look at the Wikipedia site:

http://en.wikipedia.org/wiki/Binary_prefix

User Data and Startup Scripts

You can pass any file or startup data when starting a new instance. When using the EC2 command-line tools simply add a --user-data-file parameter as shown in the example below.

```
ec2-run-instances ami-ID -n 3 --user-data-file payload.zip
```

Using the AWS management console, the user data can be passed as well as shown in the screenshot in Figure 53.

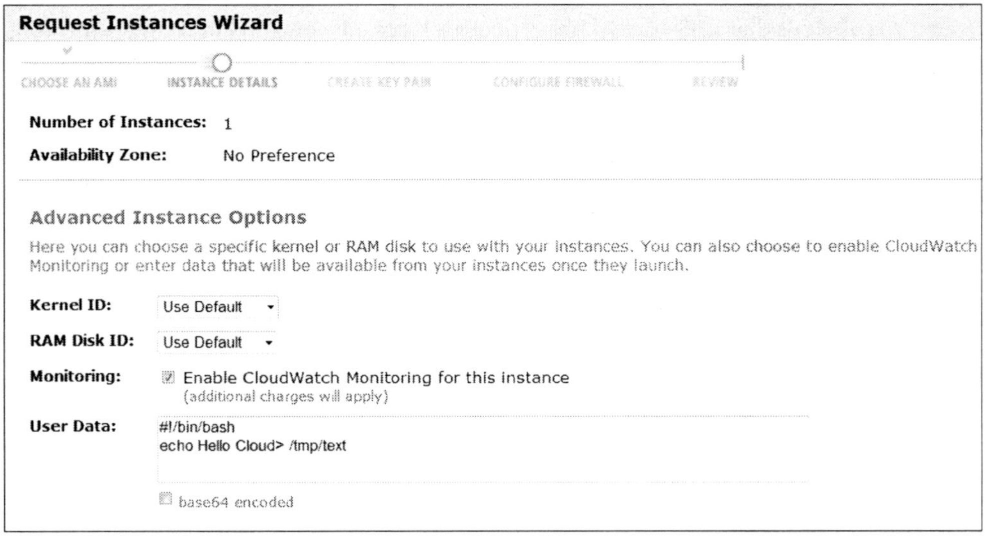

Figure 53: User Data in AWS Console

In general there is no automatic mechanism that retrieves the user data on the instance. However ,you can retrieve the data via a REST call using wget.

```
wget http://169.254.169.254/1.0/user-data -O /tmp/payload.zip
```

AMIs from Alestic and Ubuntu and the AWS Linux, implement useful additional functionality. The instance runs user-data starting with the two characters #! as the root user on the first boot.

Running a script at startup of an instance is the core mechanism to provide scripted configuration for AMIs.

runurl

Eric Hammond from Alestic published a little utility that extends the user-data mechanism even further. The runurl utility runs a remote script which is specified by a URL with the following syntax.

```
runurl URL [ARGS]...
```

The runurl utility can be installed with the following commands:

```
sudo wget -qO/usr/bin/runurl run.alestic.com/runurl
sudo chmod 755 /usr/bin/runurl
```

The advantage of this approach is that you can run any configuration script from a centralized script repository, which could be stored on any web server or on S3 as shown in Figure 54. There is no need to pass the whole script to the starting instance, just the sequence of commands for the configuration.

Centralized scripting

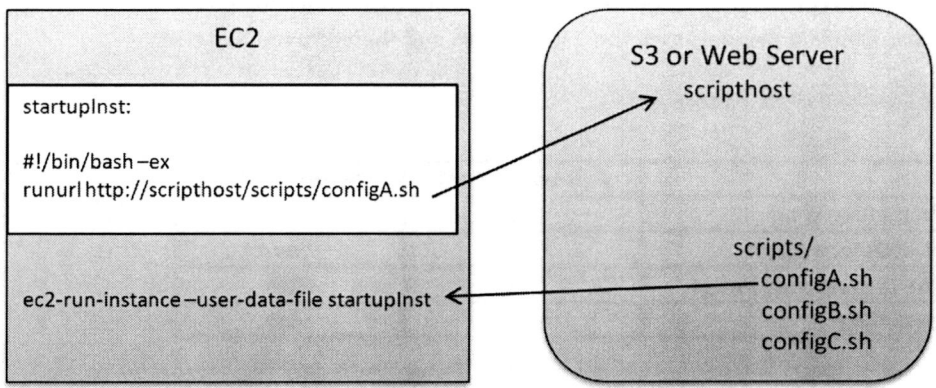

Figure 54: runurl Script for Startup Automation

Passing only the name of the script but not the script itself, also facilitates the auto scaling configuration where the startup parameters are specified in a launch configuration. When passing the name of the script only, the script itself can be changed anytime without changing the launch configuration.

Auto scaling

Configuration Model

There are two different ways to set up your AMIs. When building your first AMI you will most likely configure everything, then create a new image and happily use it.

But then, you will have to create a new AMI for every change. Be it a newer version of the Apache web server, or a new UNIX password (since you realized that the first name of your spouse isn't as safe as you thought it was, when you created the image at 2.30 am). Those fully configured AMIs are sometimes called full-baked AMIs.

The other approach is to start with a basic template containing the OS only. Based on this template you can use a script to install and configure all necessary packages.

Let's say, you start with an AWS Linux AMI, then run two different sets of scripts. One would be to set up web server AMIs, install Apache, create the users, and get the web content. And the other script would be the one that installs WebLogic, creates a domain, configures resources such as JMS queues, JDBC data sources, and finally deploys your application.

To explore things at home I have a set of full-baked AMIs that I wouldn't want to lose. For larger systems I definitely recommend a scripted approach since the maintenance overhead is lower, which in the end saves you a lot of time, and therefore reduces costs.

Table 7: Full-Baked vs. Scripted AMIs

	Full-baked AMI	Scripted AMI
Initial setup time	Low	High
Maintenance effort	High	Low
Time to start new image	Low	High
Reusability	Low	High

There are tools available that follow the scripted AMI path such as RightScale. We will examine this in more detail in the chapter 8 about cloud management.

Provisioning of Oracle Software

You most probably get your Oracle software by using a web browser and downloading it from the download section of the Oracle web site.

For a scripted setup of an image, this is rather impractical because you won't have a web browser on a server image and you cannot script the download.

I found that you can obtain the software with a simple wget as well. E.g. to download WebLogic 11g with Oracle Enterprise Pack for Eclipse, you run the following command:

```
wget --user=your_OTN_username --password=your_OTN_password
http://download.oracle.com/otn/linux/middleware/11g/
wls1033_oepe111150_linux32.bin
```

Use your web browser to interactively explore the download URLs of other products. Because of the high-speed internet connection of the EC2 instances, this approach is usually much faster than downloading the product installer from Oracle to a local repository and then uploading it again to a particular EC2 instance.

Security

After you create a template image, it will be started hundreds of times, so you'd better enforce tight security right from the start of the design process.

Consider the following items as a checklist. If you feel uncomfortable implementing them yourself consider the professional service of a specialist.

- Harden the operating system. It is best to start with the smallest possible installation, e.g. Oracle JeOS or AWS Linux, and then add only the essential packages for your installation.
- Make sure there are no unnecessary processes running.
- Use restrictive security groups. Don't open port ranges for future usage when a single port is sufficient.
- Consider encrypting your file systems. Many operating systems support encryption.
- Consider installing a virus scanner for a Windows AMI. Even if it is not running permanently for performance reasons, it can still run full system scans periodically.
- Consider installing a network intrusion detection system (NIDS) to detect unusual network patterns such as port scans or denial of service attacks. Examples for NIDS are:
    - Bro (see http://www.bro-ids.org)
    - Snort (see http://www.snort.org).
- Install a host intrusion detection (HIDS) tool for monitoring and alerting on specific file change. Examples for HIDS are:
    - TripWire (see http://www.tripwire.com)
    - OSSEC (see http://www.ossec.net).

Cleaning Up before Creating an Image

After the customization, but before the creation of a new AMI, make sure that you don't leave anything behind. During the customization of an image it is good practice not to use features of the image that won't be included in the customized image.

- Clean up log files. This means all kinds of logs. Installation logs, logs remaining from when you started WebLogic to see if it was working, syslogs from the operating system, etc.
- Delete the shell history since it will contain IP addresses and possibly even user names and passwords.
- It is best not to have a UNIX desktop such as Gnome or KDE installed, but you should at least consider removing it, if you installed one. Your image configuration should be completed by now, but even if you need the desktop again, it's only a question of minutes to reinstall it.
- Delete all browser histories in case you used the browser. Don't build images with browser links that show where you buy your stocks, go for dinner, make new friends, or which terms you have searched at Google.

6.4 Architecture Blueprint

I am well aware that you are expecting a blueprint for what to build, how Oracle Fusion Middleware looks in the cloud, and a diagram that shows all the bits and pieces of a distributed WebLogic domain in the cloud.

Distributed WLS Application

There is no single, general blueprint fitting every possible design, but let me start with a blueprint for an application built on a distributed WebLogic domain in the cloud. When building such an application, you can take advantage of the AWS cloud services; these will be introduced in the following chapters.

All these services are off-instance, they don't require any installation or maintenance, and they are inherently scalable and highly available. You can just use them without worrying about the technical details of their implementation (Please let me remind you, however, that you have to pay for them, but we will come to that later).

When using all these services for a WebLogic domain and managed servers you get around installing a load balancer, web servers and a database, as well as dealing with the WebLogic configurations for JMS and JTA availability and clustering in the cloud.

Try to visualize the blueprint in Figure 55. It shows a fictional booking system for dive cruises, based on a distributed WebLogic domain running in Amazon's Europe cloud.

Dive cruises and AWS services

The clients are located in various European countries and access the entry page of the application by its DNS name. The entry page is delivered from the nearest cache of the CloudFront content distribution network. In the entry page, the URLs for dynamic content point to the Elastic Load Balancer that is distributing the requests to the WebLogic instances across both of these two availability zones (eu-west-1a and eu-west-1b).

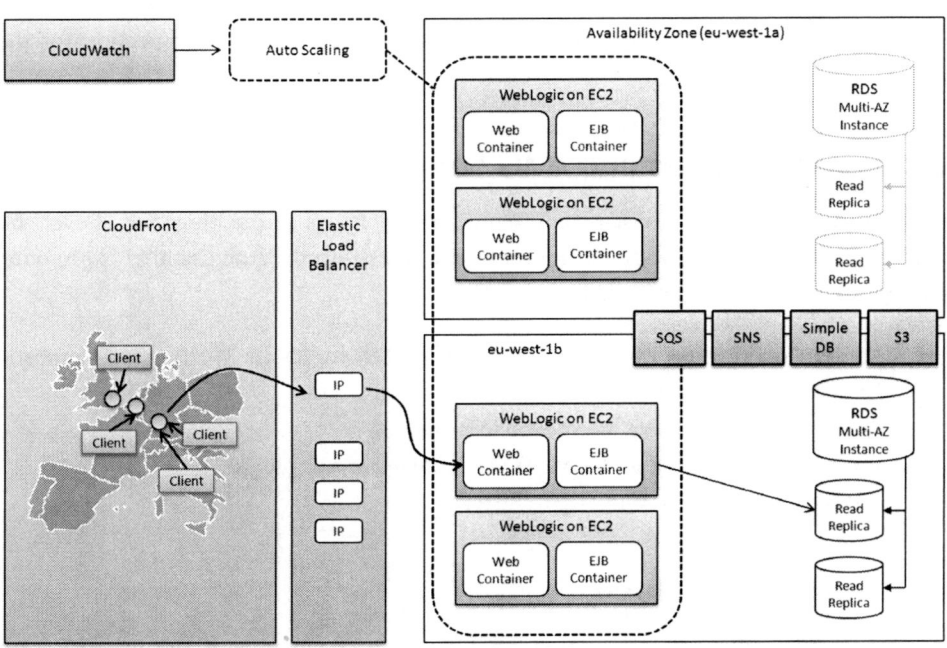

Figure 55: WLS Domain in the Cloud Blueprint

The WebLogic application uses the AWS relational database service to store the bookings, and a set of read replicas to speed up the retrieval read only data, when browsing destination catalogues of Australia, Fiji, the Philippines, and South Africa.

The booking system is decoupled from the other modules, such as billing, catalogue, and the customer loyalty program. Every module uses the simple queue service to asynchronously communicate with other modules based on persisted messages. Once a booking is completed, an email notification is sent via the simple notification service, and the booking itself is stored as a PDF file in S3.

Designing for the Cloud   133

The EC2 instances running the WebLogic domain are configured as an auto scaling group. The launch configuration of the auto scaling group specifies the setup scripts, which are executed when a new instance is created. These scripts are centrally administered and hosted off-instance in an S3 bucket. Application specific configuration data is stored in SimpleDB, and retrieved by the booking application during startup.

An auto scaling trigger defines when the number of instances is increased or decreased depending on CloudWatch monitoring metrics. CloudWatch also graphically displays the metrics of EC2 instances, the EBS volumes, and the load balancer.

I will cover every one of these services, alternatives, design-tradeoffs, and their costs in the following chapters. Use this blueprint as a reference if you build an application for the cloud.

Middleware Features and AWS Services

In addition to all the AWS services represented by the boxes in the blueprint above, you have to understand the following design trade-offs where similar functionality is provided by an AWS service and a WebLogic feature:

- Simple Notification Service vs. WebLogic JMS topics or WebLogic Diagnostic Framework Notifications
- Simple queue service vs. WebLogic JMS queues
- AWS Elastic Load Balancing vs. WebLogic web server plugin
- AWS auto scaling vs. WebLogic clustering

Middleware in the Cloud

Operating middleware products in the cloud is more challenging if the product itself requires WebLogic clustering or distributed JMS queues. Middleware products like Oracle Service Bus or SOA Suite depend on such features (for details see section 5.4).

However, an AWS service (e.g. simple queue service) cannot replace middleware features (e.g. WebLogic JMS queues) and you need to understand the technical details of highly available JMS destinations and a WebLogic cluster in the cloud. This is why the peculiarities of middleware products in the cloud are also covered in the following chapters.

7 Cloud Databases

When designing your cloud architecture, sooner or later the question about the database will arise. There are many options, and in order to make an informed decision as to which will best suit your architecture, you should know the pros and cons of at least three:

- You can start installing your database on an AMI with the operating system of your choice, or even select an AMI provided by Oracle and set up the included Standard or Enterprise Edition.

- SimpleDB is an option if you prefer the scalability and availability of a non-relational database.

- The relational database service from AWS offers a convenient and easy way to create and manage an Oracle MySQL database as a cloud service.

7.1 Oracle Database AMI

Running an Oracle database in the cloud can be as simple as selecting the right AMI from the list.

Oracle Provided AMIs

Preconfigured AMIs are available from Oracle as mentioned in section 3.1. These AMIs come with Oracle Enterprise Linux, the Oracle database, Enterprise Manager Database Control and the web based rapid development tool Applications Express (APEX).

Here is a link to Oracle's cloud offering which includes the AMIs provided by Oracle: *Oracle documentation*

http://www.oracle.com/technology/tech/cloud/index.html

As you may already know from previous chapters, I always recommend not to rely on the posted AMIs. Although they are certainly a good place to start, you have to accept that they can sometimes disappear.

If you start with one of the AMIs provided by Oracle, be sure to create your own image so that you can start it anytime, even if Oracle were to update the set of publicly available AMIs with a newer version. Yes, you do have to pay for the storage of the image snapshot.

In summary, the AMIs published by Oracle are a convenient start if you are looking for the current version of the database and the Oracle Enterprise Linux is your preferred operating system. Always use these images as a basis from which to create your own.

Custom AMIs

If Oracle doesn't provide the database version that you like to use in the cloud, or if you are not happy with Oracle Enterprise Linux, you can always start with an AMI containing just the supported operating system of your choice and install the database yourself (be sure to select a supported operating system).

Even if you choose to start with an S3-backed AMI, you will need an EBS volume for the data file.

Oracle VM with Database on AWS

At the time of this writing, running Oracle VM based images on AWS is still in the pipeline. Take a look at section 12.3 for the details.

Personally, I would like to see Oracle provide a wider range of products based on Oracle VM, including a larger variety of versions and the availability of all AMIs for all regions.

Again, don't rely on an image provided by Oracle; create your own so you can stay independent.

7.2 AWS SimpleDB

Amazon's SimpleDB service is highly scalable, highly available and even includes automatic data indexing. It is based on EC2 and S3 and therefore well suited to applications that have traditionally required clustered relational databases because of availability and performance requirements.

SimpleDB is a cloud service, so no installation is necessary, and the database does not run within your EC2 instance. You can access SimpleDB using an API (there is no integration with the AWS management console). Unlike a clustered database such as Oracle RAC, SimpleDB requires no CAPEX and no DBA for maintenance and administration.

AWS SimpleDB is a non-relational data store. The equivalent of a relational database's table is called domain. A domain stores data but, unlike with tables in a relational database, it is not possible to query data across domains in SimpleDB.

SimpleDB is another example of how a cloud service can potentially replace a complex and expensive infrastructure such as a clustered database.

The data within the domains is called attribute name-value pairs; Try to visualize a spreadsheet where the cells can have more than one value:

- The domain is specified by the spreadsheet tab.
- Items specify the rows and represent individual objects containing one or more attribute name-value pairs.
- Attributes specify the columns and represent categories of data assigned to items.
- Every cell specifies one or more values. Values represent instances of attributes for items.

	A	B	C	D	E	F
1	ID	attribute	attribute	attribute	attribute	attribute
2		color	material	size	year	price
3	sboard_01	white	fibre	6ft	2010	300
4	sboard_02	blue, white	foam	6ft	2009	290
5	sboard_03	white, blue, red	fibre	8ft	2010	350
6	sboard_04	white	fibre	6ft	2008	199

Figure 56: Simple DB as Spreadsheet

Once the data is stored, you can use select like queries or a SOAP/REST request, in order to retrieve items matching your criteria. A select query for the domain shown in the figure above can have the following syntax:

```
select * from boards where material = 'fibre'
```

Tools

There is a Firefox plugin called sdbtool for querying and updating Simple DB database domains, which can be installed directly from the following location:

```
http://code.google.com/p/sdbtool
```

AWS officially provides a Java library to access SimpleDB. Coding SimpleDB in Java is easy and compact.

A lot of folk use Typica (a Java client library) for a variety of AWS services including SimpleDB. You can obtain it from the following site:

http://code.google.com/p/typica

Costs

There is a free usage tier for SimpleDB, but do keep in mind that the total cost only covers the following items:

- SimpleDB machine hours
- Data transfer in/out
- Storage space

The first 25 machine hours and 1 GB of storage is free. On average this enables 2,000,000 GET or SELECT API requests to be completed per month free of charge.

Thereafter, $0.154 per SimpleDB machine hour consumed and $0.275 per GB-month is added to your bill.

Additional costs for the data transfer are as listed in the table below e.g. in the EU you would have to pay $0.15 per GB for up to 10 TB of data transfer:

Data Transfer**		
Data Transfer In	**US & EU Regions**	**APAC Region**
All Data Transfer	$0.10 per GB	$0.10 per GB
Data Transfer Out ***	**US & EU Regions**	**APAC Region**
First 1 GB per Month	$0.00 per GB	$0.00 per GB
Up to 10 TB per Month	$0.15 per GB	$0.19 per GB
Next 40 TB per Month	$0.11 per GB	$0.15 per GB
Next 100 TB per Month	$0.09 per GB	$0.13 per GB
Over 150 TB per Month	$0.08 per GB	$0.12 per GB

Figure 57: SimpleDB Data Transfer Pricing

7.3 AWS Relational Database Service

Amazon's Relational Database Service (RDS) is a fully featured MySQL database provided as a service. You can get started without having to use any command-line tool. The AWS management console enables the creation of new instances and the scaling of compute and storage capacity for the instances.

AWS currently supports the community edition of MySQL 5.1 with InnoDB as the default database storage engine. There is support for accessing the instances via SSL. The maximum number of database instances is limited to 20 per account. However, it is possible to request this limit be raised, by completing the form at the following URL:

http://aws.amazon.com/contact-us/request-to-increase-the-amazon-rds-db-instance-limit

Creating an RDS Instance

To create a new instance, select the Amazon RDS tab and click on launch instance. Then specify all the instance details as shown in the screenshot in Figure 58. Currently only MySQL is supported, so you cannot choose any other DB engine:

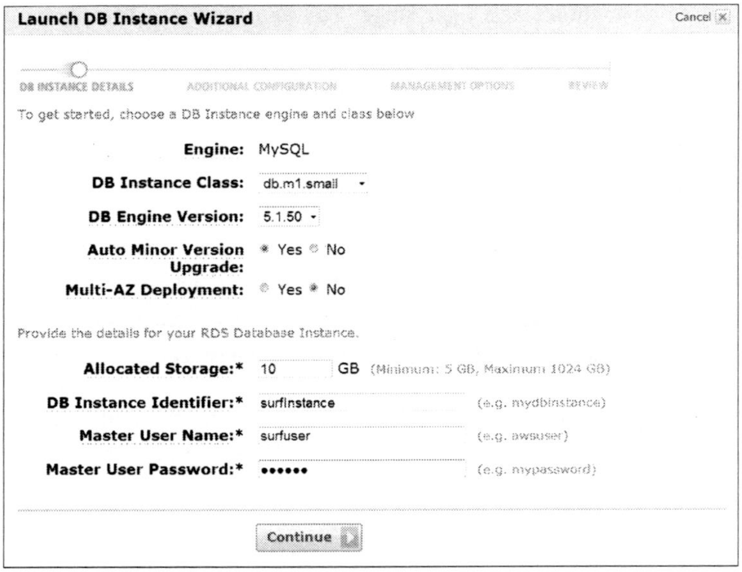

Figure 58: RDS Create Instance

Then select an instance class. At first glance, instance classes appear to match the EC2 standard and high memory instances, however there are some subtle differences.

Instance class

All database instances are 64-bit (whereas the EC2 m1.small instance type is only 32). Also, the high memory db.m2.xlarge instance provides high I/O performance (yet the EC2 instance type m2.xlarge provides only medium I/O performance). There is no micro or HPC database instance class option for the RDS service:

Table 8: RDS Instance Types

Type	bit	GB RAM	Cores	ECU	I/O perf
Standard					
db.m1.small	64	1.7	1	1	Mod
db.m1.large	64	7.5	2	4	High
db.m1.xlarge	64	15	4	8	High
High Memory					
db.m2.xlarge	64	17.1	2	6.5	High
db.m2.2xlarge	64	34.2	4	13	High
db.m2.4xlarge	64	68.4	8	26	High

It is always possible to resize an instance at a later stage. You can therefore complete all your configurations and initials tests with a cheap, small instance and then resize the instance when it is ready to serve the production load.

On the instance details screen, you can also select whether the RDS service should *automatically* perform minor version upgrades of your instances.

Multi-availability zone
The next option is yet another of those wonderful cloud features: you only need to tick the "Multi-AZ Deployment" and AWS will then silently do all the magic to get a standby copy of your instance in another availability zone. This instance runs in another data center within the same region, completely isolated and independent from the first one.

The standby copy is synchronously updated. Also, the standby copy is standby only - as the name suggests - and doesn't serve any database requests at all, not even read requests.

RDS fails over to the standby instance when the primary instance or even the whole availability zone fails, when the instance class of the database instance is changed, or when software is updated during the maintenance window provided.

This failover is automatically initiated. During the failover procedure, the CNAME record of the main instance is changed so that it points to the standby copy.

There is no button on the AWS management console forcing a failover, but changing the instance class will do so. The failover process is also logged by the RDS event log, which can be viewed from the management console.

It is not possible to assign an elastic IP address to a database instance.

I guess you will not be surprised if I say that you have to pay for the standby instance. We will look at the costs at the end of this section, but in a nutshell your costs will double as you will be charged the same fees as for the primary instance.

Next decide how much storage you want to allocate for your instance. The minimum size is 5 GB, although you can create instances as large as 1 TB.

Finally, configure database instance name, port and availability zone on the next screen as shown in Figure 59:

Figure 59: RDS Configure Instance Name, Port and Availability Zone

Don't forget to define the backup retention period. This setting determines the number of days automatic backups are stored. To disable automatic backups, set it to zero.

Backup and Maintenance

The backup window defines the UTC timeframe when the backups are taken. Minimum duration time is two hours (although this doesn't mean that your backup will actually last that long). See Figure 60 for a screenshot of the backup and maintenance settings.

Backup window

Cloud Databases 141

When using automated backups with multi-availability instances, the backups are taken from the standby instance and the primary instance continues to serve user queries.

Maintenance window During the maintenance window, AWS installs software updates and security patches etc. The minimum duration for this window is four hours. Maintenance and backups are two different things – so you have to make sure that the maintenance and backup window don't overlap.

Maintenance is applied in the least disruptive way. For a multi-availability zone instance, the maintenance is first done on the standby instance. Then a failover to the standby instance occurs. Subsequently, the maintenance is done on the previous primary instance (which by this stage is the new standby instance).

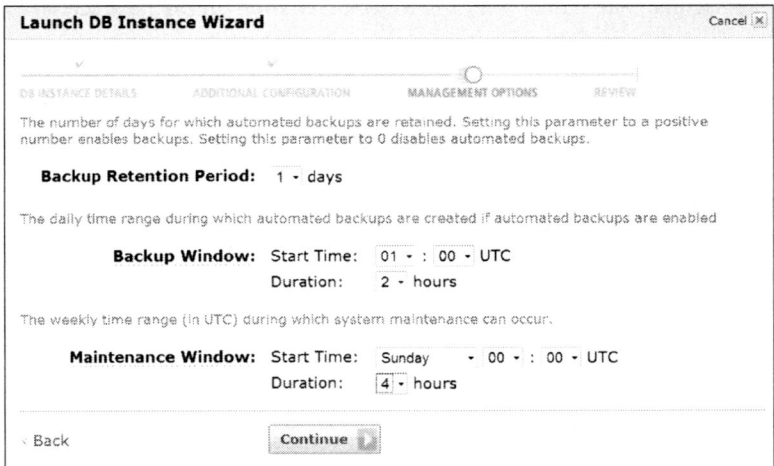

Figure 60: RDS Configure Backup Window

Finally, verify all the data in the summary. Make sure everything is okay and use the back button should you wish to correct your settings.

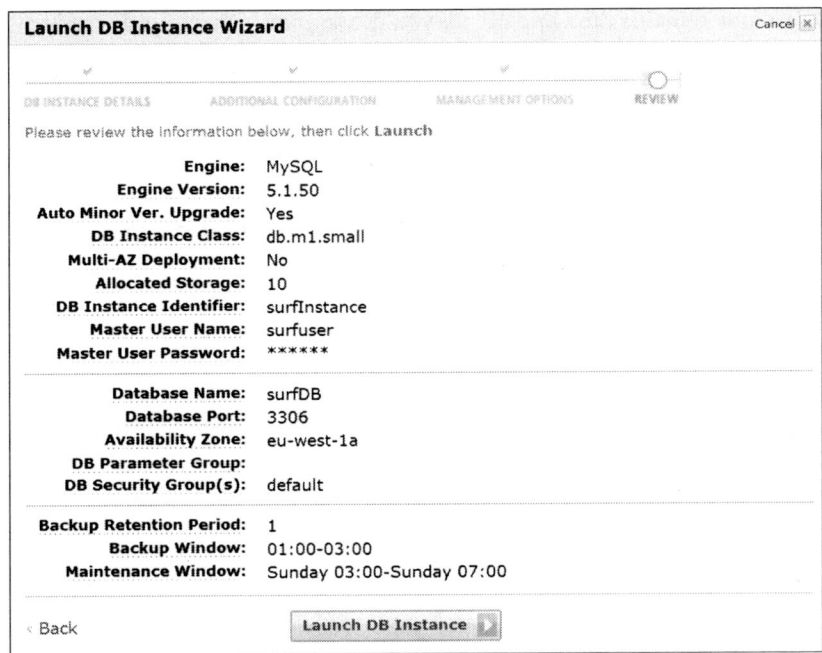

Figure 61: RDS Summary

The new RDS instance is then listed under instances with the status "creating". It will take a few minutes until the instance's state changes to "running".

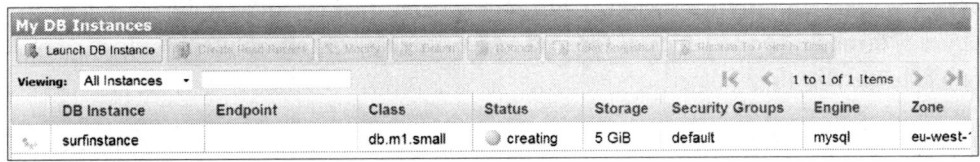

Figure 62: RDS Instance Creation In Progress

Instance Management

Once the instance is created it will display its endpoint. The syntax of the endpoint is as follows:

instancename.uniqueidentifier.region.rds.amazonaws.com

The identifier of the instance that I just created for this example is:

surfinstance.cawztecsrizb.eu-west-1.rds.amazonaws.com

This endpoint DNS name remains the same even if you delete your instance and recreate it at a later stage with the same instance name - although it might map to a different IP address.

Security groups   With the default settings, no network access is allowed to the database instances. In other words, it is secure but unusable. To be able to access the database from an EC2 instance, allow access rights for an EC2 security group by adding it to the database security group as shown in Figure 63.

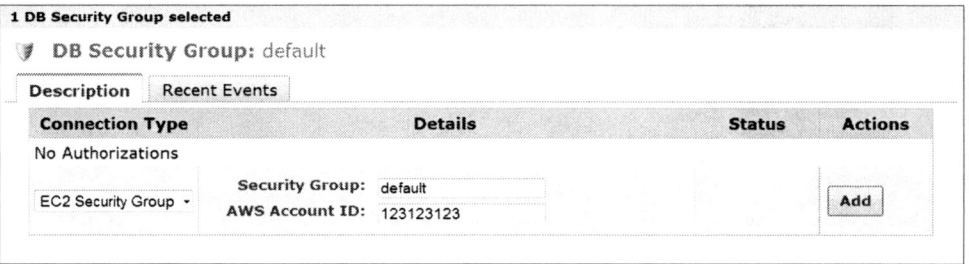

Figure 63: RDS Security Group

Be careful when adding the account-ID and don't copy any spaces, since here the AWS management console is fussy with leading or trailing space. Alternatively, you can authorize an IP address or a range of IP addresses.

Then switch to the monitoring tab. The built-in monitoring for RDS instances is done with AWS CloudWatch. Metrics such as CPU, storage and memory utilization, as well as the requests, throughput and latencies for read and write requests, are all graphically displayed for a configurable time range.

See section 11.5 to learn more about CloudWatch details such as all available metrics for monitoring, and how to retrieve statistics over time using the command-line API.

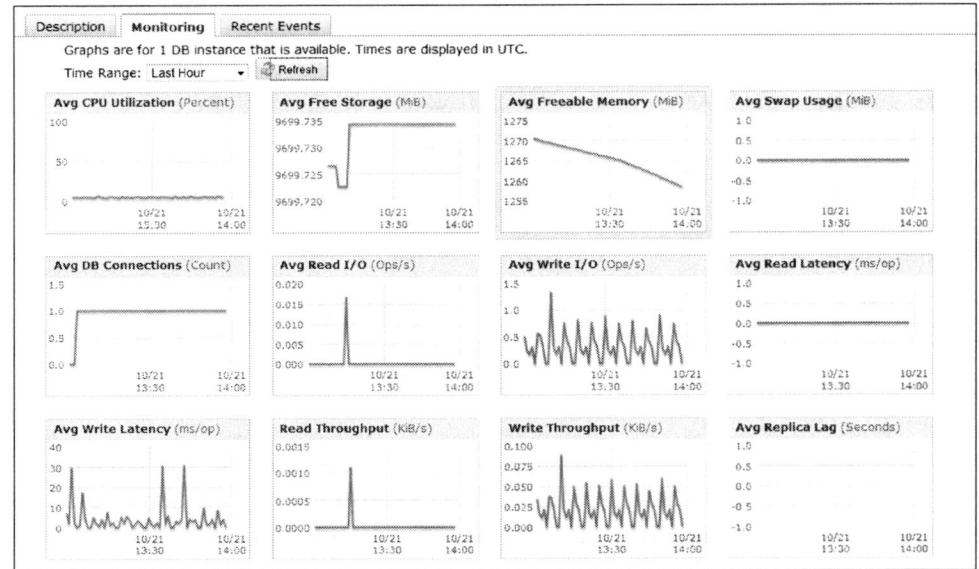

Figure 64: RDS CloudWatch Monitoring

Switch to Databases / DB Events to see the event log. The events log shows that a backup was initiated as soon as the instance was created.

Event log

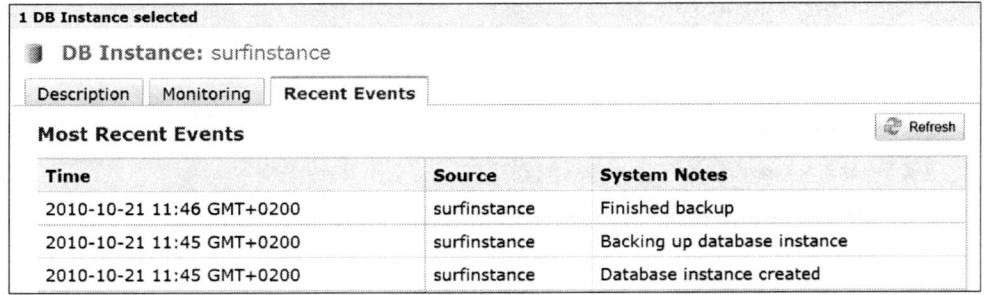

Figure 65: RDS Event Log

Even the management of existing RDS instances can be done using the AWS management console. There are a number of options for the instance management such as creating read replicas, modifying the instance settings, deleting or rebooting an instance and taking an instance snapshot.

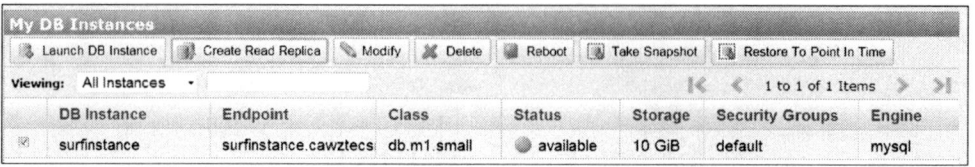

Figure 66: RDS Instance Management Options

Read replicas Let's take a look at read replicas. RDS supports read replicas that take advantage of the native and asynchronous MySQL replication. Read replicas improve the throughput for applications with a high database read ratio. You should deploy a read replica when you need to scale beyond the I/O capacity of the primary instance class. It is currently possible to create up to five read replicas for any database instance.

To create a read replica, select one of the primary database instances and click on "Create Read Replica". It is not possible to create a read replica from read replica.

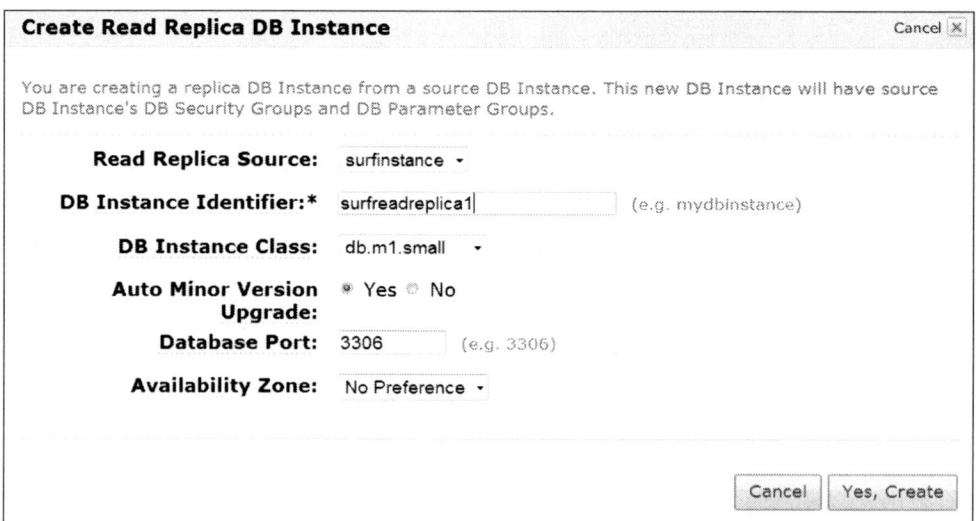

Figure 67: RDS Create Read Replica

The read replicas will automatically use the master database security group settings. For the instance class, it is recommended that the replica's instance class isn't smaller than the primary instance.

You should be aware of the conceptual differences between multi-zone instances and read replicas: multi-availability zone instances increase the availability, whereas read replicas are used for scalability.

Table 9: Comparison Multi-Availability Zone Instances and Read Replicas

	Multi-availability zone instances	Read replicas
Purpose	*Availability*	*Scalability*
Number of instances	1 primary + 1 secondary	1 primary + n secondaries
Secondaries used during normal operation?	No	Yes
Synchronization	Synchronous	Asynchronous
Use with ELB	No (only one active)	Not supported
Use with elastic IPs	Not supported	Not supported
Cost	Doubles	Per Instance

Read replicas can lag behind if the write I/O requests of the primary instance cannot be replicated early enough to the replica. The CloudWatch metric "Replica Lag" can help you to monitor the time lag.

If you combine read replicas with a multi-availability zone instance you will benefit from both. When creating a read replica from a multi-availability zone instance, you can even avoid the short I/O suspension that usually occurs because a snapshot of the primary has to be taken first.

To explore the snapshot feature, change to the instances view under Databases / DB Instance, select the image and take a snapshot of the instance. *Snapshot and restore*

Once you have taken a snapshot, you can restore the state of the database to the time of the snapshot.

When you delete a database instance you can still keep your snapshots. In fact, when you delete an instance you have the opportunity to create a final snapshot: *Delete Instance*

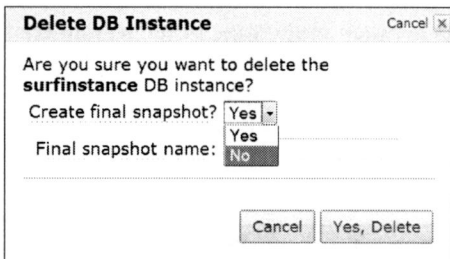

Figure 68: Create Snapshot at Delete

Are you an MySQL expert and do you feel like you need more control over the MySQL parameters? You can create a parameter group and overwrite the settings of the default parameter group shown in Figure 69 below:

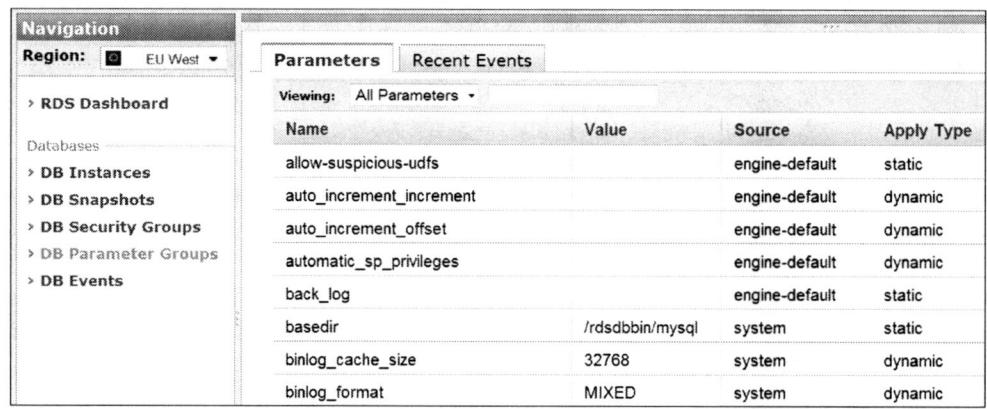

Figure 69: RDS Parameter Group

RDS Pricing

RDS is a great cloud service that comes with all the cloud benefits. Billing for RDS is complicated, so it is essential that you understand how much you are paying for this service. For multi-availability zone instances your bill will be itemized as follows:

- Per instance-hour cost primary
- Per instance-hour cost secondary
- Database storage primary
- Database storage secondary
- Backup storage
- Data transfer costs

The AWS calculator introduced in section 3.1 also includes RDS as a line item.

Standard pricing is available per hour. The smallest instance is $0.12 per hour, which equates to $1,051 per year. AWS rounds a partial instance-hour to a full hour. The largest instance class is $2.96 per hour, which equates to $25,930 per year. RDS instances cost about 30% more than running an EC2 only instance.

Standard instances

US – N. Virginia	US – N. California	EU – Ireland	APAC – Singapore
DB Instance Class (On-Demand)			**Price Per Hour**
Small DB Instance			$0.12
Large DB Instance			$0.48
Extra Large DB Instance			$0.97
High-Memory DB Instance Class (On-Demand)			
Extra Large DB Instance			$0.74
Double Extra Large DB Instance			$1.48
Quadruple Extra Large DB Instance			$2.96

Figure 70: RDS Standard Pricing

Multi-availability zone instance costs are double because AWS provides two instances (although the second one is standby only).

In addition to the instance-hours, AWS charges you $0.11 for the database storage and another $0.11 for each million I/O requests. And don't forget that AWS will also charge you for the storage of multi-availability zone instances, so your storage costs will double.

Storage and I/O costs

US – N. Virginia	US – N. California	EU – Ireland	APAC – Singapore
Storage Rate	$0.11 per GB-month		
I/O Rate	$0.11 per 1 million requests		

Figure 71: RDS DB Storage (Standard)

Similar to the concept of reserved EC2 instances, reserved database instances are also available. There's a one-time payment for each instance, and then you receive a discount on the hourly usage fee.

Reserved instances

A one-time payment for a small instance is $227.50 which cuts the subsequent usage rate in half. Instead of $0.12 you will be charged $0.059 per hour ($517 per year).

		One-time Fee		
Standard Deployment (Reserved)		**1 Yr Term**	**3 Yr Term**	**Usage Rate**
Small		$227.50	$350	$0.059 per hour
Large		$910	$1,400	$0.235 per hour
Extra Large		$1,820	$2,800	$0.471 per hour
Extra Large (High Memory)		$1,325	$2,000	$0.352 per hour
Double Extra Large (High Memory)		$2,650	$4,000	$0.704 per hour
Quadruple Extra Large (High memory)		$5,300	$8,000	$1.408 per hour
Multi-AZ Deployment (Reserved)				
Small		$455	$700	$0.118 per hour
Large		$1,820	$2,800	$0.471 per hour
Extra Large		$3,640	$5,600	$0.942 per hour
Extra Large (High Memory)		$2,650	$4,000	$0.704 per hour
Double Extra Large (High Memory)		$5,300	$8,000	$1.408 per hour
Quadruple Extra Large (High Memory)		$10,600	$16,000	$2.816 per hour

Figure 72: RDS Reserved Instances

Backup storage   We are not done yet. You will certainly want to have backups of your data. For every running instance you get backup storage equivalent to the size of your provisioned database storage for free. If you stop your database instance, the storage will be billed at $0.15 per GB. If you need more backup storage, it will show on your bill with the same rate of $0.15 per GB.

Data transfer   Last but not least, you are charged for data transfer costs in and out of RDS.

Data Transfer In	**US & EU Regions**	**APAC Region**
All Data Transfer	$0.10 per GB	$0.10 per GB
Data Transfer Out ***	**US & EU Regions**	**APAC Region**
First 1 GB per Month	$0.00 per GB	$0.00 per GB
Up to 10 TB per Month	$0.15 per GB	$0.19 per GB
Next 40 TB per Month	$0.11 per GB	$0.15 per GB
Next 100 TB per Month	$0.09 per GB	$0.13 per GB
Over 150 TB per Month	$0.08 per GB	$0.12 per GB

Figure 73: RDS Pricing Data Transfer

There is no data transfer charge for the data replication between multi-availability zone instances. For data transferred between Amazon RDS and AWS services in different regions, you are charged the Internet data transfer rate on *both sides*.

7.4 WebLogic with RDS

Have you ever wondered how you can use the RDS instance with WebLogic, the Oracle Service Bus or any other middleware product? Well, all you need is a data source.

To try it, start your favorite AMI with WebLogic. In case you don't have an AMI, check out the different options for creating one as described in chapter 3.1 about AWS basics.

Configuring a WLS Data Source

Once WebLogic is running, connect to the admin server using its public DNS address. Each of the following steps for the creation of the JDBC data source are carried out using the WebLogic admin console, rather than with the AWS management console.

Creating a data source

Using the WebLogic admin console, navigate to Domain Structure / Domain Name / Services / JDBC / Data Sources. Under JDBC create a new data source and specify the name and the JNDI name of the data source as shown in the screenshot in Figure 74.

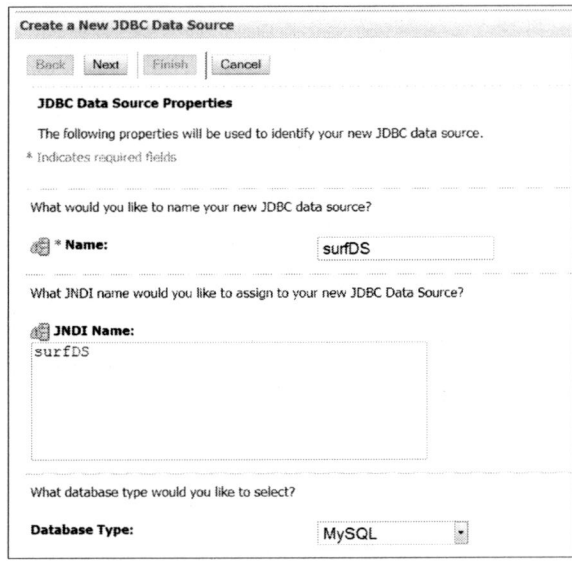

Figure 74: WLS Create Data Source

Cloud Databases 151

On the following two screens, leave all the settings for the driver class and the transactions settings with their default values, and keeping clicking 'next' until you arrive at the data source settings as shown in Figure 75.

Fill in the data source properties exactly as you specified them when creating the RDS instance. For the JDBC host name use the RDS endpoint.

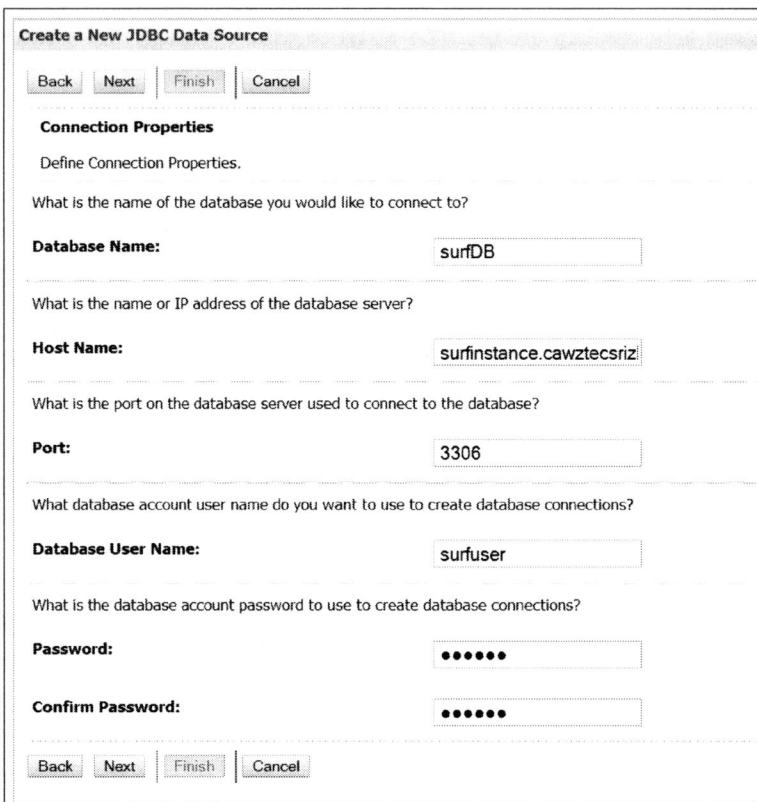

Figure 75: WLS Data Source Properties

JDBC URL   The settings for the driver class name, the JDBC URL, the user name and the password are already pre-populated. The JDBC URL will display as follows (your hostname will be different):

```
jdbc:mysql://surfinstance.cawztecsrizb.eu-west1.rds.amazonaws.com:
3306/surfDB
```

152   Cloud Databases

After checking these values, click on the "Test Configuration" button at the top of the page. If the connection to the RDS database can be established you will see a green success message in the top left of the screen.

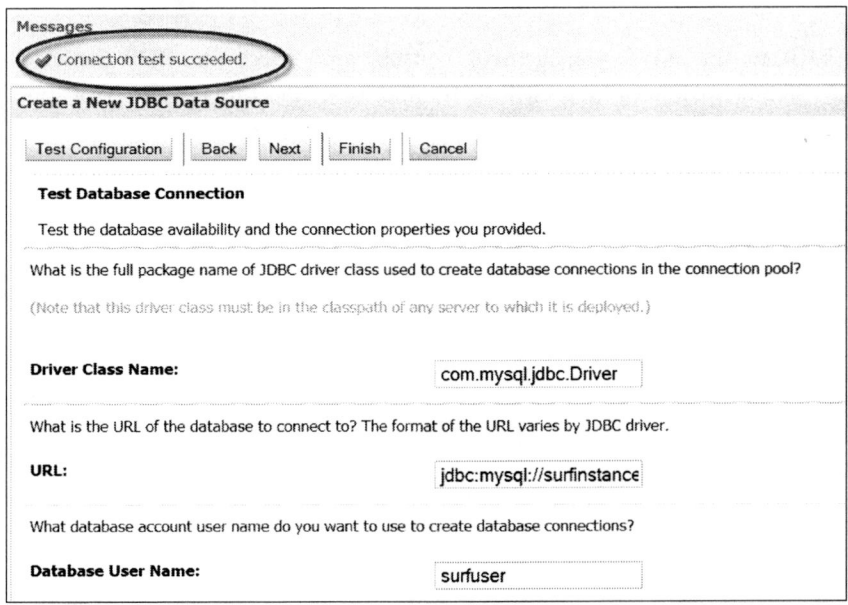

Figure 76: WLS Test JDBC Configuration

Then click finish. Re-select the data source and target the data source to the admin server as shown below:

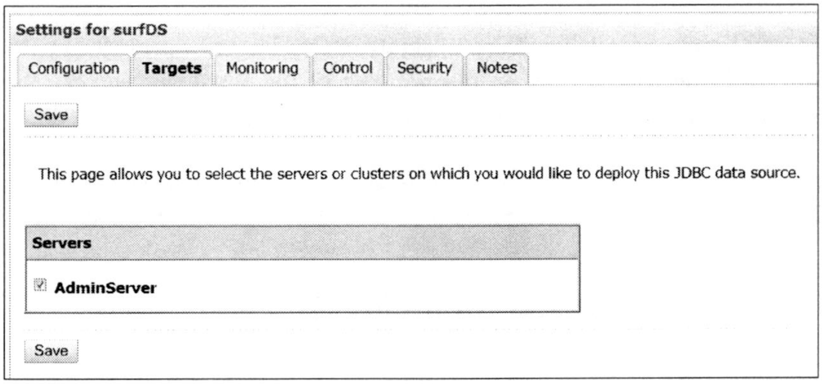

Figure 77: WLS Set JDBC Data Source Target

Verifying the RDS Connectivity

For final proof that the connection pool is actually connected to the RDS instance, increase the initial number of connections in the JDBC connection pool from 1 to 10.

Then switch back to the AWS management console and select the RDS instance's monitoring tab. Because you have increased the number of connections in the JDBC pool to 10, you will now see 10 DB connections open in CloudWatch monitoring:

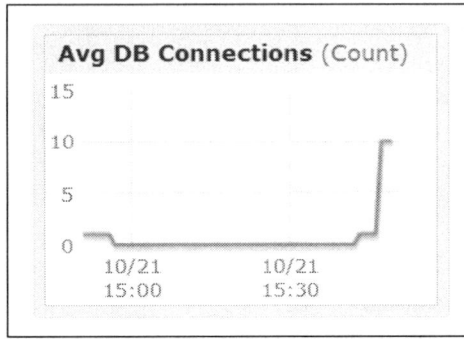

Figure 78: AWS CloudWatch WebLogic Connections to RDS

7.5 Multi Data Sources

Java Database Connectivity (JDBC) is a technology that displays some peculiarities when used in a distributed architecture. To start with, don't expect any magic to happen to your JDBC data source just because its target is set to a WebLogic cluster.

Unlike WebLogic JMS for example, where the availability of JMS has to be provided by the WebLogic domain itself (because JMS is an integral part of the WebLogic server), the actual database is not part of the WebLogic domain.

On the one hand, the database certainly has to be scalable and highly available, but on the other hand, WebLogic has to be configured in order to take advantage of such a database.

Oracle Real Application Cluster (non-Cloud)

The good news is that Oracle's Real Application Cluster (RAC) provides scalability as well as availability for the database layer in a non-cloud environment. Let me provide a high level overview of Oracle RAC from the WebLogic perspective.

Broadly speaking, Oracle RAC appears to the outer world as two or more independent nodes, which are internally synchronized and access the same shared storage. Oracle RAC is horizontally scalable, which means you can add more nodes without repartitioning the data.

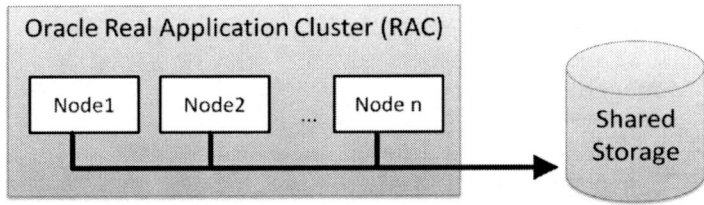

Figure 79: Oracle RAC

Although you can target a data source to a WLS cluster, this doesn't enable any failover or load balancing capabilities:

Data source deployed on cluster

The client must still look up a local JNDI name of a single data source or alternatively will receive a data source injected as a resource. Either way, all the connections in the relevant connection pool will share the same JDBC URL, and therefore access the same database instance.

To overcome this obstacle, WLS supports multi data source. The concept of multi data sources has similarities to a distributed JMS destination: The multi data source has a JNDI name and is assigned a set of data sources. When the client looks up the JNDI name of the multi data source, one of the member data sources is returned as illustrated in Figure 80. You can configure "failover only" or "load balancing" for the strategy that determines the returned data source.

Multi data source

The beauty of this approach is that it is completely transparent at the client code. The client continues to use the JNDI name which is now assigned to the multi data source.

Cloud Databases 155

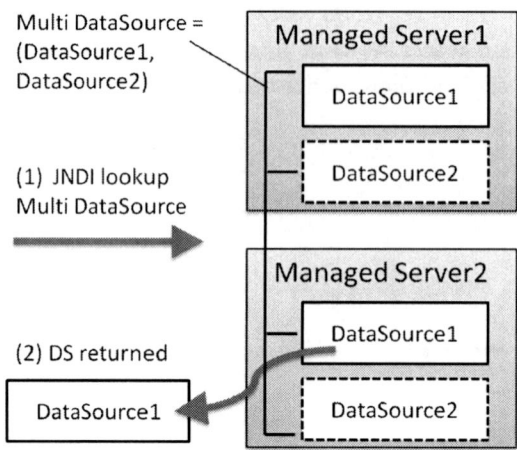

Figure 80: Multi Data Source

Connect-time Failover — There is a seemingly similar approach called connect-time failover, probably better known to those with a strong database background. With connect-time, failover load balancing occurs at the driver level when the connection is established. To configure it, you specify a list of database instances in the JDBC URL.

Oracle documentation — Although multi data sources and connect-time failover support Oracle RAC, Oracle recommends using WebLogic JDBC multi data sources for most configurations. For a detailed discussion about these alternative approaches, I recommend reviewing the WebLogic JDBC documentation at the following URL:

http://download.oracle.com/docs/cd/E11035_01/wls100/jdbc_admin/oracle_rac.html

Oracle RAC in the Cloud?

No RAC in the clouds — Here comes the bad news: there is no Oracle RAC in the cloud. Neither AWS nor RackspaceCloud support Oracle RAC.

Indeed, RAC is supported with Oracle's server virtualization Oracle VM, but Oracle VM is not an IaaS platform such as AWS or Rackspace.

Although you will shortly be able to use Oracle VM based AMIs in the Amazon cloud, these AMIs on EC2 don't support RAC either. You can find more details about the Oracle VM on EC2 announcement in section 12.3.

Multi Data Sources with RDS

Nevertheless, multi data sources do work in the cloud and they are useful even without RAC.

You can use multi data sources for scaling read requests to Amazon's Relational Database Service. RDS read replicas cannot replace all Oracle RAC features, but they can be a viable substitute for read requests.

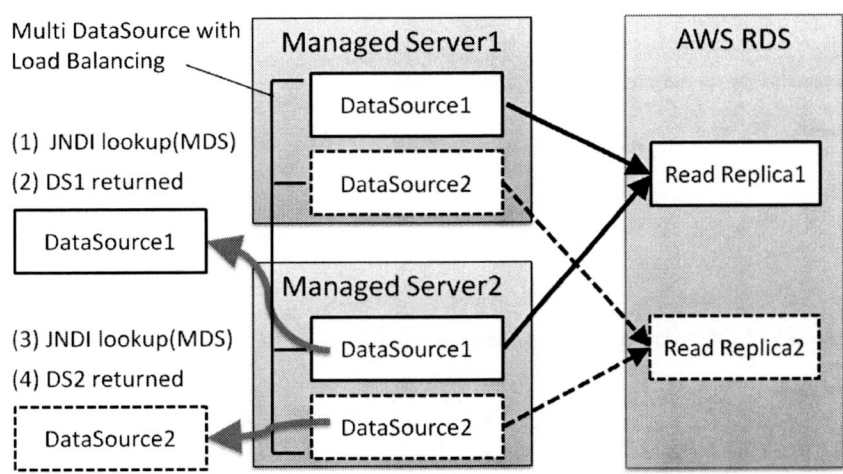

Figure 81: WLS Multi Data source and RDS Read Replicas

I reckon you remember that RDS multi-availability zone instances handle failover and that RDS read-replicas provide scalability. (In case you don't, just take another look at Table 9.) It is not a good idea to interfere with the RDS failover process because it is triggered by the RDS itself and, after the failover, the WLS connection pool will continue to use the same DNS name, which is then mapped to a RDS instance in another region.

However, a multi data source configured for load balancing can distribute read requests among any number of RDS read replicas, as shown in Figure 81.

Multi data sources for load balancing RDS read replicas

To configure a multi data source, you can use the WebLogic admin console or the WebLogic Scripting Tool. At the admin console select Services / JDBC / Multi Data Sources, then click "New". Provide a name and a JNDI name as shown in Figure 82.

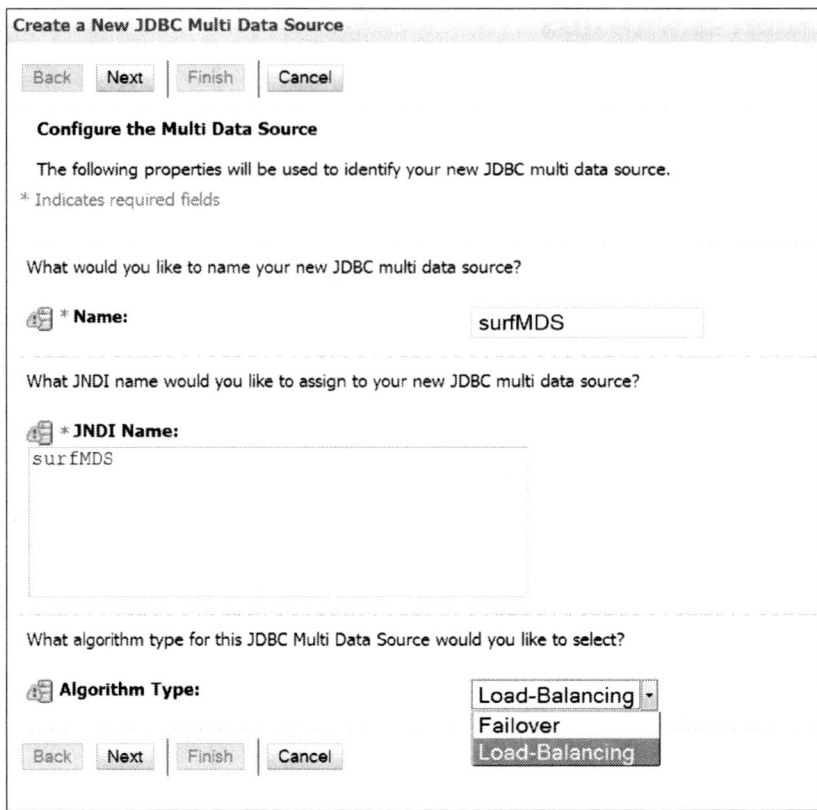

Figure 82: WLS Multi Data Source Configuration

Then select the configuration target, and decide whether you want the data source to support distributed transactions or not (XA or non-XA setting). As a final step, either create data sources that will be assigned to the multi data source, or select existing ones.

7.6 Conclusion

To conclude, you can operate and maintain your own Oracle or non-Oracle database on an EC2 instance with an EBS volume for the data file. However, this option requires basic database administration knowledge and you have to look after backups yourself.

If you are looking for an easy start with an Oracle database, it is best to check if there is an AMI provided by Oracle. Although at the time of writing, it is not possible to run Oracle's flagship database product RAC on any of the industry leading IaaS platforms.

Amazon's relational database service can be used without any database administration knowledge and requires no installation. RDS is convenient to use, easy to scale and provides failover and scheduled backups. The costs of RDS can quickly mount up, so to avoid any nasty surprises, be sure to do calculations for a month or longer using the AWS calculator.

Don't forget the other database service offered by AWS. Should a non-relational database service match your requirements, then it's worth considering the AWS SimpleDB. SimpleDB has a free usage-tier, which makes it an ideal location to store configuration data and information for bootstrapping instances.

8 Cloud Management

In this chapter, I'd like to cover cloud management aspects. I'll start with file systems and explore how shared or local file systems work with distributed WebLogic domains. Then I'll explain how distributed domains can be provisioned in a way that a managed server can be added dynamically.

Lastly, I'd like to introduce the RightScale Management Platform as an example of one of the best management products currently available for supporting multi-cloud images and multi-instance deployments.

8.1 File System

Let's explore the difference of having either a shared or a non-shared file system for a distributed WebLogic domain first.

WebLogic Domains and File Systems

In non-cloud environments I usually recommend using a shared file system for all servers in a domain when you are planning a distributed installation of WebLogic. Since a shared file system in Windows seems to be more error prone, I see this as another reason to use a UNIX operating system for production.

What speaks in favor of a shared file system? The most important reason is that there is always one single, shared configuration directory and files. Every server will always see the same configuration all the time and you don't have to worry about not having some files at some machines when distributing them manually. *Shared File System*

Another reason is log files. All log files for all servers are stored under `DOMAIN_HOME/servers/SERVER_NAME/logs`. You can easily do a recursive grep with a shared file system when looking for problems in the server logs such as stack traces.

Shared File Systems in the Cloud

EBS? But how about using a shared file system in the cloud? Every AWS instance comes with an ephemeral or EBS file system. You can't mount the EBS to more than one EC2 instance at the same time. This means you cannot create a shared file system based on EBS.

NFS? How about NFS? This is probably your next thought. It's technically possible and indeed, sometimes NFS is used with AWS. You can export a part of your local file system, make sure all necessary ports are accessible on all machines, and mount the exported file system on the other machines.

I would discourage anyone from using NFS. Looking at the design goals it becomes clear that they are against the principles of having stateless, independent machines that can be restarted quickly. In addition, the NFS server itself would be a single point of failure.

In conclusion, it is best to work with a *local* file system in the cloud. The question is if you want to go for an AMI with a persistent EBS volume, or an AMI with an ephemeral local file system. We explored the tradeoffs to answer this question in more detail in the module about AMI design (see section 6.3).

WebLogic Domains Using a Local File System

Setting up a cluster without a shared file system is possible but requires quite a bit of extra thinking. The main problem of course, is how the remote WebLogic server can possibly know about the domain configuration. There are two solutions.

Copy You can copy the domain directory over. After configuring the complete domain, including all WebLogic servers, copy the domain directory to the remote machines. Note that configuring the domain includes setting the correctly listed addresses and port numbers for the remote servers.

Remote booting Instead of copying the domain directory you can start a remote WebLogic server from an empty domain directory on a remote server. Since the domain directory is empty, obviously, there will be no start script for this domain, but there is a generic startManagedWebLogic script located in the WL_SERVER/common/bin directory. You have to pass two arguments to the script: First, the location of the admin server and second the server name of the managed server to start.

The starting managed server will contact the admin server and pull over its configuration files from the admin server's machine. After that, you will have all necessary files in your local domain directory apart from the bin subdirectory.

If you have to deal with local file systems and a rather large number of machines, I recommend using a cluster shell that runs the same command on many machines and gets back the results interactively.

Cluster shell

8.2 Provisioning of Distributed Domains

So now we have talked about setting up a distributed WebLogic domain, but there are still some peculiarities left that exist in the cloud.

Provisioning the Admin Server

To create the initial domain there are various possibilities. The best solution for yourself depends on your operational processes that already might be in place.

- In case you can create or retrieve a fully configured domain for a particular environment, then download this domain to the cloud instance using `wget` or `scp` and start with this domain.
- If you are setting up a process to provision an initial domain yourself, then consider creating an empty domain with the standard WebLogic template and the `createDomain(domainTemplate,domainDir,user,password)` scripting tool command. Once created, use the base domain and add further configurations such as JMS or JDBC using the scripting tool. Typically, you don't have to write these configuration scripts from scratch. Ask your developer to provide them, or, if you are the developer, check the Oracle documentation for examples. Another option is to record the configuration changes with the admin console to get a first version of the configuration script.

A detailed explanation of the WebLogic scripting tool can be found in section 11.2.

Provisioning a Domain with Managed Servers

In the cloud you want to plan for managed server instances that can be started and stopped anytime, e.g. because the system load changes and auto scaling kicks in. Usually, when setting up a more or less static cluster in a non-cloud environment, I recommend configuring everything first, and then, for a non-shared file system, copying over the domain directory with the configured managed servers including their IP addresses to all machines of the cluster.

Non-cloud

Cloud — This approach isn't suitable for the cloud because you won't know in advance how many managed servers there are, and you cannot configure these servers with their IP addresses because the addresses will be assigned when the instances are starting up.

So on the one hand, the standard approach is not feasible in the cloud, but on the other hand, the remote managed servers cannot boot if their configuration doesn't already exist.

Self configuration of managed servers — There is a solution for this that involves the WebLogic scripting tool. You can use a startup script for all managed servers executing the following steps:

1. Retrieve the public IP of the EC2 instance.
2. Connect to the WebLogic admin server of the domain.
3. Create a new managed server.
4. Assign the public IP of the EC2 instance to newly created managed server.
5. If it is a clustered domain, assign the managed server to the cluster.

All the steps above can be implemented with a centrally hosted, simple script, executed by the runurl utility, which takes the URL of the admin server as an input parameter.

8.3 Oracle Licensing

Licensing is an interesting topic -but not an easy one. Licensing for virtual environments is even more challenging.

Throughout this book I have emphasized the pay on demand model as an important criteria for cloud computing, and Oracle claims to be cloud ready. Yet (to the best of my knowledge), you can neither license Oracle Fusion Middleware for a customer demo that lasts a day, nor for extensive load testing that lasts a month, nor for a marketing campaign that goes along the coming World Surfing Games that may be online for half a year.

So even though you can take advantage of Amazon's EC2 instances, storage volumes, load balancers, and services such as the AWS relational database service with an hourly pay-on-demand model - the Oracle licensing breaks the cloud model at the end of the day. Interestingly enough, all the difficult technical requirements that allow hourly billing, could be successfully solved by Amazon, but the legal issues with licensing persist (it's a legal issue only, since generally there aren't license files which are technically required and checked by the Oracle products).

Oracle documentation — I cannot provide any licensing consulting here, excepting what is written at OTN. Check Oracle's official site regarding licenses:

http://www.oracle.com/us/corporate/pricing/index.html

Keep in mind that even using the Oracle provided AMI's don't include the licensing costs for the Oracle software (unlike, e.g. the AMIs with Microsoft Windows which include the Windows licenses).

However, Oracle is aware of Amazon's EC2. Every 4 virtual cores used (rounded up to the closest multiple of 4) equate to a licensing requirement of 1 socket. According to Oracle, the Standard Edition One can only be licensed on EC2 instances up to 8 virtual cores, and the Standard Edition database can be licensed on EC2 instances up to 16 virtual cores, yet there is presently no such instance. At the time of this writing, the maximum number of virtual cores is 8. There is no stated core limitation for Enterprise Edition. Standard named user plus licensing applies, including counting the minimums where applicable.

Licenses acquired under unlimited license agreements (ULAs) can be used in the Amazon EC2 environment but customers may not include those licenses in the certification at the end of the ULA term. See the following Oracle site for more details (the information provided here is a summary of this site):

http://www.oracle.com/us/corporate/pricing/cloud-licensing-070579.pdf

8.4 Backups

You should definitely consider backups. Actually, backups of your data and your images including their configuration scripts are required.

Data

It is essential for your business that you implement and test a backup plan for the database. If you use the Amazon's relational database service, it will automatically backup the data for you during a specified backup window.

If you are operating your own database you have to take care of the backup yourself. The following article in the AWS documentation explains how to automatically backup a MySQL instance on EC2:

http://aws.amazon.com/articles/1663?_encoding=UTF8&jiveRedirect=1

The Oracle Secure Backup Cloud Module can be used to create S3-stored backups of an Oracle database running either in the cloud or in a non-cloud environment. It leverages the Oracle Recovery Manager (RMAN) for compression and encryption so the backup remains encrypted when in transit on the network and on the cloud. Backing up your data to the S3 cloud storage saves you from creating tapes and storing them off-premise in a secure location.

Oracle documentation

For more information, check the following white paper:

http://www.oracle.com/technetwork/database/features/availability/twp-oracledbcloudbackup-130129.pdf

Also keep in mind that Amazon's EBS provides the ability to create point-in-time snapshots of volumes, which are persisted to Amazon S3. This way you can create regular backups of your volumes. These snapshots are incremental and they are compressed before they are stored.

AMIs

Consider backing up your AMIs as well. This is especially important for full-baked AMIs that contain all your software and configuration. If you follow a scripted approach, then you should at least have a backup of your configuration scripts.

You may wonder why it is necessary to backup your images if they are stored in S3 or as an EBS volume. The answer is, you might still lose them, although it is rather unlikely.

The durability of S3 is extremely high and the durability for EBS is still 10 times higher than a normal hard disc. Still, you may want to replicate your AMI to another region because the regions are in fact separate clouds with separate storage.

Backup EBS-backed AMIs

Surprisingly, there is no easy way to download an EBS volume or an EBS-backed AMI using the AWS management console or an AWS provided command-line tool. The best you can do is mount the volume and use the UNIX command `rsync` to copy it to your local machine.

However, there is an alternative. SecludeIT is offering a collection of scripts, e.g. for the conversion of S3-backed AMIs to EBS-backed AMIs, for the encryption of EBS-volumes, and also to download a snapshot. They provide a form-based utility where you need to type in your AWS credentials, which probably isn't everyone's cup of tea, but they also provide an AMI with all their scripts.

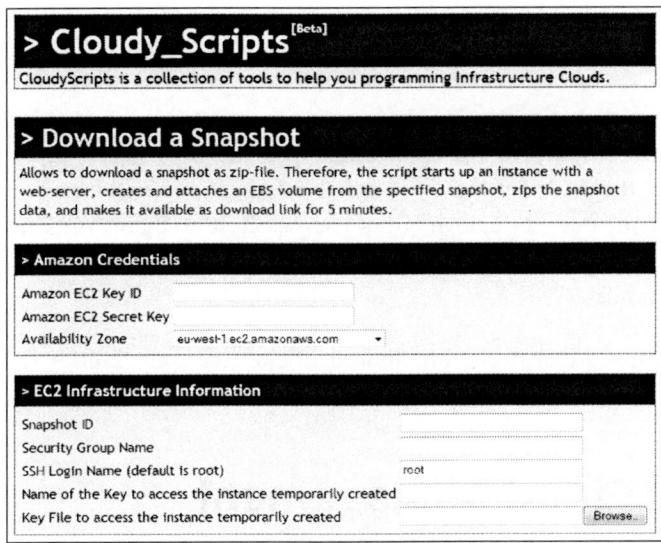

Figure 83: Download Snapshot with Cloudy_Scripts

Check their web site for the tool at the following location:

https://cloudyscripts.com/

8.5 Disaster Recovery

Disaster recovery is planning for the unplanned. Nobody likes to think about the tragedies that could happen. An oft-cited example for a disaster is that AWS is going out of business. What does the contingency plan waiting in your top drawer have listed as possible actions if this happens? Well, I agree, it's rather unlikely.

But then imagine that AWS is not going out of business but stops doing business with your company because of a dispute about your last billing statement (through no fault of your own).

With a helpful contingency plan, you will be able to estimate the worst-case scenario and get back into business again.

Failing over to another AWS region can be a first measure (unless, of course, your account is disabled due to problems with your creditworthiness) since storage is separate for every region. But you'll have to have all the images and data available already in the backup region – so it is important to plan ahead.

Failing over from AWS to Rackspace within a decent time-frame will be impossible if you are using AWS services that don't have a counterpart in the Rackspace Cloud, such as Amazon's SNS or SQS.

If you are operating a standard-based Java EE application, you are in a much better position. Standards pay off in the end. Setting up a mirrored account on Rackspace, including all configurations and the newest deployment of your application that is running on AWS, (or vice versa) is only a question of automation, but can be achieved at a very low price with the pay-on-demand model.

In general, the cloud itself is not an obstacle, but indeed offers great possibilities for disaster recovery.

8.6 RightScale Cloud Management

RightScale is definitely the company with one of the most interesting cloud management solutions. It was founded in 2006 by Thorsten von Eicken, amongst others, and still being a start-up the company closed a new round of $25 million venture funding in September 2010.

RightScale's core product is the web based cloud computing management platform, which comes in five different editions, plus 3 solution editions that are custom built for specific vertical markets such as development and testing, social gaming and grid computing. RightScale has already launched over 1.6 million servers in the cloud at the time of this writing.

There is a free edition for individual developers which includes the functionality of the AWS management console, so you can start and stop your EC instances, or create an elastic load balancer or an EBS volume, for example. Then only feature currently missing in this free edition is support for SNS, but this is by no means a deal breaker.

The standard edition, for up to five users, costs $500/month plus an initial setup fee of $2,500. The all-inclusive enterprise edition of the management platform comes with a "call-for-pricing" tag.

Usage

When you first sign up for the RightScale management dashboard, you are asked to provide the AWS account number, the access key ID and the secret access key. The RightScale management dashboard can then directly access the configurations and custom AMI images in your AWS account.

Use the following URL to get to the RightScale Cloud Management Platform login:

http://www.rightscale.com/

RightImages

RightScale publishes publically available AMIs as RightImages. RightScale ServerTemplates are built on top of RightImages.

MultiCloud Images

MultiCloud Images will work in various cloud environments. When adding a server to a deployment, the MultiCloud Image determines which image will be chosen for a particular region or cloud.

ServerTemplates

The RightScale management platform is based on configurable ServerTemplates which contain the preconfigured, scripted, software installations required to launch a fully operational server. Every server template contains the following parts:

- A base machine image with an operating system, network tools and security.
- Cloud specific configurations.
- Referenced RightScripts that can be written in shell, bash, Ruby or Python. These scripts are run at the boot process, during operation or during shutdown of the instance. They are located off-instance and can be shared for re-use across multiple templates.

Having templates that include software and the configuration scripts increases the consistency of the installations, and ensures that best-practice is applied to all images. This approach also allows their ServerTemplates to be cloud agnostic. In other words, the RightScale management platform implements a convenient, tool based approach of scripted image configuration, as explained in section 6.3 of this book about AMI design.

Furthermore, RightScale provides a library with RightScripts and ServerTemplate images. Have a look at the screenshot in Figure 84 for some examples of templates.

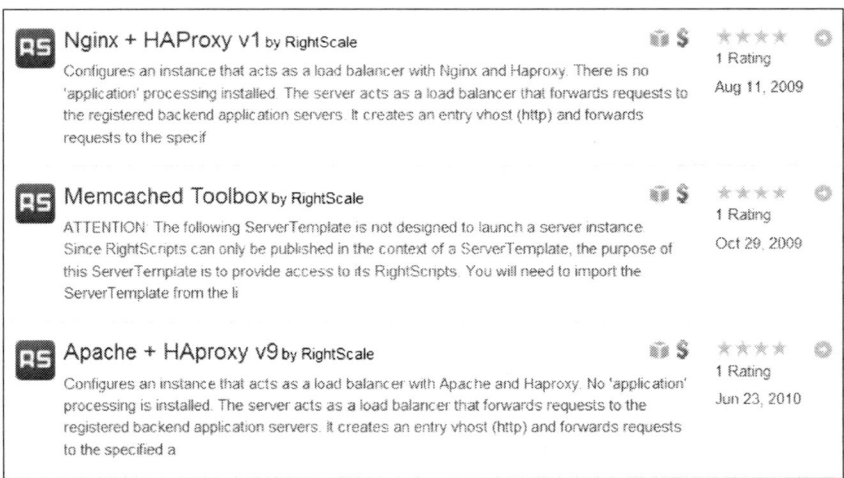

Figure 84: RightScale ServerTemplate Library

Deployments

The second key differentiator of RightScale is the grouping of servers to deployments. Deployments consist of a group of servers that work together and share common input variables and cloud configurations.

A default deployment contains servers which are launched directly from a template without first assigning them to a deployment. However, it is not possible to define input parameters for the default deployment. So, instead of using the default deployment, you typically create your own deployment and then import the server templates.

Let's assume your environment consists of HAProxy on an EC2 instance, two Apache web servers, a cluster of three WebLogic servers in a domain, and another domain running Oracle Service Bus. A RightScale deployment will treat this configuration as one single deployment.

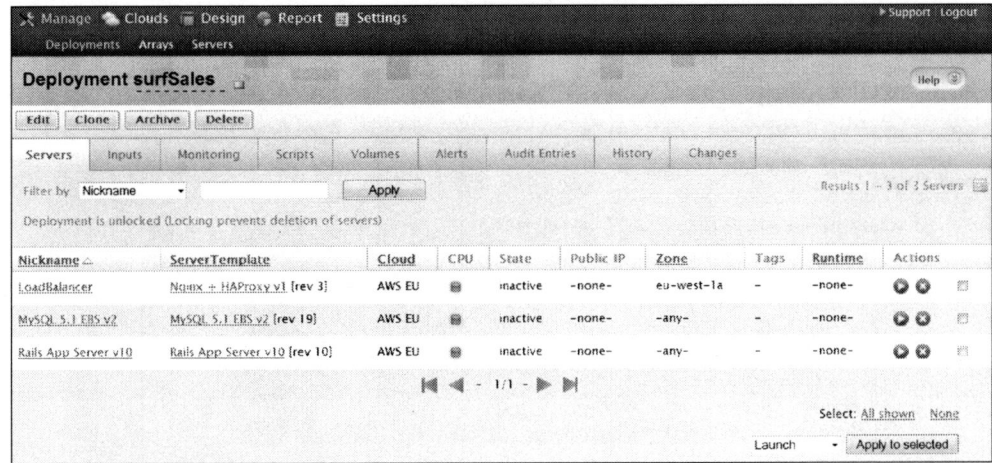

Figure 85: RightScale Deployment

Because the RightScale library doesn't contain any templates for Oracle products yet the example in Figure 85 is based on existing templates Nginx with HAProxy, MySQL and Rails.

A deployment can be managed like a single server; you can specify deployment level inputs and start, manage and stop all the servers in the deployment in one single action. An exciting feature of deployments is that you can easily clone a complete environment. So, once your load and integration tests are complete, you can clone a working environment for production use.

Deployments increase management efficiency because you configure, run *and* monitor whole environments as one single unit. With the RightScale console you can pick a template, verify all settings such as scripts (shown in Figure 86), alerts for monitoring and inputs, and then import the template to a deployment.

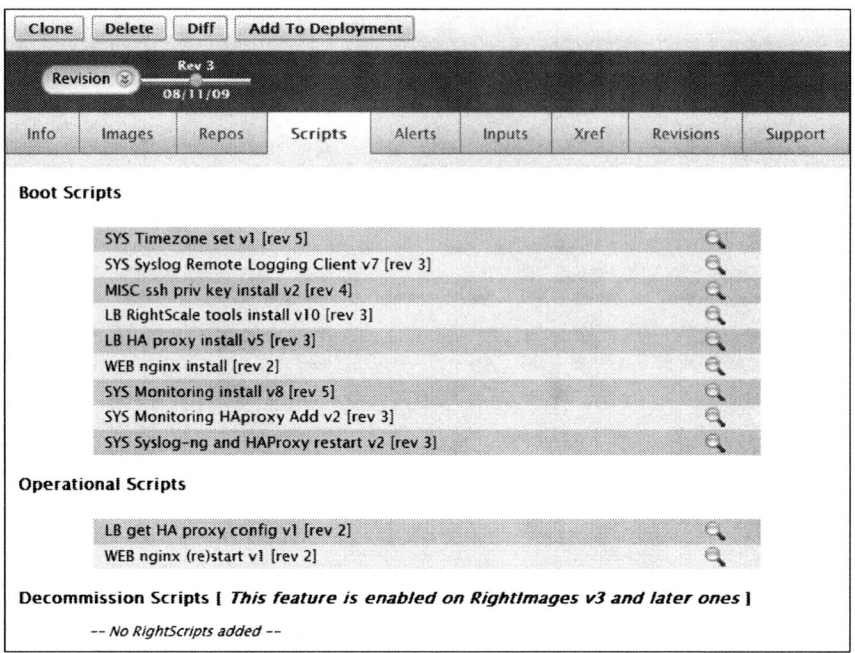

Figure 86: RightScale Server Template Scripts

Running a Deployment

When starting a deployment, you need to fill in the missing values for the scripts' input parameters. The colors in the screenshot below indicate whether a parameter is required for a script at a server, deployment or template level.

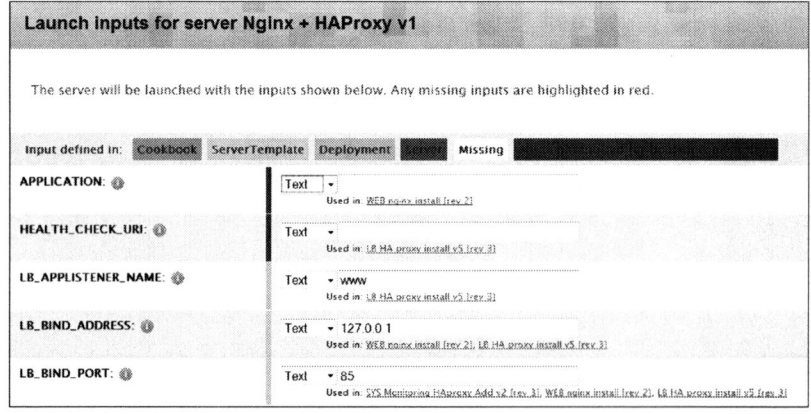

Figure 87: RightScale Launch Inputs

Cost Report and Prediction

Once the deployment is up and running, RightScale provides a detailed cost report. Month-to-date usage is displayed adjacent to the projected usage for this month and usage for the previous month.

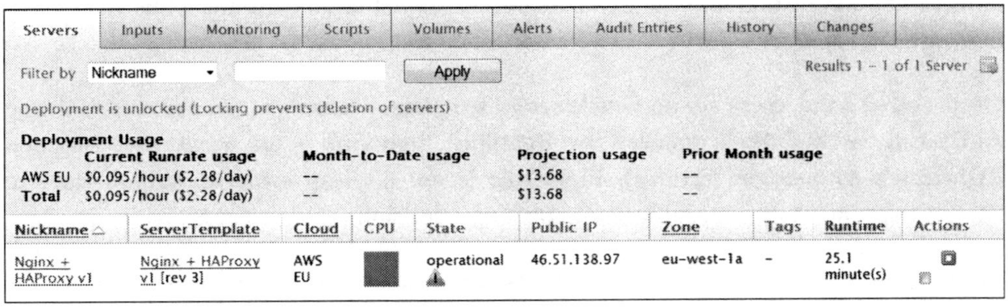

Figure 88: RightScale Deployment Usage

In addition, you can manage monthly costs per deployment: simply select Report / Usage Estimate. For instances with monitoring enabled, data-transfer rates are shown under usage estimates. To calculate these, RightScale uses the total measured traffic (but doesn't take into account the traffic within availability zones or between EC2 and S3, so it might overestimate actual usage).

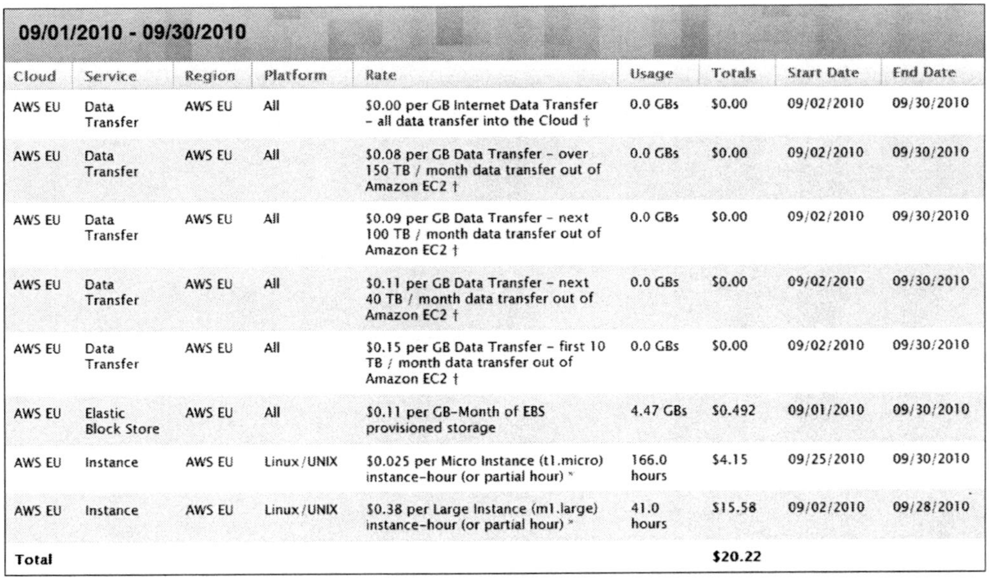

Cloud	Service	Region	Platform	Rate	Usage	Totals	Start Date	End Date
AWS EU	Data Transfer	AWS EU	All	$0.00 per GB Internet Data Transfer – all data transfer into the Cloud †	0.0 GBs	$0.00	09/02/2010	09/30/2010
AWS EU	Data Transfer	AWS EU	All	$0.08 per GB Data Transfer – over 150 TB / month data transfer out of Amazon EC2 †	0.0 GBs	$0.00	09/02/2010	09/30/2010
AWS EU	Data Transfer	AWS EU	All	$0.09 per GB Data Transfer – next 100 TB / month data transfer out of Amazon EC2 †	0.0 GBs	$0.00	09/02/2010	09/30/2010
AWS EU	Data Transfer	AWS EU	All	$0.11 per GB Data Transfer – next 40 TB / month data transfer out of Amazon EC2 †	0.0 GBs	$0.00	09/02/2010	09/30/2010
AWS EU	Data Transfer	AWS EU	All	$0.15 per GB Data Transfer – first 10 TB / month data transfer out of Amazon EC2 †	0.0 GBs	$0.00	09/02/2010	09/30/2010
AWS EU	Elastic Block Store	AWS EU	All	$0.11 per GB-Month of EBS provisioned storage	4.47 GBs	$0.492	09/01/2010	09/30/2010
AWS EU	Instance	AWS EU	Linux/UNIX	$0.025 per Micro Instance (t1.micro) instance-hour (or partial hour) *	166.0 hours	$4.15	09/25/2010	09/30/2010
AWS EU	Instance	AWS EU	Linux/UNIX	$0.38 per Large Instance (m1.large) instance-hour (or partial hour) *	41.0 hours	$15.58	09/02/2010	09/28/2010
Total						$20.22		

Figure 89: RightScale Usage Report

Cloud Management 173

Summary

To conclude, RightScale implements a cloud management approach based on multi-cloud server templates and deployments. In addition, the RightScale management platform provides extended monitoring and an alert mechanism based on events. The existing libraries and integration into the web based management dashboard make this an efficient management solution.

On the other hand, there are no Oracle server templates available at the moment (existing AMIs can be RightScale enabled by installing RightLink - an agent that supports RightScale's automation features). RightScale is not a cheap solution, so you have to analyze the benefits very carefully before making a decision.

In my opinion, if you require more than just a scripted configuration of AWS AMIs, the RightScale management platform is an interesting alternative to 'reinventing the wheel'. RightScale offers the acceleration of a PaaS application deployment environment with the full control of an IaaS environment.

When it comes to cloud portability and multi-cloud support in particular, limitations in your own scripted approach will become apparent and you will definitely appreciate the multi-cloud templates and the management platform available in RightScale's library.

9 Availability

According to the International Data Corporation (IDC) cloud services survey of 2009, availability is the number two challenge of the cloud computing model (after security, which is the number one concern) for over 83% of all IT executives.

In this chapter we cover the different aspects and strategies to provide availability of middleware in the cloud. We will start with the basics such as decoupled systems, elastic IPs and availability zones, and then have a look at clustering in the cloud, distributed JMS and other WebLogic features to increase availability, such as whole-server migration and service migration and then explain how and when to use the AWS simple queue service. The last part of this chapter explains how to keep a distributed system stable under excessive load; it's about overload protection.

9.1 Availability Basics

Decoupling Systems

The worst thing that could happen to a distributed system is that it stops working completely. The more parts the distributed systems consist of, and the tighter the coupling between those parts, the more likely this will happen. The coupling between parts increases with the number of assumptions each part has of the other. In the worst case, the whole distributed systems stops working because one service, one server, or one instance fails.

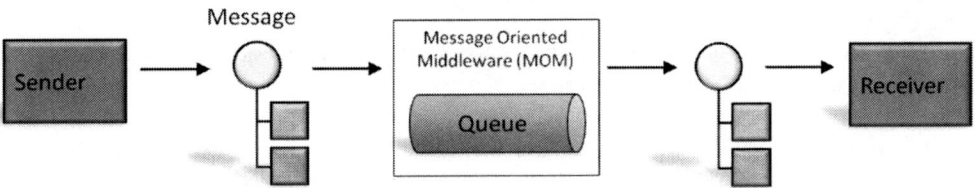

Figure 90: Message Oriented Middleware

Asynchronous messaging decreases the amount of coupling. The sender doesn't depend on the *availability* of the receiver anymore, because the message is not sent to the receiver but passed to a highly available message queue instead. Since the message queue is in between the sender and the receiver, this is called message oriented middleware (MOM).

The queue as a general concept can be implemented as an AWS simple queue service (as described in section 9.7) or as a WebLogic JMS queue (described in section 9.3).

Elastic IPs

Use elastic IPs to switch quickly between complex installations and to increase availability. A good example for the usage of the elastic IPs is the availability of the WebLogic admin server.

The admin server isn't required for processing the client requests and the operation of the managed servers, yet it is needed for monitoring, deployment and administration. If the admin server is restarted with the same IP address the managed servers discover and reconnect to it.

The elastic IP can be used to provide the same IP address after an EC2 instance failure to the new instance. In this case the admin server should listen to the elastic IP address.

Availability Zones

Another unique cloud feature is availability zones. You can increase the overall availability of a distributed system by placing its servers in two separate data centers. Selecting an availability zone is free, but you have to pay the regional data transfer rate for data transferred between Amazon EC2 instances located in different availability zones (see page 44 and following for the pricing, and page 26 for the EC2 service level agreement).

9.2 Clustering WebLogic

To recap the WebLogic section of the SOA chapter, let me quickly summarize the important features of a WebLogic cluster.

1. A cluster enables load balancing for EJBs. Replica-aware EJB client stubs are retrieved from the JNDI (which is also replicated by the cluster to all other cluster members).
2. A cluster provides in-memory session replication for failover: Session data is replicated to a second cluster instance.
3. A cluster enables server migration. With server migration, a managed server that cannot be restarted in-place is restarted on another machine.

4. A cluster enables automatic service migration. With service migration a singleton-service such as JMS, JTA or a user-defined singleton is migrated from one managed server to another managed server.
5. A cluster facilitates the deployment of applications. If you select a cluster as a deployment target, the application is automatically available on cluster nodes, which are added later.
6. A cluster is the prerequisite for distributed JMS destinations.

Clustering in the Cloud

The crucial question is, "Can we design and build a clustered architecture for the Amazon cloud?" The answer is yes; but there are some restrictions which must be understood.

AWS Cloud

The first limitation, and well-known fact, is that EC2 doesn't support multicast. You must plan and configure your cluster with unicast. The cluster communication method is typically specified when you set up the cluster using the configuration wizard or the WebLogic admin console. It is possible to change the communication method later, but it requires restarting the cluster, so it is better to select the correct one from the start.

Oracle recommends using unicast over multicast anyway, because it is a newer technology and requires less configuration effort and potentially causes fewer problems. When using unicast, you can forget about keeping records of non-conflicting sets of multicast / IP pairs and therefore lessen the burden of the operation team.

Unicast

There is little documentation about the technical details of unicast. Broadly speaking, the physical one-to-many communication of multicast is replaced by several logical one-to-one communications implemented based on TCP/IP socket connections.

WebLogic designates the server that joined the cluster first as group leader. Up to 10 members of the cluster connect to a group leader which acts as a relay point. The point-to-point connections are established between managed server ports. A new group leader for every 10 servers is chosen for clusters with more than 10 servers, and all group leaders are interconnected.

This approach is slightly more costly: Large unicast clusters tend to be a bit slower than a multicast cluster which scales inherently well.

Rackspace Cloud

It might come as a surprise, but the multicast issue is exactly the same for Rackspace Cloud servers - although it took me quite a while to figure that out, since it is not documented.

When I first talked to the "Fanatic Support" of Rackspace Cloud about this issue, I was told, "There is no reason why it shouldn't work". Even George Reese mentions in his book about Cloud Application Architectures (which I recommend anyway, don't get me wrong) that Rackspace Cloud *does* support multicast. The short story is: Rackspace Cloud doesn't. I tried to use it and failed.

After some puzzling on my side, Rackspace Cloud support finally confirmed, "It is disabled on our hypervisors to preserve network sanity".

Multicast Testing

In case you are ever tempted to setup a multicast based cluster on another IaaS provider, I recommend using the simple multicast test command line utility that comes with every WebLogic installation. Here are the instructions to reproduce the step on the Rackspace Cloud.

(1) Launch two WebLogic instances in the cloud; this should take about 3 minutes. I went for a 1GB Win2008 because I wanted to check for potential Windows problems. Note: Currently you cannot create an image from a Rackspace Windows server, which is why I started two images from the very beginning. Otherwise it makes more sense to configure one image first and then clone it later.
(2) Download and install your preferred WebLogic version.
(3) If you are using Windows instances, turn off the Windows firewall just in case. You don't want the Windows firewall to block your multicast packets.
(4) Open a command-line, then navigate to the server\bin directory of the product installation and run the setWLSEnv script to set the environment:

```
C:\Oracle\Middleware\wlserver_10.3\server\bin>setWLSEnv.cmd
```

(5) Repeat steps 2 to 4 on the other instance
(6) Then run the multicast test utility on both sides using a different name with -N for example use -N BLUE on one side and -N RED the other side:

```
java utils.MulticastTest -N RED  -A 237.0.0.1 -P 8001
java utils.MulticastTest -N BLUE -A 237.0.0.1 -P 8001
```

(7) Check the output on both machines. With multicast working correctly, both machines should detect the packages from the remote side together with their own.

9.3 Distributed JMS

It comes as a big surprise to some WebLogic users that JMS is not automatically "clustered" just because you have a cluster configured and assign the JMS server to the cluster.

SCALABILITY AND/OR AVAILABILITY?

We explore distributed destinations here in this chapter. Distributed destinations require a cluster, and the main purpose of a cluster is availability. Also, distributed destinations increase the overall availability of JMS. But then, of course, distributed destinations improve the scalability of JMS as well; that's the reason why scalability for distributed destinations is explained, too.

Even though a JMS server is running on a managed server as a part of a cluster, there aren't any cluster features for JMS, such as load balancing and failover. You can neither configure one queue to be part of two JMS servers, nor can you target a JMS server to a cluster.

The crucial point is that a particular JMS queue or topic is always assigned to exactly one JMS server. (Usually this assignment is done indirectly via subdeployments; check the WebLogic JMS documentation for subdeployments since subdeployments are beyond the scope of this book.) Therefore, even though you configured a cluster, a JMS queue without further configuration could be a single point of failure and a potential bottleneck because it only exists once.

Scalability

Distributed destinations are used to improve the scalability of the Oracle JMS architecture for WebLogic server. Such a distributed destination has several physical destinations assigned to it and comes with a JNDI name in the same way as any other destination. To send messages to a distributed destination, look up the JNDI name of the distributed destination. It will then return one of the physical destinations assigned to it as illustrated in Figure 91.

So why is this approach more scalable? The distributed destination can be configured for load balancing so the messages will be balanced across the individual JMS servers.

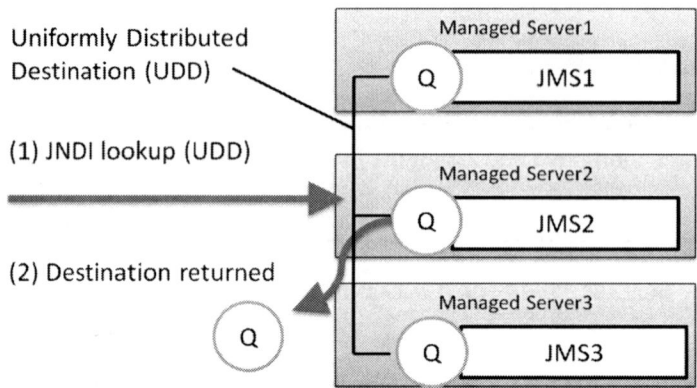

Figure 91: JMS Distributed Destinations

Typically for persistent messages, the throughput, measured in messages per second, is limited by the I/O performance of the persistence store. In WebLogic you could have two types of persistent stores. The store can either be file-based or database-based. Concerning scalability, the key question is: which one is faster? Well, even if there are no other concerns (such as availability, which is covered in the next paragraph), the only wise recommendation is to run a benchmark yourself, with your target environment, your file system and your data base. There is no rule of thumb: A fast database can easily outperform a slow file system and vice versa.

The real performance boost comes due to the fact that every JMS server is using its own persistent store now. Even if you'd like to, you couldn't share one store across two JMS servers. The I/O bottleneck is alleviated since all stores are accessed in parallel with the aggregated bandwidth.

Availability

When introducing the clustering of WebLogic in general I explained that within a WebLogic cluster there is no automatic migration of local files to another machine. So regardless of the discussion that often pops up over whether a database-based store is faster than a file store, the database-based store will be globally available with the same JDBC URL even after a server is migrated. You just have to guarantee that the database behind the JDBC URL is highly available. So looking at availability, a JDBC based store is often the better option since a shared file system such as NFS introduces more difficulties.

Now, what happens with the messages if a JMS server fails? If you didn't persist the messages, they are simply lost. This happens by design. Non-persistent messaging is much faster and whenever there is no requirement for persistence, this is the option with the higher throughput.

Failed JMS server

Quite often though, you will be dealing with applications where the loss of messages is not tolerable. Think about an ordering system for expensive holiday trips to the most exotic dive sites. Losing such a booking because the message is non-persistently stored in JMS is intolerable and ends up in a financial loss. In such a case you require reliable messaging with a persistent store.

Persistent destination

Messages which are stored in the persistent store of a crashed JMS server can only be recovered by restarting the JMS server itself. Since the stores cannot be shared, there is never another JMS server taking over the stuck messages of the crashed server automatically.

Message recovery

Now it is getting even more interesting. Assume the WebLogic server with the JMS server assigned to it cannot be restarted because the machine it was running on burst into flames due to a short-circuit. (Probably water damage is more likely - but I guess fire is the better story!) In a classical distributed architecture, which is not running in the cloud, the best solution to cope with a server failure like this is to configure WebLogic whole-server migration.

9.4 Whole-server Migration

The WebLogic whole-server migration (WSM) feature is a compelling solution for the availability of managed servers including all pinned resources on these servers. WSM was briefly introduced in section 5.3, but here comes a more detailed explanation that also demonstrates its limitation on current IaaS platforms.

Classic Non-Cloud Environment

The WLS nodemanager is a prerequisite for whole-server migration. The cluster detects that the managed server failed, and tries to connect to the nodemanager on that machine in order to restart the managed server.

Nodemanager required

If the cluster cannot detect the nodemanager (remember the previous example, where there is only a small heap of still glowing ashes left of what used to be the machine?), the cluster selects a machine from the list of potential target machines. Then the cluster contacts the nodemanager at the new target node and restarts the same WebLogic server instance there.

Floating IPs For the whole-server migration to work correctly, you have to fulfill some more prerequisites. The most important one is the availability of floating IP addresses. A managed server is listening to its floating IP address and when the whole-server migration is triggered, the IP address of the crashed server is assigned to the new target server. This is done by executing a script called `wlsifconfig.sh`, which can be found in the following location:

```
ORACLE_MIDDLEWARE/wlserver_10.3/common/bin
```

The script is triggered by the whole-server migration; it uses `ipconfig` to add or remove the floating IP for a Unix system, and the `netsh` command for Windows.

WSM simply moves the IP address to the new candidate machine before starting the managed server there. From the perspective of the managed server there is no change at all, since even the IP address is the same. The crucial point, however, is the availability of floating IP addresses that can be automatically reassigned by the `wlsifconfig.sh` script.

Oracle documentation For further details take a look at the Oracle documentation at the following site:

http://download.oracle.com/docs/cd/E14571_01/web.1111/e13709/migration.htm#BABFEFEG

So how about using WSM in the cloud?

Whole-server Migration on EC2

The EC2 instances have a public and a private IP address. You cannot get additional IP addresses, so whole-server migration isn't of much use.

In fact, you could get an elastic IP address, which is a static IP address assigned to an EC instance. Still, an elastic IP is not useful for server-migration, because assignment of the address requires the EC2 command-line and cannot be triggered from the cluster script.

Whole-server Migration on Rackspace Cloud Servers

You can get additional IP addresses for the Rackspace Cloud Servers which will be assigned by the support team. You cannot share them between servers, and to the best of my knowledge, you cannot assign them manually.

This means you cannot use the whole-server migration feature in the Rackspace cloud either.

Conclusion

You cannot use whole-server migration either for the Amazon or for the Rackspace Cloud. This is unfortunate because it would simplify the design for fault-tolerance, and it would reduce the required configurations to a server level only.

Service migration, which is described in the next section, is a viable alternative to whole-server migration.

It's worth doing a detailed ROI for those Java EE parts of WebLogic where cloud services with a similar functionality, yet inherent availability, exist.

9.5 Service Migration

Service migration provides better availability for pinned services. It migrates a failed service to another managed server, but it doesn't migrate the whole server, so you have to configure it for all relevant services.

Classic Non-Cloud Environment

Typical examples of pinned services are JTA, JMS server and its related services, such as the JMS Store-and-Forward Service, (used to persistently buffer and forward messages to remote JMS servers) or the JMS Path Service (used for the mapping of JMS messages to enforce their unit-of-order).

You can also make user-defined singletons highly available with the service migration framework. A user-defined singleton is a cluster service that is available on exactly one server at any given time. This singleton service is required to implement the Java interface `weblogic.cluster.singleton.SingletonService` with the two methods, `activate()`, and `deactivate()`, that obtain and release resources when the singleton is started or stopped. A singleton service can be packaged with an application or deployed standalone. There is a singleton master that triggers the migration of singleton services.   *User-defined singletons*

For automatic service migration you have to deploy the pinned services on a *migratable target* that groups all services that should be moved together.   *Migratable target*

For further details take a look at the Oracle documentation at the following site: *Oracle documentation*

`http://download.oracle.com/docs/cd/E14571_01/web.1111/e13709/service_migration.htm#BABGJBHD`

Service Migration in the Cloud

Service migration in the cloud Automatic service migration requires a script based nodemanager (which is only supported for UNIX platforms) but it is not based on floating IP addresses – so this solution will also work on current IaaS platforms, such as AWS or Rackspace Cloud.

9.6 WebLogic JTA

Transaction log files The JTA service depends on the transaction log file. This transaction log is written in binary format and stored in the default persistent store. At server startup the WebLogic transaction recovery service (TRS) parses the transaction log for incomplete transactions and attempts to recover them. Therefore the first attempt to recover transactions should always be to restart a failed server.

To recover failed transactions in a non-clustered environment you can manually move the transaction log to a new instance, set the path for the default persistent store to the data file, and start a new server instance.

Service migration Automatic service migration of the JTA service only makes sense if the transaction log was on a shared file system, which is not recommended in the cloud (see section 8.1 for an explanation of shared file systems in the cloud).

For a clustered WebLogic domain you can also manually migrate the transaction recovery service to another server which will take over ownership of the transaction log from the crashed server in order to recover the failed transactions.

Oracle documentation For a detailed discussion of JTA in clustered and non-clustered WebLogic domains, take a look at the following site:

```
http://download.oracle.com/docs/cd/E14571_01/web.1111/e13731/
trxman.htm#WLJTA177
```

9.7 AWS Simple Queue Service

Amazon's Simple Queue Service (SQS) is a cloud service for reliable messaging. The SQS service with its queues is located off-host. So, similar to the elastic load balancing service, or the relational database service, you can use the service without having to start an EC2 instance.

Features

SQS is available in all four AWS regions with the same pricing. All regions are independent of each other so messages can never be in-between regions. Queue names have to be unique per region.

Queues are highly available: Messages waiting in queues for their delivery are stored redundantly on multiple servers and in multiple data centers. *Highly available*

There is no limit for the number of messages or the size of a particular queue. One message body can be up to 64 KB of text in any format (default is 8KB). For larger messages you have to store the message somewhere else reliably, e.g. in S3, SimpleDB or RDS, and pass around a reference to the storage location instead of passing the message itself. *Unlimited queue size*

When a message remains in a queue (because there is no receiver removing the message from the queue), the message expires after a default of four days (or a configurable maximum of 14 days). *Message expiry*

After receiving a message from a queue, the message is locked for a configurable timeout. While the message is locked it is invisible to other receivers. SQS uses this mechanism to ensure that messages are delivered once.

It's the receiver's responsibility to explicitly delete the message when it is processed successfully. If the receiver fails before it is able to delete the message, then the message becomes visible again after the timeout, and another receiver can receive it.

Access to queues is restricted to the AWS account owners, but you can specify in an access policy statement that a queue will be shared.

Encryption is not a built-in SQS feature, but depending on your privacy requirements you can consider encrypting the content of your message at an application level. Also, there is no built-in compression feature, but you can compress large messages at an application level before sending them. *No compression or encryption*

The message delivery semantic is engineered to be "at least once". This means your applications have to cope with message duplicates. *At least once semantics*

Usage

Access to SQS is purely programmatic. Currently, there are no command-line tools from AWS, and there is no integration for SQS into the AWS management console yet.

There are language bindings for Java, PHP, Perl and C#. Also, the Java Typica library supports SQS.

SQS is ideal for decoupling systems or applications running on EC2. From a design perspective, SQS has many features in common with JMS queues. The most important differences between SQS and JMS queues are listed in Table 10.

Table 10: SQS Comparison with WLS Queues

	SQS Queues	WebLogic JMS Queues
Max queue size	Unlimited	Limit depends on JVM heap and persistent store
Best Quality of Service	At least once	Exactly-once with transactions
Configurable retries	No	Yes
Persistence	Always	Optional
Scalability	Inherent	With distributed queues
Availability	Inherent	Whole-server migration or JMS service migration
Message Order	Not guaranteed	Can be enforced even for distributed queues
Configurable quotas	No	Yes
Configurable flow control	No	Yes
Auto acknowledge	No	Yes
Time To Live configuration	1h to 14d	1 ms to ca. 2 mio years
Max message size	64 KB	Unlimited, default is 10,000 KB
Compression	No	Yes
Billing	Free usage tier, then charged per request and data transfer amount	Included with WLS

Conclusion

To conclude, SQS is an AWS cloud service that could replace WebLogic JMS queues.

Compared to JMS queues, SQS has fewer features, no auto acknowledgement of messages and no support for exactly-once message delivery. The advantage of SQS over JMS queues is SQS' inherent availability, the virtually unlimited storage for messages and the zero configuration.

The inherent availability is an especially important factor to consider when deciding between SQS or JMS queues, because the built-in features offered by WebLogic for achieving availability of JMS are restricted in today's clouds (see section 9.3 for distributed JMS).

SQS is implemented off-instance; therefore, its availability is not affected if a particular EC2 instance becomes unavailable.

Interestingly, there is a cloud service for the counterpart to JMS topics as well. The AWS Simple Notification Service allows you to send messages to more than one receiver using transport protocols such as HTTP, email and even SQS. See section 11.6 for details about the Simple Notification Service. *SNS*

In case you are wondering how this relates to Oracle Service Bus: Comparing SQS with Oracle Service Bus is like comparing apples with oranges, because in addition to the built-in JMS, service bus also supports protocol adaption, message flows with content-based routing, and most importantly, it is configuration driven. *SQS vs. OSB*

In a nutshell: SQS is a queue service for the AWS cloud to decouple systems with message passing. As a cloud service it abstracts the Java EE specific details of JMS - nevertheless SQS is specific to AWS. Currently there is no cloud messaging service offered for the Rackspace cloud. Using an AWS specific service like SQS increases the effort to migrate to another cloud provider (and limits your possibilities to quickly switch to another cloud provider as a part of a contingency plan).

Currently, there is no standard multi-cloud queue service (have a look at the discussion about "Real SaaS in the cloud" on page 13 again – a multi-cloud queue system would be the first step).

Pricing

There is a free usage tier for up to 100,000 requests per month. Beyond that, Amazon adds $0.01 per 10,000 SQS requests to your bill.

In addition, you have to pay for the data transfer as shown in Figure 92. Only data transferred between SQS and EC2 within a single region is free. Data transferred between different regions will be charged at Internet data transfer rates on both ends.

Availability 187

Data Transfer In	US & EU Regions	APAC Region
All Data Transfer	$0.10 per GB	$0.10 per GB

Data Transfer Out ***	US & EU Regions	APAC Region
First 1 GB per Month	$0.00 per GB	$0.00 per GB
Up to 10 TB per Month	$0.15 per GB	$0.19 per GB
Next 40 TB per Month	$0.11 per GB	$0.15 per GB
Next 100 TB per Month	$0.09 per GB	$0.13 per GB
Over 150 TB per Month	$0.08 per GB	$0.12 per GB

Figure 92: SQS Data Transfer Pricing

9.8 Overload Protection

Even with the most careful capacity planning in place, even with auto scaling enabled, even with carefully tuned, well-written and load tested applications which have no design flaws, you should still be prepared for instantaneous growth.

There can be various reasons for instantaneous growth.

- Increased inoffensive traffic. Unexpected demand can be great news for your business unless your business breaks down because of the overloaded system.
- Offensive traffic caused by an attacker. This is really bad news, because all of the traffic which isn't useful is just affecting the stability of the system negatively.

The better designed your application and your system architecture is, the longer you can cope even with abnormal growths without side effects. At some point with extremely high loads, you will run into trouble and the worst thing that could happen is that your system becomes unusable.

The best strategy to prevent your system from failing completely is to limit the number of requests that the system is dealing with, and to limit the amount of resources that your application will reserve for these requests.

Availability over scalability Overload protection is limiting scalability for the sake of availability. Here, the design tradeoff is obvious: You prefer to have your application running within the defined specifications and you are willing to reject additional requests instead of risking system instability or a complete breakdown.

There are a couple of measures to take in order to achieve this. None of them guarantees to protect you from overload, but these measures reduce the risk that overload will negatively affect your system.

- Reject attacks on a network level. This is certainly the most effective way to deal with offensive load coming from distributed denial of service attacks (DDOS). Firewalls can reject traffic based on DENY filters, some switches provide automatic rate-limiting for incoming traffic, and filter out bogus IP addresses; some routers come with intelligence designed to detect irregular traffic patterns.
- Protect WebLogic resources. Since WebLogic is the core infrastructure for Oracle Fusion Middleware, it is essential to understand the key settings to prevent excessive resource allocation. I summarize the important settings in the remainder of this section.
- System Architecture. Make sure you understand all possibilities and alternatives for a distributed WebLogic architecture, including the following:
    - WebLogic clustering,
    - Distributed JMS destinations,
    - Multi data sources,
    - Service migration and
    - Whole-server migration

    See sections 9.1 to 9.5 for the applicability of these measures in the cloud.

- Application Design.
    - Make sure your application is designed and built in independent modules with predetermined breaking points. Ideally you will have a service-oriented architecture in place, with independent services decoupled from their clients using Oracle Service Bus.
    - Make sure you can temporarily and dynamically disable the less important parts of your application if Armageddon is closing in. With JMX you can use a generic client (such as JConsole or WebLogic scripting tool) to change settings for your application without having to restart the application server. For a discussion of these tools, which are also used for monitoring, have a look at section 11.2.

- Test it! You are in the cloud now. You have all the resources that you need to generate even extreme load. Nobody will be able to predict the behavior of their application under massive load without testing it.

WebLogic Overload Protection and OFM

There are a number of core WebLogic settings, as well as various settings for the individual subcomponents of WebLogic (such as JMS or JDBC) that enable you to limit the effect of excessive load. I recommend using the following enumeration of topics as a checklist for your own WebLogic settings.

The basic settings are applicable for all other Oracle Fusion Middleware products which are run on top of WebLogic. Examples of these products are Oracle BPM, Service Bus, Service Registry and so on. For a brief discussion of these products see chapter 5 about SOA and Oracle Fusion Middleware.

WebLogic Administration Port

Enabling the administration port is not the same as setting a port number for the admin server. Enabling the administration port does the following: It reserves a thread and a separate port number for all administration communication within a WebLogic server domain, and it enables SSL and disables non-SSL administration communication. Using the administration port feature increases the likelihood that admin server communication will be functional under high load.
The screenshot in the figure below shows the setting which enables the administration port in the admin console under Configuration / General.

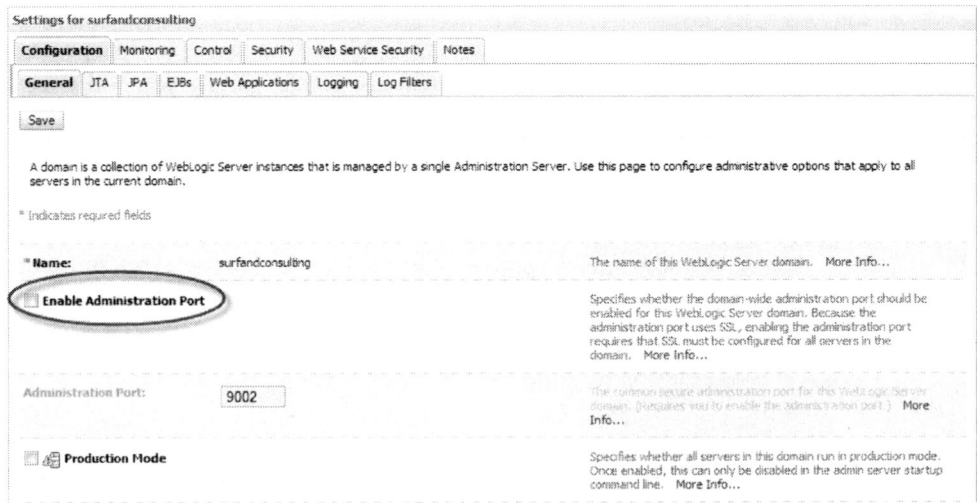

Figure 93: Enable Administration Port

Workmanager Capacity Constraint

WebLogic uses work managers with a variable and self-tuning number of worker threads. There is a default work manager, but you can define your own work manager and assign a particular application or even a part of it such as a JSP, to your custom work manager. When configuring a custom work manger you can add restrictions such as the minimum or maximum number of threads, a fair-share usage policy or a capacity constraint. The capacity constraint defines the maximum number of requests that can be queued or executed at any given point in time.

Incoming requests that exceed the number of execute threads will be queued.

Incoming requests above the capacity constraint are rejected and result in a "503- Service Unavailable" response code for web applications. This capacity constraint can be shared across multiple work managers.

Maximum Queue Length

You can define a maximum queue length shared across all work managers with the setting "Shared Capacity For Work Managers" field in the WebLogic admin console. The default value of this field is 65536. This setting does not apply for the administration port, so you will not risk the access to the admin server even if the maximum number of requests queued is reached.

Maximum Thread Poolsize

Although the work managers use a self-tuning thread pool, it is still possible to limit the maximum size of the pool. Note that in general I reckon that the self-tuning work manger is doing fine and I *do not recommend* setting a maximum number of threads. However, if your load test reveals that an excessive amount of threads will make your system slow or unstable, you could try to run your load test with a maximum constraint for the thread pool.

There is no way to set the maximum thread count directly from the WebLogic admin GUI, but you can provide an additional startup argument in your server start script:

```
-Dweblogic.threadpool.MaxPoolSize=500
```

You can achieve the same by editing the WebLogic `config.xml` in the config subdirectory of your WebLogic domain. Add the `<self-tuning-thread-pool-size-max>` element with the maximum number of threads to the `<server>` element. As always, make a backup

Availability 191

copy and stop the admin server before editing the config.xml, because a running admin server will overwrite your changes.

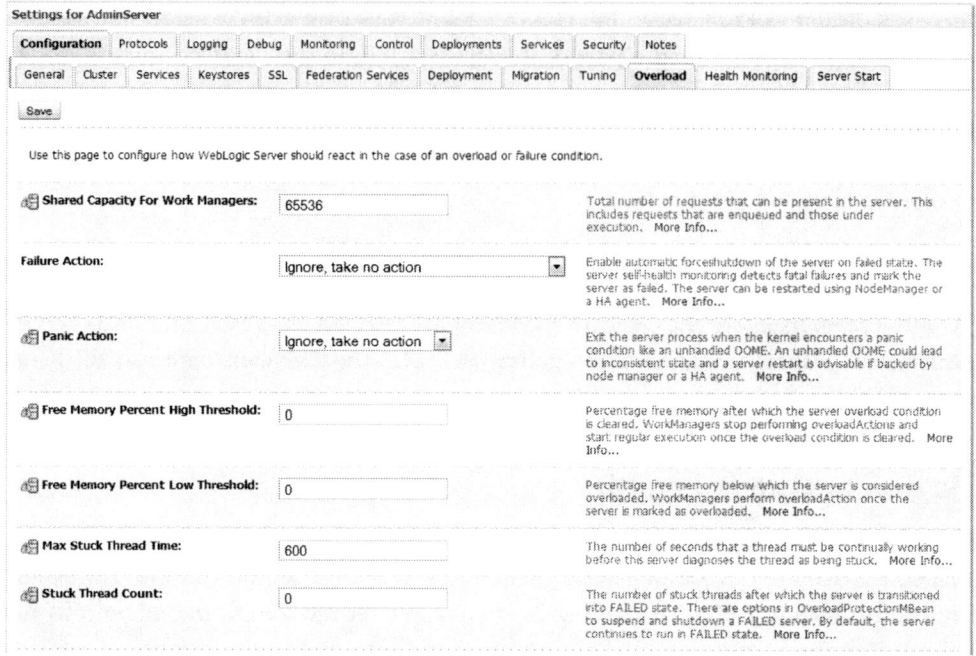

Figure 94: WebLogic Overload Settings

Maximum Heap and Panic Setting

Define the maximum heap size for the JVM with the –Xmx parameter. The maximum heap should never exceed the available physical memory in your machine since paging for virtual memory will slow the system down dramatically.

Define which percentage of free heap triggers an out of memory situation in the WebLogic admin console under Configuration / Overload (for details have a look at the screenshot in Figure 94: WebLogic Overload Settings). The "Panic Action" setting defines what action will be taken if an out of memory situation occurs. The default setting is "Ignore, take no action", but you can change it to "Exit the server process" and let the nodemanager restart your server.

Restricting the Number of HTTP sessions

For a WebLogic web application you can limit the maximum number of HTTP sessions created by setting the max-in-memory-sessions tag within the session-descriptor of the weblogic.xml file. Otherwise, creating more and more sessions due to user requests can eventually cause an out of memory exception. When this number is exceeded, a `SessionCreationException` is thrown for further attempts. This setting applies to both replicated and non-replicated in-memory sessions.

JMS quota

Limit the number of pending JMS messages on a particular destination (queue or durable topic) by specifying a quota. Use a quota resource that defines byte and messages maximums and assign the quota to the destination. With a quota setting you can calculate the maxim amount of heap space that can be consumed by your JMS destinations.

There is also a quota for destinations that do not explicitly set a value. These destinations share the quota of the JMS server.

Specifying a Blocking Send Policy on JMS Servers

For blocking send requests you can specify whether all send requests for a particular destination are queued until space is available (FIFO setting). Then, no send request is permitted to complete when there is another send request is waiting for space.

With the preemptive setting, a blocking send can preempt other blocking send operations if there is sufficient space available.

JMS Message Buffer Size

The Message Buffer Size option specifies how much of the heap memory JMS will consume to store message bodies before they are paged out to disk. There is a default value of -1 for this setting, which enables a message buffer of one-third of the maximum heap size for the JVM, or a maximum of 512 megabytes.

As shown in Figure 95, you can set the JMS message buffer size under JMS / Configuration / General for a particular JMS server.

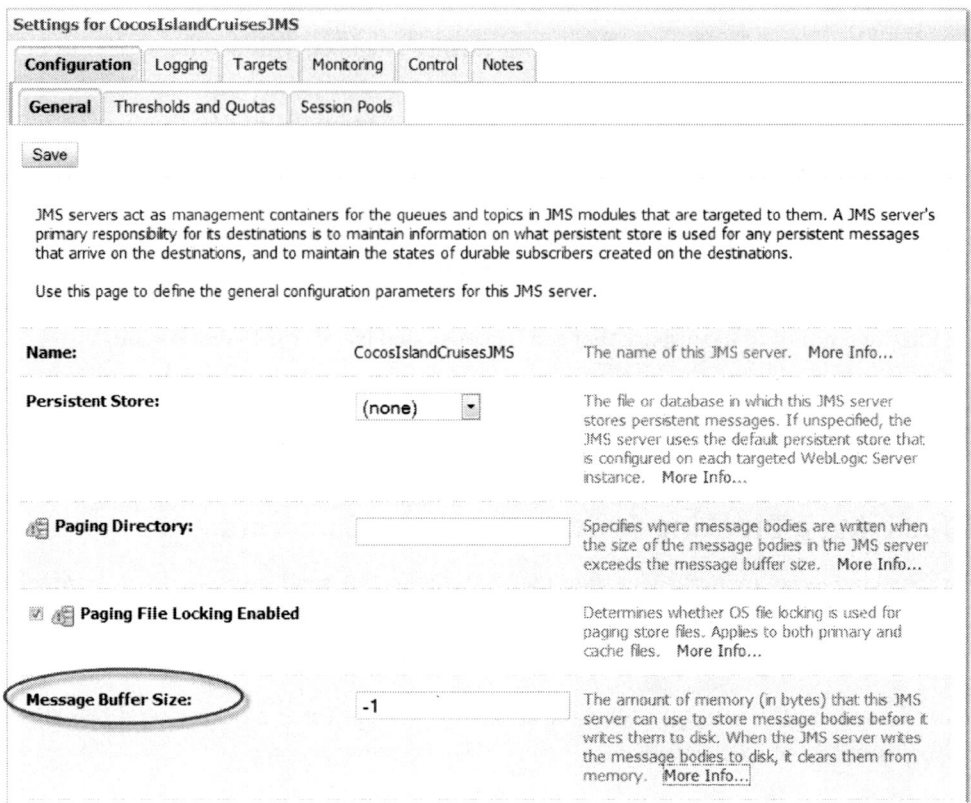

Figure 95: Set JMS Message Buffer Size

Writing JMS messages to disk will slow down JMS, but does reduce the risk of an out of memory error. You trade in performance for stability.

The JMS server will accept message even when the message buffer size limit is reached. You cannot completely prevent an out of memory exception with this setting, since new messages could arrive faster than the system can purge them to disk. To limit the maximum amount of heap space used for JMS, see the quota setting explained above.

SIZING OF JMS MESSAGE BUFFER

When restarting a WebLogic JMS server with persisted messages, the messages are read from the persistent store until the MessageBufferSize limit is reached, then messages will be paged to disk. Therefore, it is important to correctly size the message buffer to avoid out of memory exceptions when restarting.

Set a large message buffer to avoid paging for a maximum of performance, but keep it small enough in relation to your heap settings.

Maximum Number of JDBC Database Connections

Set the maximum number of connections to the value determined by load testing the application (maximum number determined during load test plus some safety margin). Set the initial size of the connection pool to the number of used connections.

Note that the WebLogic JDBC pinned to thread feature is particularly dangerous in overload situations. With pinned to thread enabled for a connection pool the connections are not returned to the pool but remain attached to the execute thread. The pinned to thread feature will save connection wait time if there is a high competition for database connections for a busy connection pool, but the number of database connections increases beyond the maximum number of connections set for the connection pool.

10 Scalability

This chapter is about the scalability of cloud architectures. We will cover basic strategies such as horizontal and vertical scaling, the process of capacity planning (and the reasons why it is still necessary in a cloud environment), various load balancers with their limitations, and auto scaling in the cloud.

10.1 Basics

Granularity

Scaling is not continuous: Regardless whether you replace a running cloud instance with a smaller or a bigger one, or whether you add another instance to a cluster; you have to request the most suitable instance type that is available from your IaaS platform provider. Nowadays it is not possible to ask for an arbitrary increment or decrement of CPU power or RAM in the cloud.

Scaling is more fine granular in the cloud because of the large selection of available instance types. Due to the rapid elasticity of clouds, scaling also happens a lot quicker.

Granularity of scaling

Horizontal Scalability

Horizontal scaling is the classical way to scale web applications. Horizontal scaling means that you add another server to your server farm or cluster to improve the overall performance of the system. This approach works well if the overall system is designed carefully, and scales almost linearly with the number of servers.

To achieve this kind of scalability, shared-nothing architectures are preferable. As soon as there is a single system in your architecture that doesn't scale when adding another server, you are in trouble. For example, if the throughput limit is due to a single backend database, adding another application server won't help to improve your overall system throughput.

Linear scalability is not only to be expected in shared-nothing architectures. Even a WebLogic cluster doesn't slow down significantly when the number of servers is increased, although the state of an HTTP session is shared. However, the session state is replicated only once to a second server instance. Therefore, the overhead cost doesn't increase with the number of servers.

Horizontal scalability requires a load balancer that distributes incoming requests to all instances. There are different kinds of load balancers around. A stand-alone web switch that usually copes with very high loads is one example. Software based load balancers can become a bottleneck in the cloud when there is a very high number of clients accessing multiple load balanced servers. This load balancer bottleneck can be avoided by using a highly scalable load balancer that is not running on a dedicated general-purpose cloud instance. Have a look at the end of section 10.2 for a detailed discussion about load balancers and their scalability. Horizontal scaling adds to the availability of the overall system, but has some limitations if an atomic single task needs several resources on one machine.

Vertical Scalability

Vertical scalability is the process of increasing the size of a particular machine. This is a desirable solution for tasks that cannot be split and run on two or more machines. Imagine a complex algorithm processing a large data set; it would require more RAM or CPU cycles whenever no scalable parallel implementation exists. Sometimes parallel implementations of algorithms do not scale at all, or they provide a very poor speedup because the communication or synchronization overhead is too high.

Vertical scalability does not increase the overall availability of the system, because one instance is replaced by a larger one, (or by another smaller one, if you down-scale vertically).

Also, scaling vertically becomes more expensive with the number of processors per machine. Symmetrical multi-processor machines (SMP) have more than one processor and are more complex to build. They are therefore more expensive than multi-core based, single processors. Complexity and costs led to the network of workstations movement, which was started in the 90s with the idea to replace large computers with a cluster of small commodity of the shelf (COTS) machines – a trend which is still valid today; just think about the Intel-based blade systems used for webhosting.

A closer look at vertical scaling reveals that it is usually a special case of horizontal scaling. For a running virtualized instance, neither the amount of RAM can be increased, nor additional processors added, while the instance is running. You must scale horizontally first, (add a new machine), then migrate your applications and data to the new machine, and lastly, shut down the smaller machine.

I described the technical details on how to scale vertically to a bigger EC2 instance in a command-line example in section **3.4** titled "Resize an Instance".

Vertical scaling is not dynamic, either in the Amazon, or in the Rackspace cloud: One instance is stopped, and a larger or smaller instance is started. Actually, I assume this will change in the future. If virtualization becomes better integrated with the hardware and the OS, adding a small amount of extra RAM or another CPU core will be possible.

Resource Ceilings

Nailing down the root cause of a scalability problem is not an easy task. This task gets even more challenging if different infrastructure servers, such as an application server and a database, or a web server and an application server, share the same cloud instances. If there is more than one server running on an instance, it's no longer possible to draw conclusions from system monitoring (which is the easiest and most available monitoring approach).

Having separate machines for separate infrastructure systems leads to more useful system and application monitoring data. Tuning and scaling then become easier.

The difficult decision is when and what to scale. You must have a good understanding of the resource ceilings of your application in order to answer this question. To be more precise, it is typically not about the application or the system as a whole, but the resource ceilings of the individual infrastructure components involved in the application architecture: the load balancers, the web servers, the application servers, the database, and so on.

So how can you detect a ceiling? I am hesitant to provide you with an answer because it requires a lot of work, work that has to be done very carefully.

Detecting the ceiling involves running stress and load tests with increasing amounts of load to determine the limiting resource, such as CPU, RAM, disk I/O, network bandwidth, Java heap, or JMS performance that prevents the application from coping with even more load. At a certain level of load, you will see saturation for one resource. When the middleware installation is distributed and the infrastructure components don't share a common server, this test will also show you whether the database, the application server, or any other system is the bottleneck.

Now, to measure the resource usage, you have to have system and application monitoring in place. See chapter 11 for a discussion about monitoring in the cloud.

I am aware of the fact that even the basic application level load tests (without increasing loads and careful resource monitoring) are often not done. There is a long list of rationalizations for this ignorance; starting with missing hardware, missing load generators, missing requirements, up to missing time allotted. Just do it! Testing is cheap and easy in the cloud.

Determining the ceiling of your servers is definitely more exhaustive than a basic load test. In addition, it needs to be done separately for each of the individual components of your system architecture.

The output of this stress/load test is the load level at which a particular resource becomes the limiting factor. This in turn, tells you when to scale, and what to scale.

User Experience Metric

Knowing your ceilings is an important first step. It is even more important though, to derive a metric for the resulting user experience when the system hits the resource ceiling. For example, if your company books scuba diving cruises, and page navigating on your website becomes so slow that users leave it in search of a competitor's, or the website cannot support any more cruise bookings because the system is overloaded, then your company quickly starts losing money. For this effect, you would try to derive a metric such as the mean time to submit a booking, or the maximum number of bookings per hour.

Let's assume you have already figured out that the throughput for your application servers is determined by the heap size, which is de-facto limited by the amount of RAM available on a particular machine for a 64-bit JVM.

The information that you should direct to your management is not, "we could support more booking with a larger EC2 instance," but instead, "the current system does not support more than 50,000 bookings per hour. If we add another cloud instance with 17.5 GB, this will cost us an extra $10 per hour and support another 10,000 bookings per hour". You have to know your numbers to provide such a statement, of course.

Economy and Procurement

It is important to understand that scaling is directly related to money. Scaling horizontally or vertically, scaling up or down – every change in capacity means that the cost on the bill at the end of the month will change. Obviously, your procurement process has to consider expenditures related to scaling, and it certainly makes sense to have an upper boundary for the maximum amount of money to be spent on scaling up your cloud architecture. Based on the budget, you can derive technical parameters such as the maximum number of instances that can be started for an auto scaling group.

Scaling in the cloud is as cheap as it gets for several reasons:

- Depending on the size of your instances and local labor costs, hiring a performance tuning consultant for a day might cost you as much as adding another cloud instance to the system for half a year or even an entire year. Please note, this is no excuse at all for badly designed or implemented application software or system architecture. Scalability options in the cloud can neither replace a good design, nor compensate for a bad one.
- Due to the rapid elasticity of clouds, scaling takes place more quickly. You can immediately get rid of unused machines and stop paying for them. If your application requires more resources, you can procure them within a few seconds.
- The instances that you pay for match the actual resource requirement much better, due to the reduced granularity of scaling in the cloud.

To figure out the best way to scale, you have to consider cost versus user experience metric.

At the same time, keep in mind that the system availability increases when scaling-up horizontally, whereas the management of a system becomes easier when scaling-up vertically, because you are dealing with fewer instances.

Capacity Planning

Capacity planning is proactive. It is about determining the future trend for the resource requirements. The goal is to find out how much capacity you will need in the future. The planning task becomes less guess-work if there is historic data available. Still, the whole process of capacity planning is both an art and a science.

In fact, you will never know all of the factors that influence the demand for capacity unless you have a crystal ball. On the other hand, this exercise can become as scientific as you like.

From a mathematical perspective, you are fitting a curve based on a formula with several degrees of freedom to match your historic data points as accurately as possible. Once the curve and all the parameters are known as a mathematical function, you can use this information to extrapolate future values.

Keep these two issues in mind when modeling you resource requirements:

- Remember that you have to know your ceilings, because capacity will not grow unless you scale the system accordingly.
- External factors that cannot be anticipated are beyond your control, but affect the capacity requirements. Even the most accurate mathematical resource model that perfectly fits your historic monitoring data, is no guarantee for future capacity requirements.

Capacity Planning vs. Auto Scaling

You are probably wondering if capacity planning is necessary in modern cloud architecture with auto scaling. It is important to understand that capacity planning is not superseded by auto scaling. Actually, in most of the bigger cloud environments you should expect to see a combination of both.

There are a couple of reasons why auto scaling doesn't save you from the tedious work of capacity planning:

- Capacity planning is a proactive, manual process, whereas auto scale can be an automated, reactive process.
- Capacity planning is necessary to predict costs.
- Capacity planning helps to predict limits for auto scaling.

John Allspaw's classic book titled "The Art of Capacity Planning" is a recommended and pragmatic read without too many statistical details.

10.2 Load Balancing

Load balancing is often thought of as a feature of a WebLogic cluster. Typically, this is not true. When using the web container of WebLogic, load balancing is not provided by the cluster itself. Load balancing for the web container is neither done by the WebLogic cluster, nor by the admin server, which is not part of the cluster. Load balancing has to be provided by an external load balancer.

Single Entry Point

Load balancing makes a set of clustered servers look like one single unit to the outside world. You can use load balancing to provide an IP address for a set of managed WebLogic servers without creating a WebLogic cluster at all. This would save you the cost of a cluster license.

However, without the WebLogic cluster you lose all features described in section 5.3 about clustering, such as session replication for HTTP sessions and stateful session beans, uniformly distributed JMS destinations, whole-server migration, deployments with cluster target and so on. In summary, this may reduce the overall availability of your system.

The situation is different when looking at EJBs or JMS. EJB and JMS clients use a replica-aware client stub, which is injected by the container (or retrieved by doing a JNDI-lookup). So there is no external load balancer needed for JMS or EJB.

There are two major types of load balancers according to the network layer at which they operate (as defined by the Open Systems Interconnection Reference Model, better known as OSI):

- Layer 4 load balancers distribute requests based on the network layer (IP) and transport layer (TCP, UDP).
- Layer 7 load balancers also include the application layer protocol (HTTP) and use HTTP header/content or cookie data for the load balancing criteria.

The load is often balanced in a simple round robin order because it is easy to implement, there is no measureable overhead for the algorithm itself, and it is fair, at least for a large number of clients and requests.

There are many different solutions for load balancing in the cloud. The following list includes the ones covered in this book, but this is still only a subset of all the important options available for load balancing:

- DNS round robin
- Hardware load balancer
- WebLogic HTTP Proxy Servlet
- WebLogic Web Server Plugin
- HAProxy
- AWS Elastic Load Balancer

All the options above are suitable for load balancing, of course. Some provide HTTP session failover such as the WebLogic HTTP proxy servlet and the WebLogic web server plugin, both of which come with the WebLogic installation, without any additional costs. Others are free as well, but have to be downloaded separately, installed, and operated on a cloud instance such as HAProxy. The AWS Elastic Load Balancer requires no installation and no separate cloud instance, but the service has to be paid for.

There are many other options, which I cannot explain in detail here. For example, have a look at the software load balancer nginx, which is used for many large projects such as WordPress.com, GitHub, and SourceForge. For further details see the nginx web site:

http://nginx.org.

DNS Round Robin

DNS round robin returns a list of IP addresses for a single DNS name. This list is permutated for subsequent lookups. Clients typically connect to the first IP address on the list.

DNS round robin provides an additional level of indirection because you can flexibly change the assignment between the DNS name and the IP addresses returned. This technique is used, for example, to assign a DNS name for a whole WebLogic cluster, which, in turn, can be used within a JNDI lookup to retrieve a distributed JMS destination.

This is the same for most other companies. To give you an example, Amazon uses DNS round robin to provide a load balanced and fault-tolerant list of the machines behind amazon.com.

You can use the UNIX command `dig` to retrieve the details about the servers, which are assigned to a DNS entry:

```
frank@ubuntu:~$ dig amazon.com

; <<>> DiG 9.6.1-P2 <<>> amazon.com
;; global options: +cmd
;; Got answer:
;; ->>HEADER<<- opcode: QUERY, status: NOERROR, id: 62456
;; flags: qr rd ra; QUERY: 1, ANSWER: 3, AUTHORITY: 7, ADDITIONAL: 0

;; QUESTION SECTION:
;amazon.com.            IN   A

;; ANSWER SECTION:
amazon.com.     36   IN   A 72.21.210.250
amazon.com.     36   IN   A 72.21.207.65
amazon.com.     36   IN   A 207.171.166.252
```

The downside of DNS round robin is that you have to take care that DNS lookups aren't cached, and that they occur often enough on the client side to provide decent load balancing.

At larger companies, DNS is often not within the responsibility of the team dealing with middleware, so there might be some organizational overhead costs involved.

A disadvantage of using DNS for load balancing is that it will not detect if one of the servers in the returned list of IP addresses isn't accessible anymore, so requests will be still directed to this instance.

Hardware Load Balancers

Companies such as CISCO or F5 provide hardware load balancers. Hardware load balancers are not within the scope of this book because they cannot be moved to the cloud. In the cloud, you can either install your own software based solution, or use a load balancer provided by the IaaS provider, such as Amazon's Elastic Load Balancer.

WebLogic Proxy Plugin Servlet

When you use the WebLogic domain configuration wizard to create a clustered domain, and you specify an additional managed server (e.g. with the name loadBalancerServer) that is not part of the cluster, the wizard will ask you whether you want to create an HTTP proxy.

This HTTP proxy is a servlet based load balancer, which supports round-robin load balancing, and transparent session failover for HTTP sessions in the case of a replicated session in a cluster.

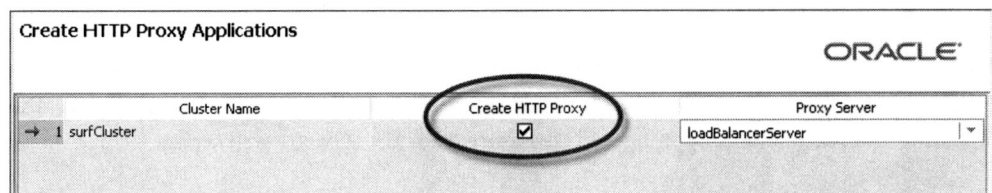

Figure 96: Create a HTTP Proxy with Domain Wizard

If you decide to create a HTTP proxy, a web application will be automatically deployed to the selected load balancing server. It may come as a surprise when you examine this web application that there is no code at all, such as a servlet, a JSP or a jar file, but only the two deployment descriptors. Actually, the servlet code is already in WebLogic's classpath, so there is no need to put it into the web application deployment.

Then, configure the load balancer with the initial cluster configuration and define which requests should be forwarded to the application server by modifying the `web.xml` deployment descriptor. Once configured, the HTTP proxy servlet is self-learning and will detect failed or new application server instances in the cluster.

The proxy servlet is a quick way to demonstrate the load balancing and session failover for a cluster. By using a shopping-cart application with in-memory session replication enabled, you can easily demonstrate the failover from a failed instance to the instance with the backup session. This failover is done by the proxy servlet and it is transparent for the client.

Session failover

I remember the times when BEA didn't recommend the proxy servlet for production use, but apparently this has changed. Personally, I like to use the WebLogic HTTP proxy servlet for demonstration purposes only.

WebLogic Web Server Plugin

WebLogic comes with another option for load balancing; a plugin for the most common web servers. This plugin is used in many production systems as a front-end installed in Apache 2.0 or 2.2. The Apache plugin is called mod_wl. There is also support for SunOne and Microsoft web servers.

The web server plugin actually has the same function as the proxy servlet, which means it will also provide transparent session failover for HTTP sessions. The plugin is a native, compiled code, so you have to carefully select the right one for your operating system and web server.

The plugin is located under the following directory of a Fusion Middleware installation: MIDDLEWARE_HOME/wlserver_10.3/server/plugin. You have to install it on the machine where Apache is running and configure it for the Apache web server.

Decentralized Load Balancing — Sometimes the WebLogic web server plugin is used on two or more web servers to increase the throughput and the availability of the web server layer. Such a decentralized load balancing solution has to be managed carefully. Make sure that all plugins use the same configuration.

It's best that you test your WLS plugin based load balancing solution to verify what happens when one of the backend servers fails.

You can easily forget to upgrade the plugin when upgrading the WebLogic or Fusion Middleware installation since it is running on the web server machines. However, this is necessary since the plugin is only backward compatible to older WebLogic versions.

Apache is known to be vulnerable to denial of service attacks such as slowloris. For more details, have a look at: http://ha.ckers.org/slowloris/. Insteadof exposing the WebLogic web server as a frontend to the Internet, it might be a good idea to put it behind a hardware load balancer or a software based solution such as HAProxy.

HAProxy

HAProxy is an event-driven, single process load balancer solution for HTTP and TCP. It was mainly developed by Willy Tarreau with the help from a small community of contributors, and distributed under GPL 2. At the time of this writing, HAProxy is available for Linux, Solaris, FreeBSD and OpenBSD, and MacOSX.

HAProxy is a very fast and reliable software load balancer. Many large web sites such as Twitter, Fedora, GitHub, and Stackoverflow use it.

HAProxy can be downloaded from http://haproxy.1wt.eu

The single process model enables a higher rate of connections without the memory and system scheduler limits or the lock contention of multi-threaded software. It may sound surprising at first, but actually, it is not that uncommon for professional software to be implemented as a single threaded process, or with a very limited number of threads. Apart from load balancers, this is also the case for some JMS servers.

Reliability

HAProxy stands out due to its extreme reliability. The stable version has never crashed in a production environment on sites which serve millions of pages per day. According to Willy Tarreau, users generally forget about it, and some have even reported uptimes of 3 years without a single reboot. No bug has required an emergency update in the last 8 years.

Scalability

HAProxy scales extremely well and supports tens of thousands of concurrent connections running on modern hardware (e.g. a single core Pentium PC). Parsing an average HTTP request takes only 2 microseconds.

HAProxy internals

To save memory bandwidth and CPU cycles, it avoids memory copies as much as possible, which means that it tries to forward traffic directly between the network interfaces when the underlying OS permits it (TCP splicing). It makes use of single-buffering without copying between reads and writes. The protocol parsers are designed to avoid scanning input bytes more than once. For instance, HTTP headers are indexed while they are being parsed. Typically, more than 90% of HAProxy's CPU time is spent in the kernel, so choosing the right operating system and tuning it as recommended in the HAProxy documentation makes sense.

Performance

All these design choices have an effect on performance. Typical numbers for a 2.66 GHz dual core system indicate about 40,000 forwarded connections per second, an ability to forward traffic at 10 Gbps with less than 25% of CPU usage, and an average HTTP request parsing time of less than 1 microsecond.

There are two limitations due to the design choices of HAProxy:

- HAProxy doesn't currently support SSL since SSL would cause the load balancer to become a bottleneck. In order to use SSL, an SSL-aware reverse proxy is required in front of HAProxy, such as Apache mod_ssl, nginx, pound or stunnel. In this case, the reverse proxy accepts the SSL on its SSL port, terminates it, and forwards the non-encrypted request to HAProxy. If high loads are expected, then multithreaded or multi-process components such as Apache or pound should not be mixed with HAProxy on the same CPUs. HAProxy is a single threaded component, so it would only get its share of the CPU once in a while.

- HTTP keep-alive is not supported because their state has to be stored per client. Storing the state reduces the maximum number of concurrent sessions. Not supporting keep-alive connections increases the maximum number of concurrent connections that can be supported, but also slightly increases the latency when fetching several parts of a page.

HAProxy offers cookie-based server affinity. You can configure it to insert a cookie once a request returns from a backend server. An incoming client request with the attached cookie will then always be assigned to the same backend server. However, the cookie is removed before the request is forwarded, to keep this mechanism transparent for the server. It is also possible to prefix an existing cookie, such as the JSESSIONID cookie, for the same purpose.

Overload protection   Another HAProxy feature worth mentioning is request queuing based on the limit of the maximum number of concurrent connections on the server. When using this setting, you configure the maximum number of concurrent connections to a server. Keeping excessive load off the server improves the server throughput in critical situations. Requests that exceed the maximum number of connections acceptable by the server are serialized. Excess requests are either distributed to other servers or queued. As soon as a server completes a request, it takes another one from the HAProxy queue, making the whole process transparent to the user.

This is a great way to ensure that a server is not overrun by a distributed denial of service attack.

AWS Elastic Load Balancing

Amazon provides Elastic Load Balancing (ELB) as a part of AWS. ELB is an example of how an expensive and highly effective device, such as a hardware load balancer, becomes a simple, zero-installation, pay-on-demand service in the cloud.

ELB Costs   You are charged for the usage time as well as for the data transferred through ELB. Billing is done for each partial or full hour of usage time at the end of a month. Usage time for ELB will cost you $0.025 per hour (which adds up to $18 per month or $216 per year). In addition you will be charged $0.008 per GB data transferred. For small to medium sites, the data transfer fee will usually be less than the fee for the usage time, since $18 gives you a volume of more than 2 TB of transferred data.

Advantages   ELB comes with a number of advantages compared to the other load balancing approaches described above:

- ELB bandwidth is not limited by the network bandwidth of a single EC2 instance. As described below, ELB will scale automatically with the increased load and add more instances for the load balancing.
- ELB will work with your EC2 account. No additional software installation is required (apart from the API tools) and you don't have to start another EC2 instance for it.
- ELB is monitored by AWS CloudWatch, and works hand in hand with AWS auto scaling.
- More often than not, ELB will be even cheaper than running a software based solution such as HAProxy on a small EC2 instance: The cost per hour for ELB is about one third of the cost for the smallest EC2 instance. For an exact comparison you have to consider the data transferred through ELB versus the Internet data transfer in and out.
- ELB will distribute traffic across different availability zones without any additional costs. Using other approaches, you will be charged for traffic across different availability zones.
- One can assume it is at least as reliable as using a software solution on an EC2 instance.

Elastic Load Balancing is a key building block for increasing the overall availability of your system architecture, because load balanced instances can be located in different availability zones. ELB checks the health of the assigned instances, automatically skips unhealthy instances, and distributes the incoming load to the remaining healthy instances.

Since ELB distributes the traffic equally across the availability zones, the same number of instances in each availability zone is recommended.

ELB AND REGIONS

ELB supports load balancing in different availability zones such as eu-west-1a and eu-west-1b. Load balancing across regions such as Europe and the US is not supported.

Use the regional service endpoint to create a new Elastic Load Balancer for a particular region. All availability zones have to be in the region of the load balancer.

Implementation details about the inner functionality of ELB are not officially documented, but take a look at this blog entry about benchmarking load balancers from Rightscale, which includes a lot of useful information on the topic:

http://blog.rightscale.com/2010/04/01/benchmarking-load-balancers-in-the-cloud

How it works ELB itself, is highly scalable because there are two levels of indirection or scalability:

1. When you configure ELB, it returns a DNS name. Clients should regularly do a DNS-lookup for this name. It is important to use the DNS name here, and not the IP address, since ELB will automatically scale to higher load by adding more ELB instances. This scaling is done by assigning the additional IP addresses of the newly added instances to the pool of IP addresses related to the DNS entry.
2. The client then connects to the returned IP address of the DNS lookup belonging to one of the ELB instances. ELB forwards the request to one of the assigned load balanced backend instances.

ELB is truly elastic and will size itself automatically according to increased or decreased load. Due to the first level of indirection, there is no bottleneck imposed by a single instance regarding the bandwidth or the number of requests per second.

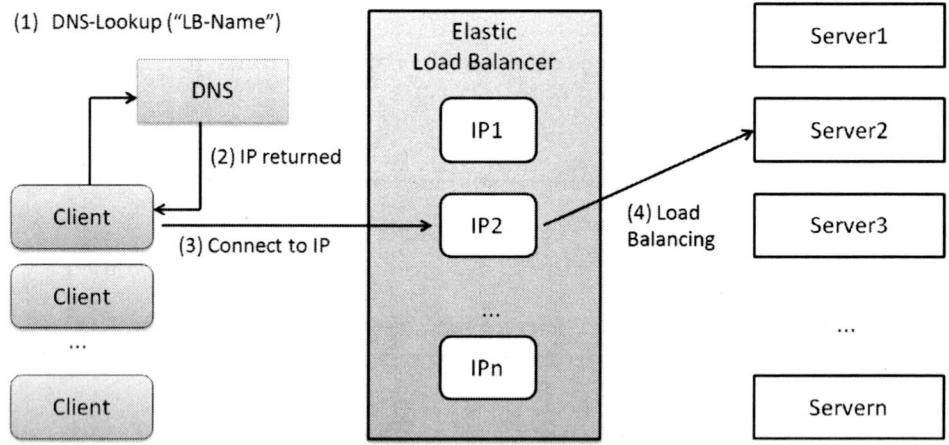

Figure 97: Elastic Load Balancer

In his detailed and interesting blog entry, Shlomo Swidler writes about doing regular DNS lookups on the client side, the blog entry can be accessed from the following site:

```
http://www.shlomoswidler.com/2009/07/elastic-in-elastic-load-balancing-
elb.html
```

Shlomo explains, in his blog posting, that caching can be disabled by setting `sun.net.inetaddr.ttl=0` at the command-line starting the Sun JVM. The same could be achieved for Sun and JRockit JVM, by setting a property `networkaddress.cache.ttl=0` in the `java.security` file, which is located in `JAVA_HOME/jre/lib/security`.

Since the DNS name returned from ELB is in the form `surfLB-1542392149.eu-west-1.elb.amazonaws.com`, you do not want to expose it to your customers. Instead, use the DNS tool provided by your ISP to create a CNAME for it. A CNAME is like a synonym for a DNS entry that you choose, e.g. `divecruises.something.com`. It is possible to assign multiple CNAME records to a single DNS entry.

ELASTIC LOAD BALANCER WITH MYDOMAIN.COM

Depending on your hosting provider, it should be rather easy to set up a CNAME record that maps the load balancer DNS name to `www.mydomain.com` or `some_other_subdomain.mydomain.com`.

However, CNAMEs are not allowed on the root apex, e.g. you cannot have a CNAME for `mydomain.com`. For some companies this is a real showstopper since `mydomain.com` is often used interchangeably with `www.mydomain.com`.

Also, you cannot assign an elastic IP address to the ELB due to its internal mechanism to scale for high loads. The only way out is to configure the root domain to a service that redirects mydomain.com to www.mydomain.com. If you decide to build such a solution yourself, make sure you will not introduce a single point of failure with this service...

ELB limitations   There are some design trade-offs due to the way ELB is implemented.

- Clients have to do DNS lookups regularly. Without the DNS lookups the client won't profit from the scalability of ELB.
- ELB needs time for scaling and adding more internal IPs. It is probably not very well suited for spiky load patterns.

Support for sticky HTTP sessions with ELB was added in April 2010. It is now possible to always assign a particular client to the server instance where the HTTP session (or some other user state) is stored. Note that there is no support for sessions under HTTPS. Also, there is no support for WebLogic in-memory session failover to a second instance as described in section 5.3 of the WebLogic introduction.

ELB session stickiness can be based on cookies generated by ELB by specifying the details for the lifetime of the sessions. Optionally, ELB can be configured to respect application generated cookies.

SSL support   Until October 2010 ELB could only support SSL traffic by setting the listening protocol to TCP. Now, however, there is support for SSL termination and sticky sessions. SSL certificates are centrally stored and managed at the ELB layer. Currently, it is not possible to change the SSL settings for a running ELB instance with the AWS management console. However, if you use the management console to create a new instance with HTTPS, you can choose an existing SSL certificate, or upload a new certificate.

Figure 98: ELB SSL Termination

CloudWatch automatically persists and displays ELB monitoring data, such as request count and request latency.

Similar to Amazon's CloudWatch, the ELB is considered a separate project, which is why you have to download and unzip the ELB API tools, in addition to the EC2 command-line. Click on "Developer Tools" to get to the download at the following site:

Download / Install

http://aws.amazon.com/elasticloadbalancing

Make sure to set an environment variable AWS_ELB_HOME that points to the location of your unzipped tools, and add AWS_ELB_HOME/bin to your path.

A quick look at the WSDL file for the ELB reveals that the web service interface consists of fewer than 10 methods:

- Create/DeleteLoadBalancer
- Register/DeregisterInstancesWithLoadBalancer
- ConfigureHealthCheck
- DescribeInstanceHealth
- DescribeLoadBalancers
- Enable/DisableAvailabilityZonesForLoadBalancer

After the installation process, you can verify the availability of the ELB command-line tools with elb-describe-lbs:

Command-line usage

```
frank@ubuntu:~$ elb-describe-lbs

No LoadBalancers found
```

Then, after starting a distributed WebLogic installation over three EC2 instances, create a new Elastic Load Balancer with the following command:

```
frank@ubuntu:~$ elb-create-lb surfLB  --region eu-west-1 --availability-
zones eu-west-1b --headers   --listener "protocol=http,lb-
port=80,instance-port=7001"

DNS_NAME   DNS_NAME
DNS_NAME   surfLB-1542392149.eu-west-1.elb.amazonaws.com
```

The --region option is necessary if you don't want your load balancer created in the default region. The option --availability-zones specifies the availability zones. The returned DNS name is specific to the region. Clients will use this logical name to address your system hidden behind the load balancer:

surfLB-1542392149.eu-west-1.elb.amazonaws.com

Scalability 213

Assign backend instances
Next, you have to assign the backend instances to the ELB. For a hardware based load balancing solution, this typically requires the IP addresses of the instances. In the AWS world, you have to supply the IDs of the EC2 instances to the ELB:

```
frank@ubuntu:~$ elb-register-instances-with-lb surfLB --region eu-west-1
--headers --instances  i-fc90fb8b,i-fa90fb8d,i-f890fb8f
INSTANCE_ID   INSTANCE_ID
INSTANCE_ID   i-fc90fb8b
INSTANCE_ID   i-fa90fb8d
INSTANCE_ID   i-f890fb8f
```

It is not possible to use the ELB from AWS as a general service and point it to other servers running at your local datacenter, because the instances are, unfortunately, registered with their EC2 IDs.

Next, specify how the ELB should check for the health of the assigned backend instances:

```
frank@ubuntu:~$ elb-configure-healthcheck surfLB --region eu-west-1 --
unhealthy-threshold 2 --timeout 3 --healthy-threshold 2 --interval 30 --
target "http:7001/ping"

HEALTH_CHECK  http:7001/ping  30  3  2  2
```

This health check is set up to verify the status of each load balanced node every 30 seconds on port 7001. A node is removed from service if it fails more than twice. The parameter `healthy-threshold` defines how many consecutive successful checks are required before a node is marked as "in service".

Now you can use the `elb-describe-instance-health` command to check for the health of the assigned instances. The example below shows the output of the command if one of the instances has crashed:

```
frank@ubuntu:~$ elb-describe-instance-health surfLB --region eu-west-1
INSTANCE_ID   i-f890fb8f   InService      N/A N/A
INSTANCE_ID   i-fc90fb8b   InService      N/A N/A
INSTANCE_ID   i-fa90fb8d   OutOfService   Instance has failed at least the
UnhealthyThreshold number of health checks consecutively.
```

Then, use the `elb-describe-lbs` command-line to check for configured ELBs and their assigned DNS names:

```
frank@ubuntu:~$ elb-describe-lbs --region eu-west-1

LOAD_BALANCER  surfLB  surfLB-1711782566.eu-west-1.elb.amazonaws.com
2010-08-08T22:30:25.920Z
```

ELB is also nicely integrated into the AWS management console. You can configure your ELBs or check existing ones by selecting the "Load Balancers" link on the left side of the navigation frame. An overview window with the ELB status, port configuration, and assigned availability zones will display as shown on the following screenshot:

Using ELB from AWS console

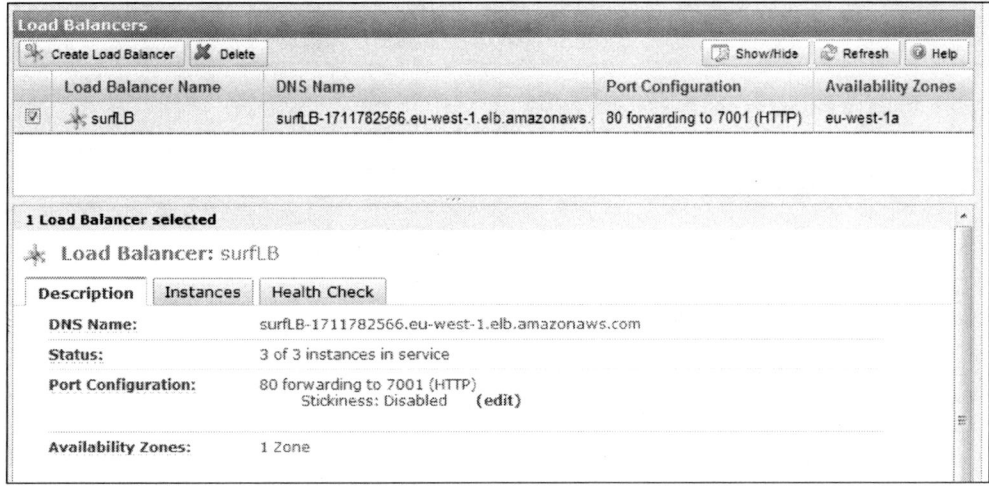

Figure 99: ELB Description

From the "Instances" tab it is possible to remove or assign new instances or availability zones.

On the screenshot in Figure 100, there is one availability zone without any instances. Remember that ELB distributes the load equally across availability zones. About every second request in this scenario will fail, because eu-west-1b has no instances assigned. The failed request will then be redirected to a eu-west-1a.

Select the "Health Check" tab to get to the details for the health check performed on the instances – in this case the web based management console is a rather nice substitute for the lengthy `elb-configure-healthcheck` command-line (see Figure 101).

Scalability   215

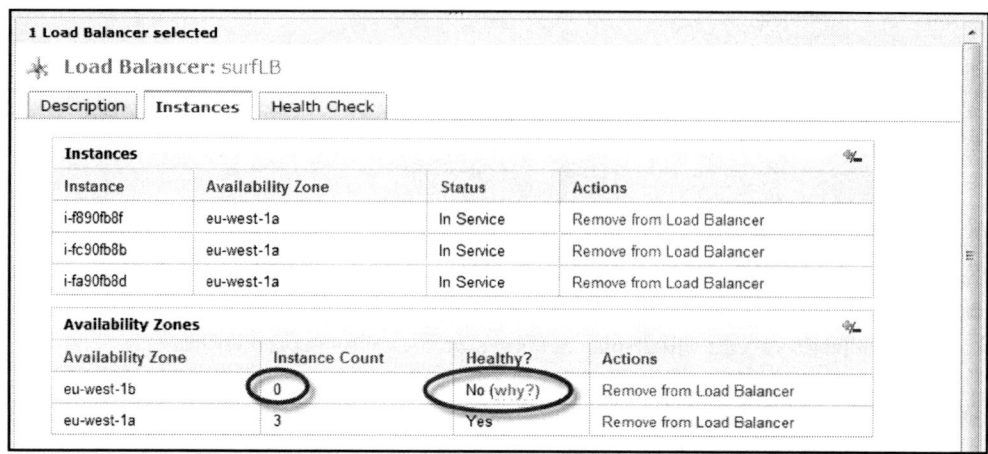

Figure 100: ELB Instances and Availability Zones

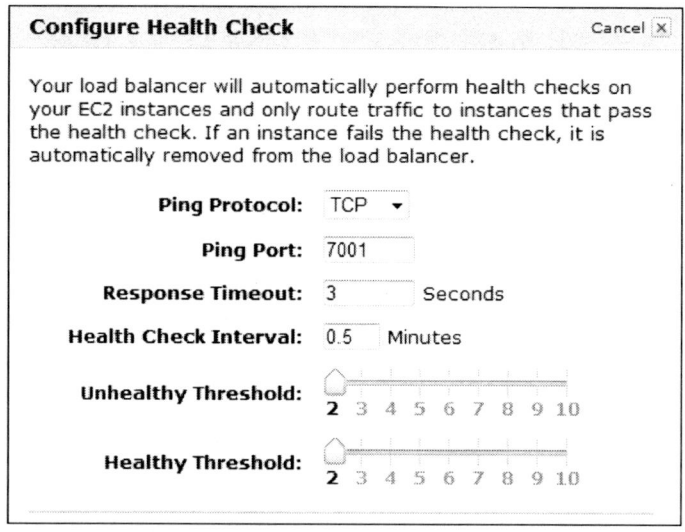

Figure 101: ELB Health Check Configuration

Load Testing Load Balancers: HAProxy and ELB

Brian Adler, from RightScale, has done extensive load testing with ELB. He has published a paper about it, which can be downloaded from RightScale after signing in to their web site. The title of the paper is called "Load Balancing in the Cloud: Tools, Tips, and Techniques".

Brian compared ELB with HAProxy and two others (Zeus Load Balancer and aiCache Web Accelerator - both partner with RightScale). His paper contains some interesting findings.

In Brian's initial test, HAProxy version 1.3.19 was configured for round-robin load balancing and running on an m1.large EC2 instance with two virtual cores, 7.5 GB of memory, and a 64-bit platform.

1 Load Generator
5 Web Servers

Five identically configured web servers were used as targets for the load balancers. All were running Apache 2.2.3, and serving a small page of 147 bytes text-only. The main idea behind using a small web page, was to allow the web servers to scale for a high request rate. CPU was measured on both the load balancer, and the web server sides, to make sure the CPU was not a bottleneck.

Almost 5,000 responses / second were measured for HAProxy. After tuning the kernel, this result was improved to 5,200 responses / second.

When running the same test cases with ELB, surprisingly, only 2,300 requests / second were measured, less than half of the HAProxy responses. Initially, ELB seemed inferior when only looking at raw numbers. However, if you think about the design of ELB and the way the test was done, it is obvious that there was no chance for ELB to scale, because the test didn't require the test client to search for the DNS name for ELB.

Brian then did a new test with 25 backend web servers and 3 load generating servers, each of them generating about 500 requests / second. For this test, several iterations were completed with a DNS lookup at the beginning of each iteration. ELB processed about 1,000 requests / second, and a DNS lookup showed 3 IPs being used.

3 LG
25 WS

Increasing the number of load generating servers to 25, which in total generated 12,500 requests / second, caused ELB to use between 11 to 15 IPs. Due to restart times for the tests, a response rate of 10,500 was measured.

25 LG
25 WS

Finally, a total of 45 load generating servers were started; this caused ELB to use between 18 and 25 IPs, and to generate a response rate of 19,000 / second.

45 LG
25 WS

Trying to run a similar test with HAProxy revealed more interesting results: No increased performance was seen for HAProxy after adding more than 10 load generating servers, so the test was done with 16 load generating servers only, instead of the 45 used with ELB. The web server backend was the same as for the ELB test.

Only 5,000 responses / second were measured, which was increased by 10% after some optimizations. Further analysis showed, interestingly enough, that neither bandwidth nor CPU was the bottleneck, but that the network stack on the virtual instance could not handle more than 110,000 packets of total throughput (input + output).

This limitation indicates that *virtualization* is the bottleneck here, because the packets move through two network stacks. This bottleneck was also confirmed with the ttcp testing utility for network throughput.

I'd expect HAProxy to perform better today, since version HAProxy 1.3.19 did not either support keep-alive or TCP optimizations. Since the limit in virtualized environments is the number of packets per second, every packet saved per connection means a higher request rate.

SUMMARY OF LOAD TESTING RESULTS:

ELB seems to scale almost unlimited if load is ramped up gradually, and clients do DNS lookups regularly when connecting to ELB.

AWS virtualization does well for CPUs and memory. However, virtualization becomes the bottleneck when network intensive solutions with a very high packet rate are running on EC2 instances.

A network-intensive component, such as HAProxy on an EC2 node, runs 8 times slower than on a dedicated $500 PC. However, you cannot move that $500 PC into the cloud. Also, remember that the ELB solution required 25 IPs to support the peak load of the test.

10.3 AWS Auto Scaling

Auto scaling sizes your capacity according to the actual load - so your capacity becomes elastic. For auto scaling you define a criteria that triggers the scaling, as well as the minimum and maximum number of servers.

Auto scaling is reactive scaling, which means the scaling action always happens after some condition is met, e.g. a load spike occurred. John Rees calls it *"a powerful rope you can easily hang yourself with"* in his book, "Cloud Application Architectures". I mentioned that auto scaling is reactive, because it will not save you from doing proper capacity planning (as explained in section 10.1).

There is no additional fee for auto scaling. Since auto scaling depends on CloudWatch metrics, you should enable it for your instances. For a detailed discussion about CloudWatch, see the monitoring chapter in section 11.5.

No extra charges

Even if there is no additional fee for auto scaling, you should be aware of the consequences it can have with relation to the bill that your cloud provider will send you at the end of the month. Make sure that the total costs caused by auto scaling don't break your budget.

AWS Auto Scaling Overview

To use auto scaling you have to download its command-line tools. I guess you are used to this by now – wouldn't it be nice if there was one distribution containing all API tools?

Here is quick overview of the three steps involved to set up auto scaling:

1. Create a launch configuration with the *as-create-launch-config* command. A Launch Configuration defines all the parameters needed to launch new cloud instances.
2. Create an auto scaling group with the *as-create-auto-scaling-group* command. The auto scaling group defines those cloud instances to which certain scaling conditions apply. Usually an auto scaling group represents a distributed application running on multiple cloud instances.
3. Then define the trigger that starts a scaling action. Use the *as-create-or-update-trigger* for the conditions based on any metric collected by CloudWatch.

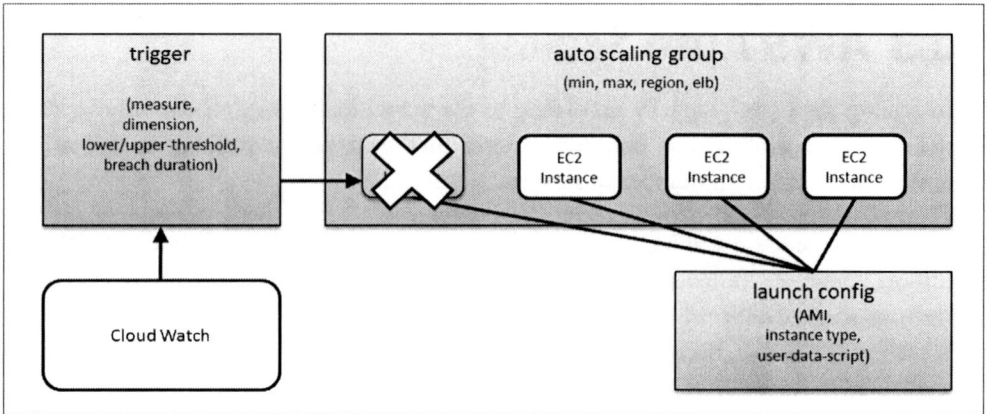

Figure 102: Auto Scaling Overview

Auto Scaling with ELB
Auto scaling can be combined with Elastic Load Balancing. Such a setup can guarantee that there is always a minimum number of *healthy* load balanced cloud instances available. If one of the instances changed its state to unhealthy, this would be detected by the CloudWatch and another instance would be started by the auto scaling mechanism. Note that auto scaling only adds instances to the load balancer if the ELB name is specified in the auto scaling group.

Auto Scaling Installation

Since setting up auto scale requires several lengthy commands, I would like to provide a hands-on example.

Installation command-line tools
If you haven't installed the auto scale tools, then it is time for that now. Navigate to the following URL, and click on the link for Amazon EC2 API tools to download the auto scale command-line tools:

http://aws.amazon.com/autoscaling/

Unzip the file, have a look at the instructions, and make sure you set the AWS_AUTO_SCALING_HOME variable. Also include this directory in the path.

Then, verify the installation with the command as-cmd --help, which will output a list of all available auto scaling commands:

```
frank@ubuntu:~$ as-cmd --help
Command Name                         Description
------------                         -----------
as-create-auto-scaling-group         Create a new auto scaling group
as-create-launch-config              Create a new launch config
```

Usage Example

For this example it is assumed that there is a load balancer already running. So if you do not have a load balancer running, follow the steps in section 10.2 under Elastic Load Balancing (or follow the example without a load balancer).

To verify that the load balancer is configured, use the `elb-describe-lbs` command, which will return the name and the time of the creation of the load balancer:

```
frank@ubuntu:~$ elb-describe-lbs   --region eu-west-1

LOAD_BALANCER  surfLB   surfLB-1711782566.eu-west-1.elb.amazonaws.com
2010-08-08T22:30:25.920Z
```

The first step for the auto scaling configuration is to create a launch configuration that defines which image will be used during a scaling activity and what instance type will be started from this image. I will use an AMI that I have prepared before with the id ami-b2d5ffc6. For the instance type I will use the new micro instances since they are the cheapest to experiment with. The parameter `--key` can be used to pass the access key to the launch configuration:

Create a launch configuration

```
frank@ubuntu:~$ as-create-launch-config surfLaunch
--region eu-west-1 --key xess --image-id ami-b2d5ffc6
--instance-type t1.micro

OK-Created launch config
```

After creating the launch configuration, an auto scaling group is needed. The important parameters to create the auto scaling group are the minimum and maximum size of the group. If you list the load balancer as well, then the newly created instances will be attached automatically:

Create an auto scaling group

```
frank@ubuntu:~$ as-create-auto-scaling-group surfScale --launch-
configuration surfLaunch --region eu-west-1 -availability-zones eu-west-
1a,eu-west-1b --min-size 2 --max-size 4 --load-balancers surfLB

OK-Created AutoScalingGroup
```

You can supply an additional parameter cooldown; this specifies the time in seconds after a scaling activity has been completed and before any other scaling activity can start.

AUTO SCALING COSTS

When using Elastic Load Balancer and creating an auto scaling group, instances will be started according the definition in the auto scaling group.

So, be prepared ; your bill will change after using this command. The auto scaling service itself however, is free of charge.

When checking with the `as-describe-scaling-activities` command, right after the creation of the auto scaling group, you can see the instances being added to the group:

```
frank@ubuntu:~$ as-describe-scaling-activities surfScale
--region eu-west-1
ACTIVITY   e6d04329-cef2-41ee-b385-338312f550b2   InProgress
ACTIVITY   f9b2b01d-80cc-4f07-9e72-91541595bd22   InProgress
```

Last but not least, you create a trigger. The trigger defines the metrics together with their thresholds, and that starts the scaling process.

```
frank@ubuntu:~$ as-create-or-update-trigger surfTrigger
--region eu-west-1 --auto-scaling-group surfScale
--namespace "AWS/EC2" --measure CPUUtilization
--statistic Average -dimensions "AutoScalingGroupName=surfScale"
--period 60   --lower-threshold 40 --upper-threshold 60
"--lower-breach-increment=-1"
"--upper-breach-increment=1"
--breach-duration 120
```

Apart from the parameters, which are well known by now, the trigger specifies the statistic from CloudFront on which the scaling action is based. The statistic used here is the average CPU utilization, which is computed for the auto scaling group. When the CPU utilization goes below the `lower-threshold`, the number of instances is changed by the value of `lower-breach-increment`. Since the value for `lower-breach-increment` is -1, the actual number of instances is reduced by one. The same happens accordingly for the upper-threshold and upper-breach-increment.

The attribute breach-duration defines how long a metric has to go beyond the defined limit before the trigger fires.

For more explanation about the statistics that can be used for the scaling, have a look at section 11.5 about CloudWatch. Another possible value for the dimension is the latency of the load balancer, which can be specified as follows.

```
--dimensions "LoadBalancerName=the-load-balancer"
```

I am certainly aware that your system architecture is much more complex than this simple example. Anyway, I always recommend testing a simple example with the easiest possible configuration first. Once you have shown that the configuration is working correctly, you should certainly test it with a realistic load test.

To prove that auto scaling is working at all, I suggest the following little trick to generate CPU load on the EC2 instances. There is no need to install a load generator. Use the Unix binary calculator, (bc) and compute the 2 to the power of 123456789:

```
ubuntu@ip-10-48-137-224:~$ bc
2^123456789
```

This will keep the EC2 instance busy long enough to trigger the scaling activity. If you want to occupy more than one CPU, run it again in another shell.

Once the calculation is running longer than the value set for the breach duration, which is 120 seconds in our example, check for the scaling activity. You should see two scaling activities that ramp up the number of instances from two to four:

```
frank@ubuntu:~$ as-describe-scaling-activities surfScale --region eu-
west-1 --show-long
ACTIVITY,a88f8be3-ec20-45f7b808d363bb5248f4,(nil),InProgress,(nil),
"At 2010-09-27T21:00:39Z a breaching trigger explicitly set group desired
capacity changing the desired capacity from 3 to 4.

At 2010-09-27T21:00:39Z trigger surfTrigger breached high threshold value
for CPUUtilization, 60.0, adjusting the desired capacity from 3 to 4.

At 2010-09-27T21:01:00Z an instance was started in response to a
difference between desired and actual capacity, increasing the capacity
from 3 to 4.",0,Launching a new EC2 instance,
2010-09-27T21:01:00Z
```

```
ACTIVITY,66b55a1a-fae2-4e4c-881a-cab2b540bfd9,2010-09-
27T21:00:23Z,Successful,(nil),

"At 2010-09-27T20:58:39Z a breaching trigger explicitly set group desired
capacity changing the desired capacity from 2 to 3.
At 2010-09-27T20:58:39Z trigger surfTrigger breached high threshold value
for CPUUtilization, 60.0, adjusting the desired capacity from 2 to 3.

At 2010-09-27T20:59:00Z an instance was started in response to a
difference between desired and actual capacity, increasing the capacity
from 2 to 3.",100,Launching a new EC2 instance:
i-f3793784,2010-09-27T20:59:00Z
```

Once the load generation is terminated, you will see a scaling activity that reduces the number of instances again. The auto scaling group will size itself to the minimum number of instances, since the CPU load falls below the minimum threshold:

```
frank@ubuntu:~$ as-describe-scaling-activities surfScale --region eu-
west-1 --show-long

ACTIVITY,ff4ffa20-a479-4042-96c2-1a3186118e00,2010-09-
27T22:48:51Z,Successful,(nil),

"At 2010-09-27T22:45:41Z a breaching trigger explicitly set group desired
capacity changing the desired capacity from 3 to 2.
At 2010-09-27T22:45:41Z trigger surfTrigger breached low threshold value
for CPUUtilization, 40.0, adjusting the desired capacity from 3 to 2.

At 2010-09-27T22:46:10Z an instance was terminated in response to a
difference between desired and actual capacity, shrinking the capacity
from 3 to 2.

At 2010-09-27T22:46:10Z instance i-f3793784 was selected for
termination.",100,Terminating EC2 instance i-f3793784,2010-09-
27T22:46:10Z


ACTIVITY,108216f1-cbf0-462f-99dd-eb1d9e3ce91b,2010-09-
27T22:44:49Z,Successful,(nil),

"At 2010-09-27T22:41:40Z a breaching trigger explicitly set group desired
capacity changing the desired capacity from 4 to 3.
At 2010-09-27T22:41:40Z trigger surfTrigger breached low threshold value
for CPUUtilization, 40.0, adjusting the desired capacity from 4 to 3.

At 2010-09-27T22:42:10Z an instance was terminated in response to a
difference between desired and actual capacity, shrinking the capacity
from 4 to 3.
```

```
At 2010-09-27T22:42:10Z instance i-d97937ae was selected for
termination.",100,Terminating EC2 instance i-d97937ae,2010-09-
27T22:42:10Z
```

So the output above is basically the log file for the auto scaling activities.

The capacity can be changed without using any trigger at all. For an auto scaling group, you can set desired capacity between the minimum and maximum setting, and the group will scale itself accordingly. To set the capacity use the following command:

```
frank@ubuntu:~$ as-set-desired-capacity surfScale --desired-capacity 3 --
region eu-west-1
OK-Desired Capacity Set
```

After changing the desired capacity, check for the necessary scaling activities to fulfill the request.

```
frank@ubuntu:~$ as-describe-scaling-activities surfScale --region eu-
west-1 --show-long

ACTIVITY,26d643b0-49ff-4cfd-8dbef1b8cf875035,(nil),InProgress,(nil),
"At 2010-09-28T05:54:00Z a user request explicitly set group desired
capacity changing the desired capacity from 2 to 3.
At 2010-09-28T05:54:18Z an instance was started in response to a
difference between desired and actual capacity, increasing the capacity
from 2 to 3.",0,Launching a new EC2 instance,2010-09-28T05:54:18Z
```

Description Commands Example

There are a number of commands that help to analyze a configured auto scaling setup. You can use the command as-describe-launch-configs, to find out about existing launch configurations:

describe-commands

```
frank@ubuntu:~$ as-describe-launch-configs --region eu-west-1

LAUNCH-CONFIG  surfLaunch  ami-b2d5ffc6  t1.micro
```

The as-describe-auto-scaling-groups command describes all configured auto scaling groups for a particular region:

```
frank@ubuntu:~$ as-describe-auto-scaling-groups --region eu-west-1
AUTO-SCALING-GROUP  surfScale  surfLaunch  eu-west-1a,eu-west-1b  surfLB
2  4  2
INSTANCE  i-2b19565c  surfScale  eu-west-1b  InService
INSTANCE  i-2919565e  surfScale  eu-west-1a  InService
```

Adjacent to the name of the load balancer SurfLB, the minimum, maximum, and the number of actually running instances is printed.

To verify the configured trigger, use the `as-describe-triggers` command as shown in the following example. The parameter `--headers` in the example is used to print the column headers.

```
frank@ubuntu:~$ as-describe-triggers surfScale --show-long --region eu-west-1 --headers

TRIGGER,TRIGGERNAME,GROUP,STATUS,NAMESPACE,MEASURE,STATISTIC,PERIOD,LOWER-TH,UPPER-TH,LOW-BR-INCR,UP-BR-INCR,BR-DURATION, DIMENSIONS, UNIT

TRIGGER,surfTrigger,surfScale,NoData,AWS/EC2,CPUUtilization,Average,60,40.0,80.0,-1,1,600,{AutoScalingGroupName=MyAutoScalingGroup},(nil)
```

Remove Auto Scaling Example

Auto scaling instances will simply be restarted if you terminate them with the AWS management console. You cannot delete an auto scaling group while there are instances associated with it. Stopping instances and quickly deleting the group is not possible, because immediately after stopping the instances, a scaling activity occurs which again prevents removing the auto scaling group.

Delete Trigger — To correctly shut down an auto scaled and load balanced application, remove the scaling trigger first and then set the auto scaling group minimum and maximum to zero:

```
frank@ubuntu:~$ as-delete-trigger surfTrigger --region eu-west-1 --auto-scaling-group surfScale

Are you sure you want to delete this trigger? [Ny]y
OK-Deleted trigger
```

Set auto scaling min, max =0 — Once there are no more triggers for the auto scaling group, set the minimum and maximum number of instances to zero:

```
frank@ubuntu:~$ as-update-auto-scaling-group surfScale --min-size 0 --max-size 0 --region eu-west-1

OK-Updated AutoScalingGroup
```

Verify that the instances are shutting down and no instances are left in your auto scaling groups:

```
frank@ubuntu:~$ as-describe-auto-scaling-groups surfScale
--region eu-west-1

AUTO-SCALING-GROUP  surfScale  surfLaunch  eu-west-1a,eu-west-1b  surfLB
0  0  0

INSTANCE   i-fb99d68c   surfScale   eu-west-1a   Terminating
INSTANCE   i-fd99d68a   surfScale   eu-west-1b   Terminating
```

REDUCING GROUP SIZE

It is not possible to configure a specific instance for removal if you reduce the group size of an auto scaling group.

Remember that all instances are identical images.

You can follow the scaling activities that happen after reducing the number of instances to zero with the command as-describe-scaling-activities:

```
frank@ubuntu:~$ as-describe-scaling-activities surfScale --region eu-west-1 --show-long

ACTIVITY,515a3587-2917-449c-b8fd278279fc52cf,(nil),InProgress,(nil),

"At 2010-09-27T20:16:39Z a user request update of AutoScalingGroup constraints to min: 0, max: 0, desired: 0 changing the desired capacity from 2 to 0.

At 2010-09-27T20:17:03Z an instance was terminated in response to a difference between desired and actual capacity, shrinking the capacity from 2 to 0.

At 2010-09-27T20:17:03Z instance i-ebb8f79c was selected for termination.

At 2010-09-27T20:17:03Z instance i-e9b8f79e was selected for termination.",0,Terminating EC2 instance i-e9b8f79e,2010-09-27T20:17:03Z
```

Delete auto scaling group Once there aren't any instances in the auto scaling group left, you can finally delete the auto scaling group itself. To remove the group, use the command as-delete-auto-scaling-group:

```
frank@ubuntu:~$ as-delete-auto-scaling-group surfScale --region eu-west-1

Are you sure you want to delete this AutoScalingGroup? [Ny]y
OK-Deleted AutoScalingGroup
```

Delete launch config After that, it is time to get rid of the launch configuration. To remove it, use the command as-delete-launch-config:

```
frank@ubuntu:~$ as-delete-launch-config surfLaunch --region eu-west-1

Are you sure you want to delete this launch configuration? [Ny]y
OK-Deleted launch configuration
```

Fixed Size Cloud

Keeping a distributed cloud architecture at a fixed size is a special case of scaling, and can be achieved using the AWS auto scaling feature.

10.4 Content Distribution Network

A Content Distribution Network (CDN) is another cloud platform related technology that helps to scale your system architecture. Actually, a CDN is not a compulsory feature of a cloud and there were CDNs such as Limelight around even before we had clouds. However, most cloud platforms also offer a CDN service.

A good CDN has a large number of distributed caches close to all major client sites with a fast connection to the Internet. When clients access cached content, they benefit from latencies and a high bandwidth.

Content Distribution Networks

I'd like to use Amazon's CDN CloudFront as a detailed example of the architectural discussion of content distribution networks. In section 4.2 I already explained Rackspace's CDN solution, called Cloud Files.

CloudFront is exciting because it is another simple cloud service like ELB that offers scalability far beyond non-cloud architectures. CDNs can, in general, replace a traditional architecture where static pages are off-loaded to web servers, as shown in Figure 103.

This extra layer of web servers takes the load off the application server layer although the application servers could of course technically handle static content. Every request for non-static content is forwarded by the web server plugin to one of the application servers. This self-learning plugin balances the load and provides failover for HTTP sessions. It starts off with an initial list of the available servers, and then continuously updates it with new information about recently added or failed application server instances.

Imagine a swimwear fashion online-shop application with tens of thousands of CSS, images and video files showing different designs and colors. With the additional web server layer, all these requests are already served by the web servers and don't cause any load on the application servers.

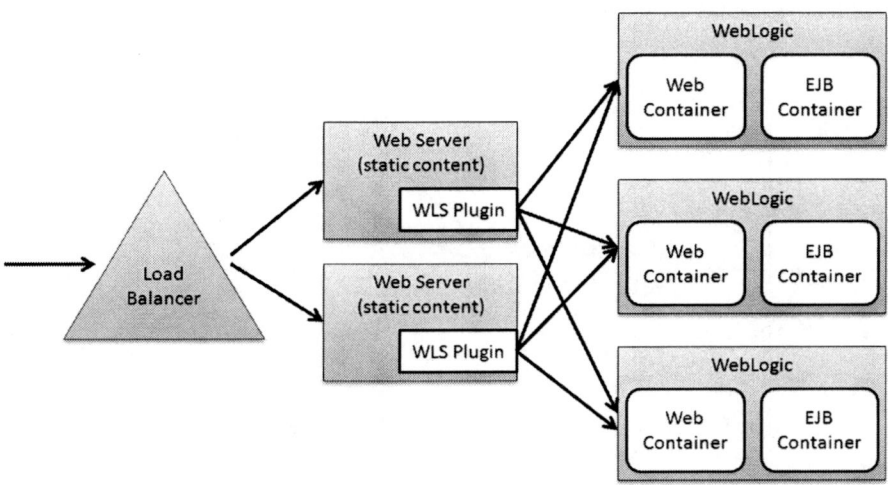

Figure 103: Usage of Web Servers to Offload Static Content

Using a CDN instead of a web server for the static content has a number of advantages:

- You save the operational overhead costs of running a web server. Using a CDN is much easier than operating a web server farm. The CDN is operated by the IaaS platform provider, but running web servers requires installation, monitoring, security updates, etc.

- Network latencies can be much smaller when using a CDN compared to a centrally located web server, since the CDN will deliver the static content from the closest location.
- The CDN is more scalable because the content is delivered from a local cache. Amazon claims to support 1,000 megabits per second, and claims peak request rates of 1,000 requests per second.
- Due to the distributed caches located worldwide, the CDN offers lower latencies.
- Using a CDN could cost you less; however, this depends on details. To figure out the exact cost difference, compare the CDN (data transfer, HTTP requests, invalidation requests, and hosting the file on the origin server) with the costs for running the required number of EC2 instances with the web servers and the operational costs.

AWS CloudFront

Amazon CloudFront offers a global network of 13 caches worldwide for the delivery of static content (8 caches are located in the US, 4 in Europe, and another 3 are in Asia).

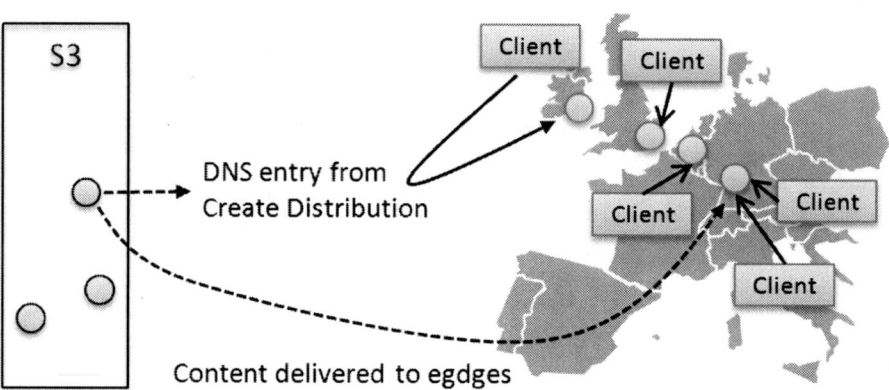

Figure 104: CloudFront Distribution Creation and Edge Access

The streaming of Flash content using the Real Time Messaging Protocol (RTMP) is also supported. Amazon calls these CloudFront caches edge locations. The content on the origin server has to be enabled for the delivery via CloudFront, then it's served from the edge location located nearest to the client.

SLA CloudFront comes with an SLA that guarantees an uptime of at least 99.9% during any monthly billing interval. You are eligible to receive a service credit for *future* payments if AWS doesn't meet the SLA. For an uptime of less than 99.9% but more than 99%, you receive a service credit of 10%, for an uptime of less than 99% you receive 25% service credit.

A small example: If all your customers' requests fail with an error rate of 100% on a particular day from 10am to 5pm, (a total of 7h, i.e. less than 1% monthly downtime) you are entitled to a service credit of 10% on your next bill. You still receive only 10% service credit if every second request fails for up to 14h.

CloudFront Usage

Your standard EC2 account does not include the CloudFront usage. To use CloudFront you first have to sign up for it under:

http://aws.amazon.com/cloudfront

Once signed up, using CloudFront is a piece of cake. First, you must put your content on an origin server. CloudFront supports S3 buckets or any other origin servers hosted on EC2, and even servers in your own data center.

For S3 you can use any of the S3 tools explained in the AWS chapter in section 3.2 of this book. In this example, I will use the S3 AWS. Remember that all S3 content is assigned to regions, so you have to select a region for your bucket.

You can use any file to try this yourself. I will use the shark.mpg file that served in the Rackspace CDN example in section 4.2. First, you need to upload the file with the S3 browser on the AWS management console.

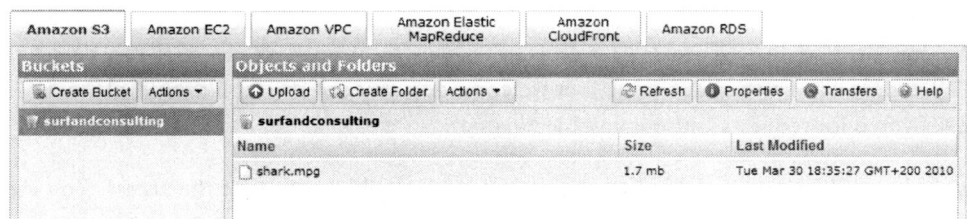

Figure 105: CloudFront Example File in S3 Browser

In the second step, you create a distribution, which then returns the DNS domain name of the distribution. This is the name that you will use on the client side to access the content via the distribution network.

Scalability 231

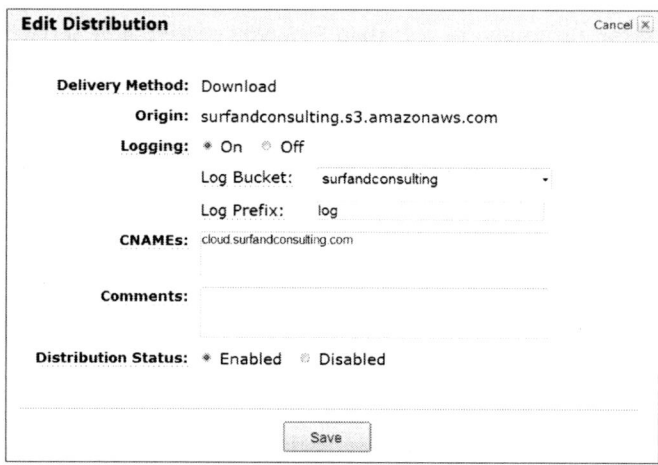

Figure 106: Create a CloudFront Distribution

After creating the distribution for your bucket, switch to the CloudFront tab in the AWS console. Here you can check for the domain name that is used on the client side to gain access to the content via the distribution network.

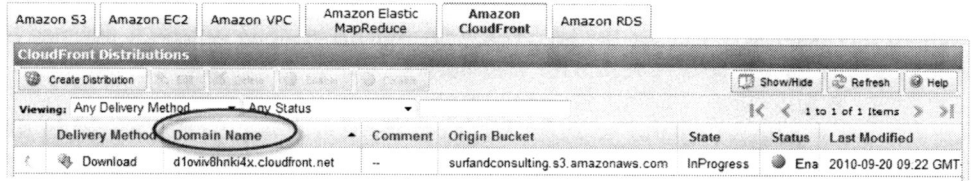

Figure 107: CloudFront Domain Name and Settings

The content is delivered via HTTP or HTTPS, but the transport protocol can be set to HTPPS only. Similar to a web container welcome-file, you can specify a default file that will be delivered for requests without an object name.

Typically, all files are readable by anyone, but it is possible to restrict the access. You can invalidate all cached files simultaneously. For a better understanding of the traffic patterns, access logs can be activated and stored in an S3 bucket.

After enabling the bucket for the CDN distribution, you should run a test to compare routing and the number of hops for the original S3 bucket to the content delivered via the CloudFront CDN.

Here is a test that I was running from my home in Munich. The example is compelling because it shows the advantage of the CDN in a real world case: the routing from my home to access data that is stored in the Amazon's S3 location for Europe.

The routing to the S3 origin storage is the routing that happens if there is no CDN configured. See below: the output from my laptop running Windows 7 to the destination of the S3 bucket, surfandconsulting.s3.amazon.com.

```
C:\Users\frank>tracert surfandconsulting.s3.amazonaws.com

Tracing route to s3-3-w.amazonaws.com [87.238.86.131]
over a maximum of 30 hops:

  1     2 ms     *      2 ms  fritz.box [192.168.178.1]
  2    28 ms     *     27 ms  mdsl.ac2.muc1.m-online.net [82.135.16.21]
  3     *      26 ms    *     gi3-12.r1.muc1.m-online.net [212.18.6.201]
  4    26 ms     *     26 ms  xe-0-3-0.r3.muc7.m-online.net [212.18.6.97]
  5    27 ms     *     27 ms  62.140.24.49
  6    32 ms     *     33 ms  ae-4-4.ebr1.Frankfurt1.Level3.net [4.69.134.2]
  7    41 ms     *     34 ms  ae-61-61.csw1.Frankfurt1.Level3.net [4.69.140.2]
  8    34 ms     *     34 ms  ae-62-62.ebr2.Frankfurt1.Level3.net [4.69.140.17]
  9    36 ms     *     36 ms  ae-47-47.ebr1.Dusseldorf1.Level3.net [4.69.143.173]
 10    36 ms     *     37 ms  ae-1-100.ebr2.Dusseldorf1.Level3.net [4.69.141.150]
 11    40 ms     *     40 ms  ae-48-48.ebr1.Amsterdam1.Level3.net [4.69.143.209]
 12    39 ms     *     39 ms  ae-1-100.ebr2.Amsterdam1.Level3.net [4.69.141.170]
 13    47 ms     *     47 ms  ae-45-45.ebr2.London1.Level3.net [4.69.143.70]
 14    48 ms    51 ms   *     ae-100-100.ebr1.London1.Level3.net [4.69.141.165]
 15    60 ms    61 ms  59 ms  ae-5-5.car1.Dublin1.Level3.net [4.69.136.89]
 16     *        *      *     Request timed out.
 17     *        *      *     Request timed out.
 18     *        *      *     Request timed out.
 19     *        *      *     Request timed out.
 20     *        *      *     Request timed out.
 21   213.242.106.86   reports: Destination net unreachable.
```

The journey starts at my router at home, and makes stops at my Munich Internet provider, then in Frankfurt, Düsseldorf, Amsterdam, and London, before finally ending in Dublin!

On the other hand, the traceroute to the CDN, which I mapped via a CNAME entry to cloud.surfandconsulting.com, is much shorter; there are only 10 hops instead of 21.

```
C:\Users\frank>tracert cloud.surfandconsulting.com

Tracing route to cloud.surfandconsulting.com [216.37.61.31]
over a maximum of 30 hops:

  1    2 ms     *        4 ms  fritz.box [192.168.178.1]
  2   27 ms     *       27 ms  mdsl.ac2.muc1.m-online.net [82.135.16.21]
  3    *       27 ms     *     gi3-12.r1.muc1.m-online.net [212.18.6.201]
  4   26 ms     *       38 ms  xe-0-3-0.r3.muc7.m-online.net [212.18.6.97]
  5   43 ms   171 ms     *     62.140.24.49
  6   32 ms     *       33 ms  ae-4-4.ebr1.Frankfurt1.Level3.net [4.69.134.2]
  7   36 ms     *       45 ms  ae-61-61.csw1.Frankfurt1.Level3.net [4.69.140.2]
  8   52 ms     *       35 ms  ae-1-69.edge4.Frankfurt1.Level3.net [4.68.23.12]
  9   33 ms     *       34 ms  212.162.24.70
 10   34 ms     *       35 ms  server-216-37-61-31.fra2.cloudfront.net [216.37.61.31]

Trace complete.
```

After leaving my home network, the network packets are delivered from my Internet provider straight to the edge location in Frankfurt.

This example shows how accessing data via the CDN dramatically shortens the routing and the number of hops. In the map, the whole journey across the northern part of Europe is replaced by the first leg from Munich to Frankfurt.

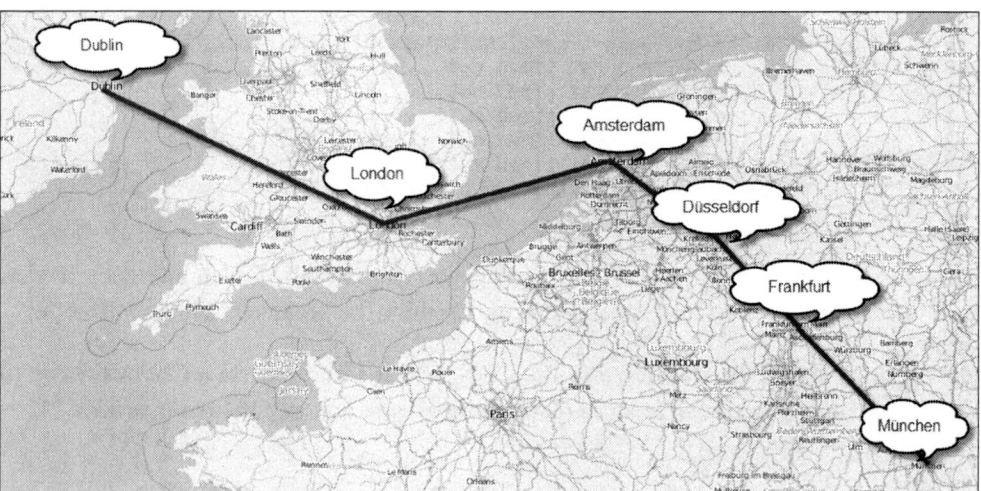

Figure 108: Routing with CloudFront (Munich to Frankfurt) versus direct S3 access (Munich to Dublin)

CloudFront Pricing

As usual, you have to pay extra for every AWS service that you use, and CloudFront is no exception to that rule. The costs for the usage of CloudFront consist of the following:

- The costs for the CloudFront service start at $0.150 per GB for the first 10 TB / month of data transfer out.
- In addition $0.0090 per 10,000 HTTP requests will show up on your invoice if you are located in Europe (prices for other regions differ only slightly).
- The first 1,000 files that you request for invalidation each month are free, then an additional charge of $0.005 per file occurs.
- If S3 is used for the storage of the origin files, you pay the regular rates for the S3 usage as well, e.g. to fetch the data from S3 that is delivered to the edge location.

CloudFront with WebLogic Server

The complete design when using Amazon's CloudFront in conjunction with the Elastic Load Balancer and WebLogic is illustrated in Figure 109. Requests from clients for static content will be forwarded to the nearest edge location. The static content at the edge location uses URLs that point to the ELB, which is the entry point to the WebLogic domain. The ELB and the WebLogic instances are located in the eu-west availability zone in this example (both are drawn off the map of Europe for illustrational purposes).

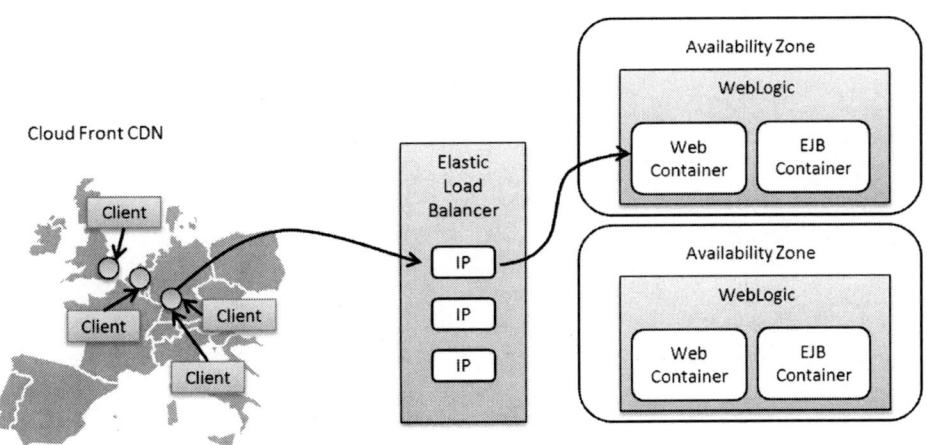

Figure 109: CloudFront, Elastic Load Balancer and WebLogic

More CDN Use Cases

A number of compelling usage cases exist for a content distribution network:

- A CDN is an interesting choice for the distribution of software because of its compelling performance data. An increasing number of software is downloaded straight from Cloud File. The popular file manager TotalCommander is just one of many examples.
- A CDN is an excellent web cache - not only for web and Java EE application server architecture. There are very convenient tools available for blog-sites and content management systems (CMS). For example, W3TotalCache is a plugin for the popular website and blogging software Wordpress. This plugin can upload the static pages of a blog onto the Amazon's CloudFront CDN.

11 Monitoring

This chapter explains the monitoring options for the cloud. We will explore solutions for system, middleware and application monitoring, as well as taking an in-depth look at Amazon's CloudWatch. The AWS Simple Notification Service is also explained is this chapter, since it is a service that can be used to implement a monitoring solution (among other things). Further, a number of common monitoring solutions that can be used in the cloud as well as in non-cloud environments will be introduced.

11.1 Overview

Whenever I have the opportunity to become involved in exciting software projects, I ask my client about monitoring. Unfortunately, a frequent response is that the project manager hasn't had sufficient time to investigate monitoring options, *even though* the application is usually so critical that any failure will be immediately apparent to the end-user.

I strongly believe that your operations team should be aware of any failures *before* the customer – albeit literally only the second prior to picking up the phone to answer the dreaded call from the angry customer with the failed system.

The monitoring process adopted in the cloud doesn't *have* to be any different from that adopted in non-cloud environments. However, the former is arguably more crucial because the instances in public clouds are further away, thus reducing your physical control over the process and entailing the need to ensure that the cloud platform provider meets its Service Level Agreement (SLA).

In this chapter, we will look at different monitoring approaches. Firstly, we will cover monitoring of the WebLogic server (which applies to any other middleware product running on top of WebLogic) i.e. deep monitoring of the middleware. For example we will take a look at how to monitor the amount of free heap in the JRockit JVM, the number of busy connections in your production data source, and the length of the JMS queue for the billing system.

Secondly, when looking at the cloud on a higher level, you'll no doubt be interested in verifying whether a particular EC2 instance is up and running. Alternatively, you will want to measure the CPU and disk usage of some instances in the cloud. This second category is a shallower, higher level, system monitoring, that is agnostic of the application itself, of the middleware and of the database.

At the end of the day, you should be looking at a combination of both approaches. For every application in production, you should ensure monitoring is installed for the key runtime values of WebLogic. Running your application in the cloud makes no difference; in the cloud you have to plan and monitor for instance failures.

Other monitoring approaches include Amazon's CloudWatch, which is unique in that auto scaling is reliant upon monitoring data produced by CloudWatch.

Table 11 provides an overview of the monitoring tools I will mention in this chapter - two of which I would like to focus on:

- WebLogic Scripting Tool and WebLogic Diagnostic Framework can both be used in the cloud. These tools are free and included with the WebLogic distribution, eliminating the need for individual installation.
- AWS CloudWatch plays an important role in system monitoring, because it provides the metrics for auto scaling and stores historic data off-instance.

Unfortunately, it is not possible for me to provide detailed information about all the different tools and frameworks available for the monitoring process, as this would fill a book at least twice the size of this one. Nevertheless, my passion for monitoring meant I simply couldn't stop myself from including some brief comments at the end of this chapter on other popular monitoring tools and frameworks.

Table 11: Monitoring Tools and Frameworks

System Monitoring	Middleware Monitoring
Amazon CloudWatch	SNMP
Ganglia	**WebLogic Scripting Tool**
RDD	**WebLogic Diagnostic Framework**
	JMXShell, JMX4Perl
	Hyperic
Nagios (with JMX4Perl)	
Oracle Enterprise Manager Grid Control	

11.2 WebLogic Scripting Tool

WebLogic Scripting Tool (WLST) is an easy to use, command-line and scripting interface, forming part of the WebLogic installation. It is certainly the most efficient way to access monitoring data or to implement configuration changes (unless you are using the WebLogic admin console). The good news is that using WLST requires no additional licensing or installation.

From a design perspective, it is a good option for middleware layer monitoring:

- Middleware layer monitoring is independent of the cloud and the operating system. WLST scripts inherently provide multi-cloud support so you don't have to change the scripts when you move your applications to another IaaS provider.
- On the middleware layer there are more metrics available than on a system layer.
- The metrics available describe the application state more accurately than any other system metric currently available.

JMX Basics

WLST itself is implemented in Jython, which is an implementation of the popular scripting language Python on top of the JVM.

WLST is a great abstraction layer for the Java Management Extensions (JMX) interface; you could even program a JMX client in Java to accomplish the same task instead of using WLST. However, trust me, programming JMX in Java is extremely time-consuming and therefore ill advised; numerous lines of Java code can be replaced by just two or three lines of a WLST script.

WLST is also a fantastic example of the benefits to be gained from using a domain specific language (DSL). DSLs address a problem domain by using a high level language, which has been specifically tailored to address the problem. They have become very popular in recent years, so chances are that you will have come across them if you have attended computer conferences during the last three years.

Domain Specific Language

The problem domain that WLST addresses is configuration and monitoring of WebLogic. The WLST solution uses the language features of Jython.

WebLogic MBeans

The JMX API enables you to communicate with MBeans which represent the management information on the server side. Different types of MBeans exist, yet all share the following features:

- MBeans have attributes. For example, the listen address of a managed server is an MBean attribute.
- MBeans have operations i.e. methods that you can call. For example, there is an MBean with an operation named shutdown(). If you call this operation the application server will shut itself down.
- MBeans have children. You can navigate from a parent MBean to a child MBean. All MBeans together span a directed graph.
- MBeans use notifications (as this is irrelevant to monitoring, it will not be covered in this book).

MBean Server   WebLogic uses an MBean server for configuration. These MBeans represent the configuration data that is stored in the config.xml file under DOMAIN_NAME/config and all linked system modules in the subdirectories of the config directory. Configuration attributes are read/write and you are able to alter the attributes of a configuration MBean during a change session.

The runtime MBean server is the most interesting for monitoring purposes. It hosts the runtime MBeans that have attributes that represent all runtime values (runtime attributes are read-only). Usually, it doesn't make any sense to change them, but unfortunately they cannot be reset to zero should the need arise.

One of the best graphical JMX clients that you will ever see is the WebLogic admin console. As there is no secret shortcut for the admin console, internally the console uses JMX to display and to change the MBean values.

Another JMX client which is more generic and comes with every JDK installation, is the JConsole tool. Assuming you have a JDK installed and the path correctly set, you can start with the command jconsole and use it to take a look around. Starting with WebLogic 10.3.3, you should be able to view the WebLogic MBeans straightaway when connecting locally. (In earlier versions, the WebLogic MBeans are hidden and you first have to enable this behavior). Please see Figure 118 for a screenshot of JConsole.

Monitoring with WLST

WLST is basically a thin layer of Jython on top of JMX. You can start WLST after setting the correct environment, e.g. by running the `setDomainEnv.sh` script of an existing domain with the following command:

`java weblogic.WLST`

`wls:/offline>`

WLST will respond with an offline prompt to indicate that you not connected to a running domain and are therefore working in offline mode.

Many exciting tasks can be accomplished in offline mode, such as creating a new WebLogic domain or connecting to nodemanager process and setting up a domain. However, as far as monitoring is concerned, it is preferable to connect to a running instance in the cloud.

Offline Mode

Next start your favorite WebLogic image in the cloud. A running admin server of any domain will be adequate for this example (even one of the sample domains that comes with the WebLogic installation).

Ensure that the listen port of the admin server is in the AWS management console's settings for the security group. You always connect to the WebLogic admin server, as it hosts the runtime values for the whole WebLogic domain.

Group Name:	default				
Description:	default group				
Allowed Connections:					
Connection Method	Protocol	From Port	To Port	Source (IP or group)	Actions
All	icmp	-1	-1	default group	Remove
All	tcp	0	65535	default group	Remove
All	udp	0	65535	default group	Remove
SSH	tcp	22	22	0.0.0.0/0	Remove
RDP	tcp	3389	3389	0.0.0.0/0	Remove
-	tcp	(7001)	7003	0.0.0.0/0	Remove

Figure 110: Enable Connection to Admin Port for WLST

To connect, use the `connect(username, password, URL)` command with the elastic IP address that you assigned to the admin server. Alternatively, you could connect to the

Online Mode

public IP or DNS name of the EC2 instance, although using an elastic IP will make the monitoring more robust.

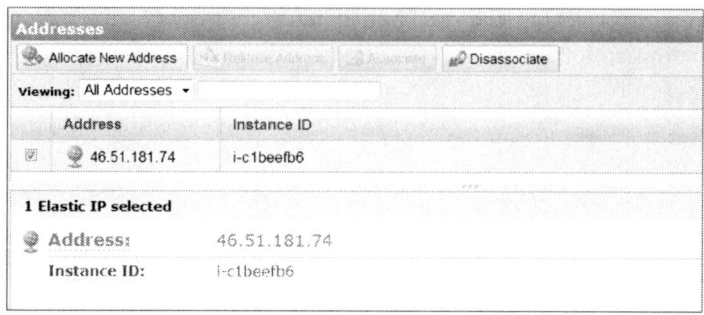

Figure 111: Elastic IP of WebLogic Admin Server

If the admin server should fail, simply run another EC2 instance, re-start the admin server and assign the elastic IP to the new EC instance. With elastic IPs you can simply use the script shown below (no changes required):

```
wls:/offline> connect('weblogic','weblogic1','t3://ec2-46-51-181-74.eu-west-1.compute.amazonaws.com:7001')
```

```
Connecting to t3://ec2-46-51-181-74.eu-west-1.compute.amazonaws.com:7001
with userid weblogic ...
Successfully connected to Admin Server 'AdminServer' that belongs to
domain 'fm'.

Warning: An insecure protocol was used to connect to the
server. To ensure on-the-wire security, the SSL port or
Admin port should be used instead.This shows that we successfully
connected to our instance running in the cloud. You could use t3 over SSL
to get red rid of the security warning.
```

Interactive WLST Once WLST is up and running, you can use it interactively to retrieve runtime and configuration data from a WebLogic server domain. To change to the server runtime MBeans, type the command `domainRuntime()`, then navigate to the admin servers runtime environment and from there to the JVMRuntime. The interaction here is shown step-by-step for illustrative purposes only – in reality, the last three commands can be amalgamated into one.

Use `cd()` and `ls()` to navigate in the MBean hierarchy and display attributes, or use `get('attributeName')` to retrieve the value of an attribute. Take a look at the following script that retrieves the free heap from the JVM:

```
domainRuntime()
cd('ServerRuntimes/AdminServer')
cd('JVMRuntime/AdminServer')
get('HeapFreePercent')
```

The script in the example above didn't retrieve any WebLogic specific runtime data, since I wanted to keep it as generic as possible. However, you can try it with any domain. Runtime data for WebLogic resources only exists after the resource is created, the target of the resource is set and, of course, only if that particular server is running.

Let's look at another example. Imagine you created a data source with the JNDI name emergencyDB. To retrieve the current capacity of the associated connection pool, you will need to run the following command after changing to the server's runtime MBean server:

```
get('JDBCServiceRuntime/AdminServer/JDBCDataSourceRuntimeMBeans/
emergencyDB/CurrCapacity')
```

To monitor a value over a period of time, you must continuously wrap the command in a Python loop, add a sleep statement that lasts a couple of seconds, and voilà, that's all there is to a very basic monitoring script. The new script can be used to observe the heap usage of a deployed application on a WebLogic cloud instance. System integrators like such scripts to observe the memory usage patterns of a new application and to look for memory leaks over a longer period of time.

You can write a script to monitor a JMS queue, the transaction manager, an EJB pool or any other MBean attribute, and every runtime value found in the WebLogic admin console can be read via JMX or WLST.

Finally, in order to create a real script, first copy the interactively used commands, then save them in a file named script.py and execute the script as follows:

```
java weblogic.WLST script.py
```

Now, before you start implementing such a script I recommend you read the following section in the book, which covers WebLogic Diagnostic Framework, as there is an even easier way to achieve the same result. I covered the scripting tool first because some experience with JMX makes it easier to understand the WebLogic Diagnostic framework.

Scripting

11.3 WebLogic Diagnostic Framework

WebLogic Diagnostic Framework (WLDF) was a new feature of WebLogic 9. It facilitates and unifies logging and monitoring of WebLogic server and any other Oracle middleware product running on top of WebLogic server. As with WLST, no additional license or installation is necessary and it can be used for monitoring WebLogic based middleware servers running on *any* cloud platform.

A steep learning curve is required for WLDF. However, once you are able to navigate your way around the Framework, you can use it to monitor applications running on WebLogic or even to monitor WebLogic server itself.

Collected Metrics

The easiest thing to do with WLDF is to replace the example with the Python loop. By the way, did you by any chance stop to wonder why I didn't include a complete script for the monitoring with the WLST example? Here is why: you don't even have to write a script.

Instead of writing such a script (which will regularly read an attribute of a runtime MBean and then wait for a few of seconds), you can simply configure a collected metric with the WebLogic Diagnostic Framework in the WebLogic admin console. The effect is the same, yet it is configuration only, with no scripting required.

File or JDBC archive A collected metric defines an attribute of a certain MBean instance or type which is written to an archive at regular intervals. The default archive is a file, but you can easily change it to a database that is accessed via a data source.

Collected metrics provide deep monitoring and can log the execution time of a particular method of a SOAP web service (which is part of an SOA based application). The following screenshot shows the selection of the average, high and low execution time of the web service operation runtime MBean belonging to a SOAP web service.

In order to arrive here, you need to create a diagnostic module and then navigate to Diagnostics / Diagnostic Module / Configuration / Collected Metrics in the WebLogic admin console.

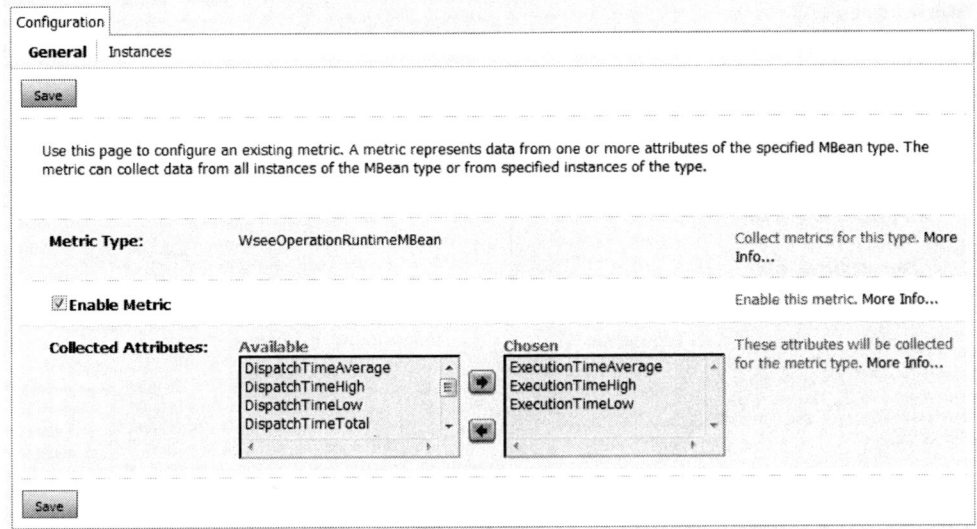

Figure 112: WLDF Define Collected Metrics Attribute

Watches and Notifications

You are not completely wrong if you think that there could still be a better solution, as often, collecting runtime values at regular intervals is not necessarily the best solution. Indeed, attributes of runtime MBeans aren't particularly interesting if their value is within the normal range: exciting data is abnormal data.

Watches define a condition based MBean attribute. Although there is a rule language for the watches, usually the rule is specified by logically combining expressions in the WebLogic admin console. Figure 113 shows the configuration of a watch.

The notification can use one or more of the following transport protocols:

- Java Management Extensions (JMX)
- Java Message Service (JMS)
- Simple Mail Transfer Protocol (SMTP)
- Simple Network Management Protocol (SNMP)

In addition you can use a notification to trigger the creation of a Diagnostic Image.

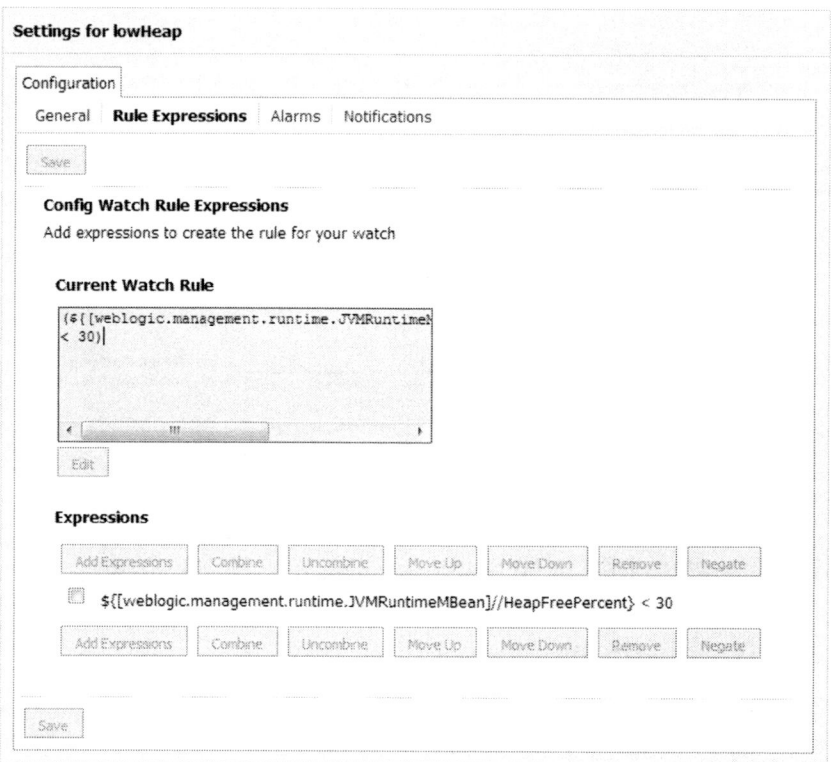

Figure 113: WLDF Watch Configuration

You define the watch on an instance in the cloud, and the notification will then be delivered to any receiver that you specify. For example, you can stay informed via email if the free heap of a cloud instance falls below 10%.

Instrumentation

To discover more about what happens at runtime, you can instrument either your application or WebLogic server itself; instrumentation means that you insert a certain piece of diagnostic code at particular locations. It's a powerful tool that is based on aspect-oriented programming (AOP). In contrast to AOP however, instrumentation in WLDF cannot actually execute an arbitrary piece of code, but only run certain predefined actions.

To set up instrumentation you need to configure a diagnostic monitor, which will define *when* the monitoring happens. A diagnostic action defines *what* happens when the monitor is executed.

There is a long list of predefined monitors to instrument EJB, JDBC, JMS, JNDI, Servlets and HTTP sessions, which can all be used for monitoring a particular application, as shown in the screenshot below:

WLDF Monitor

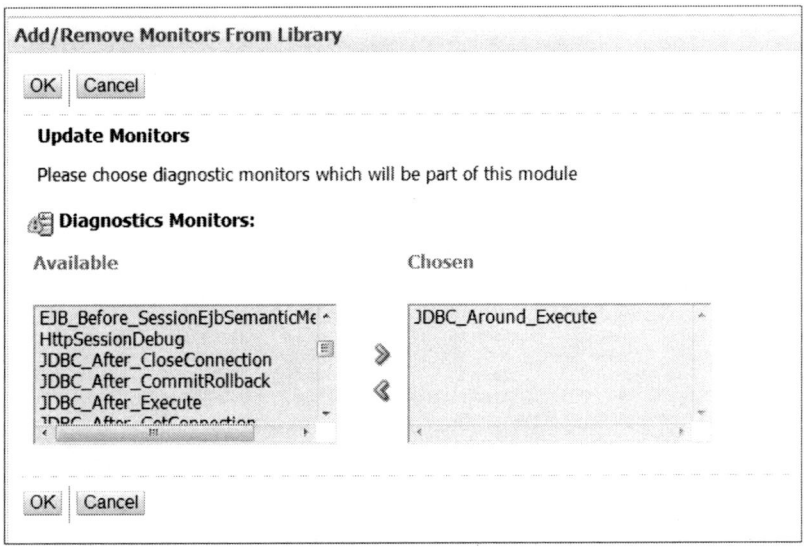

Figure 114: WLDF Instrumentation Monitors

A number of different steps are required to display the arguments of a method, to create stack or thread dumps and to trace time or memory consumption of a method invocation:

WLDF Action

- `DisplayArgumentsAction`
- `StackDumpAction`
- `ThreadDumpAction`
- `TraceAction`
- `TraceElapsedTimeAction`
- `MethodInvocationStatisticsAction` (since 10.3)
- `MethodMemoryAllocationStatisticsAction` (since 10.3.3)

These actions generally write to the WLDF event log.

However, there is one exception, the `MethodInvocationStatisticsAction` updates method invocation statistics on another MBean without the I/O overhead of writing to an archive. These statistics can be retrieved via JMX or WLST.

Method Invocation Statistics Mike Cico has written a small web application that retrieves the method invocation data and displays it in a tabular format, as shown in the screenshot below:

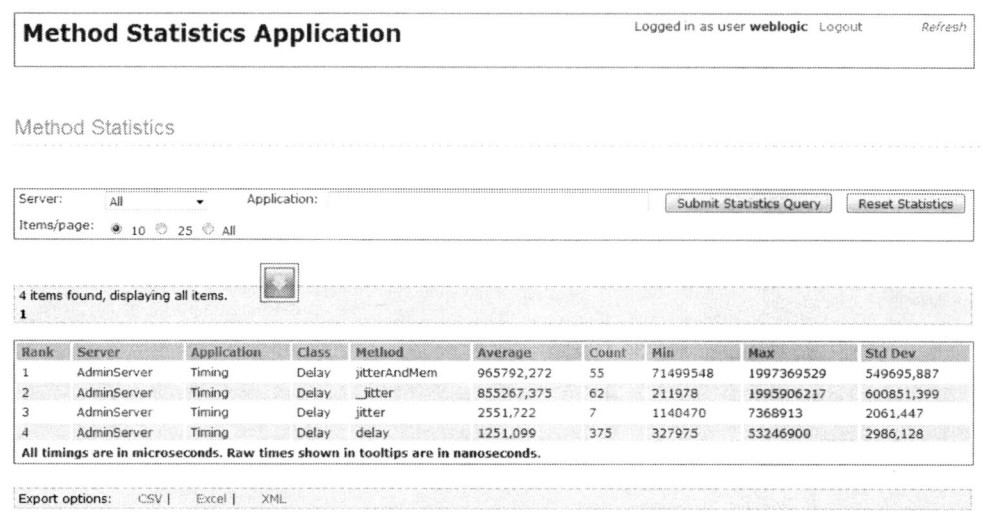

Figure 115: methodstats Web Application for MethodInvocationStatistics

Oracle documentation Mike's article is an interesting overview of WLDF, which can be found together with links to the web application and the source files at the following location:

http://crmondemand.oracle.com/technetwork/articles/cico-wldf-091073.html

Server Instrumentation The exciting part of the instrumentation is that you don't need to have any knowledge about the structure or the way in which the application is built. You can simply choose a `JDBC_Before_Execute` monitor and attach a `DisplayArgumentsAction` to monitor the JDBC statements of an unknown application that are sent to the database. Simultaneously, you will see the file with the line number and the name of the method executed. A part of the output data is shown in the figure below:

Module:	Emergency.war
Monitor:	JDBC_Before_Execute
File Name:	__dbaccess.java
Line Number:	100
Class Name:	java.sql.Statement
Method Name:	executeQuery
Method Descriptor:	(Ljava/lang/String;)Ljava/sql/ResultSet;
Arguments:	weblogic.jdbc.wrapper.Statement_com_pointbase_net_netJDBCStatement@10, select id, first_name, middle_name, last_name, phone, email from physician

Figure 116: WLDF Instrumentation Event

Not always you have to deal with an application with a completely unknown structure. Quite often you already know a set of critical methods and you want to observe their execution times. WLDF can instrument certain locations in your application. These locations are called pointcuts. The following expression instruments all methods in the package com.surfandconsulting that start with bookTicket, have an arbitrary number of parameters, any return value type and public visibility.

Application instrumentation

```
execute ( public * com.surfandconsulting* bookTicket* (...) )
```

Dashboard

Last but not by no means least, the time has come for me to mention the new dashboard, which is a new feature of WebLogic 10.3.3. and replaces the older WLDF console extension. As the dashboard is no longer built as a Java applet, there are less potential problems with the JVM in the client browser.

In addition to the technical enhancements, the new dashboard is also much more aesthetically pleasing, and can be located via the following URL when accessing the WebLogic admin server:

```
http://host:port/console/dashboard
```

The dashboard can display a set of graphical views showing a variety of runtime data, over a fixed time period. The example below shows a faulty JDBC application that isn't returning connections to the connection pool. The current capacity of the connection pool will therefore continue increasing until the maximum capacity is reached. Once this happens, connections will be waiting and the failed request count will increase.

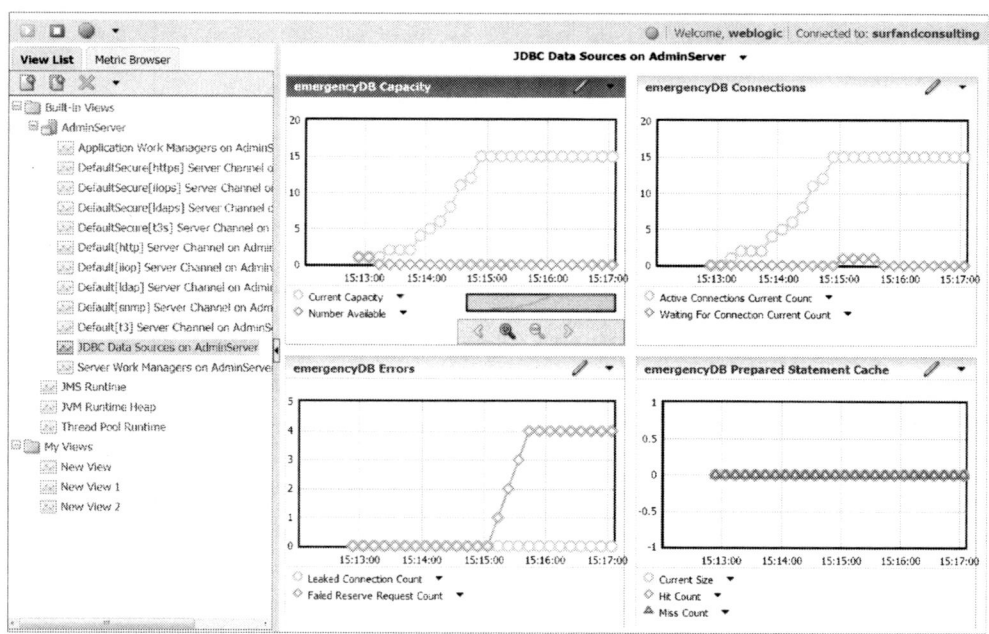

Figure 117: WebLogic Dashboard

11.4 JMX4Perl and JMXShell

JMX4Perl is a Perl module that is often used as a plugin for Nagios in order to obtain access to JMX data on application servers. It provides an efficient and convenient way to retrieve JMX data and it supports an extensive list of application servers.

JMX without Java

JMX4Perl uses HTTP to talk to the application server, thus avoiding the overhead cost of starting a JVM on the client side (a small web application is all that needs to be deployed on the application server).

A Perl client, or a simple REST request, communicates with the deployed web application j4p.war, which in turn uses JMX to access the MBeans. The web application is already included in the JMX4Perl distribution, so you don't have to build it yourself. You can take the web application from the distribution and deploy it for a first test on the WebLogic admin server.

JMX4Perl was developed by Roland Huss. The latest version can be obtained from CPAN, at the following location:

`http://search.cpan.org/~roland/jmx4perl`

REST based JMX Monitoring

With the j4p.war application deployed, you can use the following URL to request the heap memory usage:

`http://localhost:7001/j4p/read/java.lang:type=Memory/HeapMemoryUsage`

You will immediately notice how much faster this request returns compared to starting WLST in a JVM on the client side. Saving the overhead of starting a JVM really pays off when the invocation is triggered regularly by a monitoring tool such as Nagios.

To access a WebLogic specific value (e.g. to retrieve the listen port of the server) try the following REST request:

`http://localhost:7001/j4p/read/com.bea:Name=AdminServer,Type=Server/ListenPort`

The request returns the following JSON structure:

```
{"timestamp":1287229335,
 "status":200,
 "request": {"mbean":"com.bea:Name=AdminServer,Type=Server",
      "attribute":"ListenPort",
      "type":"read"},
 "value":"7001"
}
```

There is also a Java library that you can use instead of sending REST request with the browser or `wget`.

As you can see, the most challenging task is finding out the correct name of the MBean. Once you know the MBean's name, it is very easy to read an attribute. There are different ways to discover the correct name. If you are an experienced WLST user, you can interactively navigate to the right level and then print out the current managed object cmo:

`wls:/surfandconsulting/serverConfig/Servers/AdminServer> print cmo`

`[MBeanServerInvocationHandler]com.bea:Name=AdminServer,Type=Server`

Alternatively, you can use JConsole to navigate your way to the right MBean and then obtain its name from the MBean info tab:

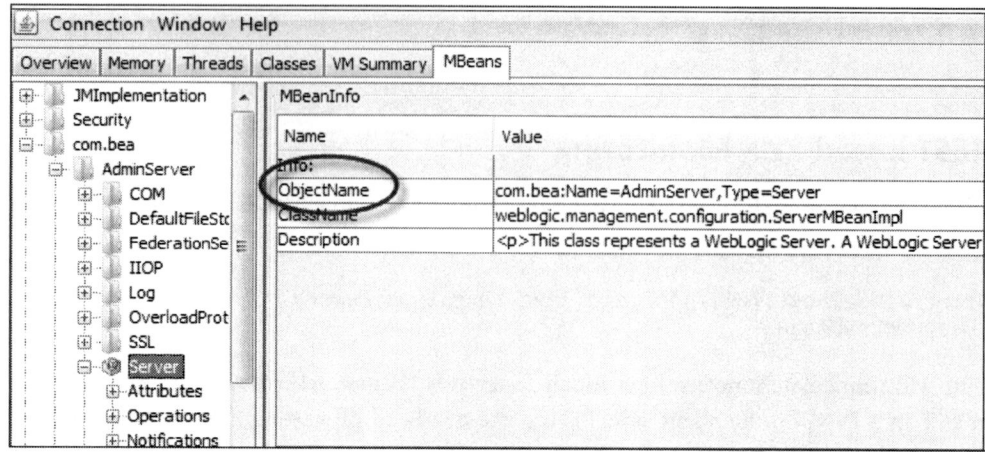

Figure 118: Using JConsole to Access WebLogic MBean Name

JMX Shell j4psh

Have you ever thought that WLST is "so Eighties"? It's running from a DOS-box or a Unix shell, there are no such comforts as tab completion of commands and there is no syntax-highlighting. Although, to be fair, in case you didn't notice, you can always retrieve the last command with the cursor-up key.

Don't get me wrong, I am in fact a big fan of WLST, as it's a good example of how useful a domain specific language can be. However, I do receive a lot of queries from Oracle customers asking whether all the accomplishments of 20 years of software development have somehow passed unnoticed by the WLST development team?

There is a better way. JMX4Perl comes with a JMX shell called j4psh. It's an interactive shell with context sensitive command-line completion, syntax-highlighting with color scheme support, history saved across sessions and Emacs key bindings.

It is certainly useful for interactively exploring the JMX world of WebLogic, but it cannot replace WLST for scripting (do still give it a go though for reading and writing MBean attributes, or to call MBean operations). I was using a very early version (0.7) but I am pretty sure there will be more documentation around once this book is published.

A thought: wouldn't it be a nice idea if Oracle took some of the j4psh ideas and included a WLST shell with command-line completion and syntax highlighting? Or maybe even a Eclipse plugin for WLST?

Hello Oracle ...

11.5 AWS CloudWatch

Amazon's CloudWatch is the monitoring solution provided by AWS. On a high level, it can be used directly from the AWS console, although it also comes with a command-line interface and an API.

Basics

The main benefit of CloudWatch is that it's capable of monitoring EC2 instances, EBS volumes, the AWS elastic load balancer and the relational database service. The monitoring data is graphically displayed in the AWS web console. Using the CloudWatch command-line you can create alarms invoking SNS notifications or auto scaling events.

Basic monitoring data is always collected - there is no need to install or start a separate monitoring process on the cloud instances.

Costs

CloudWatch has a free usage tier: Basic monitoring with a granularity of 5 minutes and up to 10 alarms per month is provided free of charge. Also, monitoring is free for the relational database service, the elastic load balancing, and EBS volumes.

If you select the detailed monitoring (at a 1-minute frequency), every EC2 instance that you monitor is charged at a rate of $0.015 per hour, which adds up to an extra $ 10.80 per month.

CloudWatch can be enabled from the AWS console as soon as you start one or more instances or, alternatively, it can be enabled for running instances at a later stage.

When starting an instance from the command-line with the `ec2-run-instances` command, you can provide the option `--monitor` to enable monitoring right from the start.

For instances which are already running, you can use the `ec2-monitor-instances` command to enable the monitoring and `ec2-unmonitor-instances` to disable it again.

Once CloudWatch is enabled, you can view the statistical data by selecting the 'Instance' and clicking on the 'Monitoring' tab:

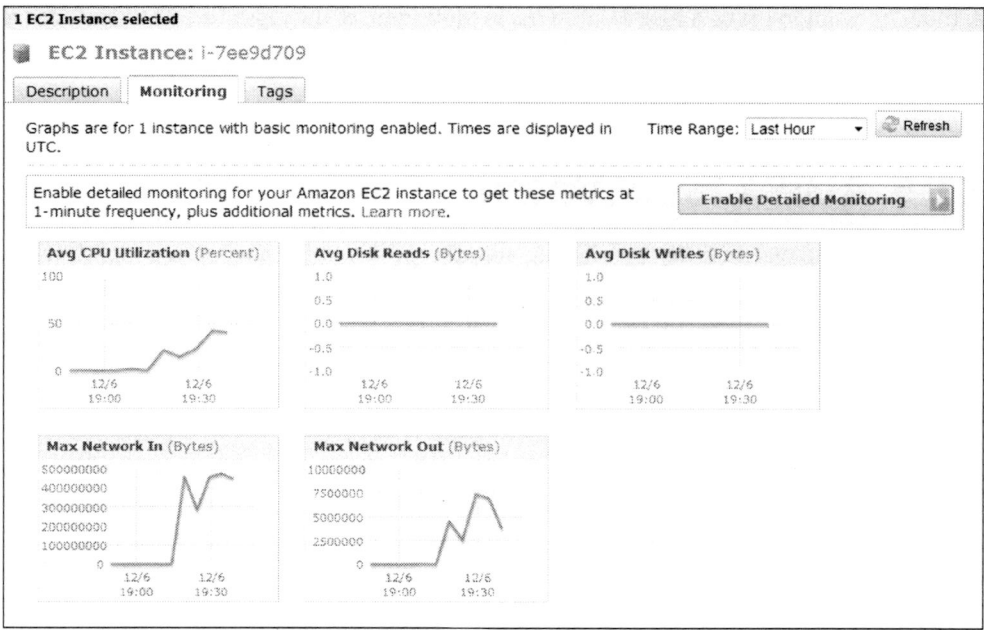

Figure 119: CloudWatch EC2 Basic Monitoring

Let me quickly explain what happens behind the scenes: CloudWatch is collecting raw data which is called *measures*. Every measure has a name, a value, a unit, a namespace and associated dimensions:

```
measure = (name, value, unit, namespace, dimensions)
```

Measures are buffered at one minute intervals and aggregated into *metrics*. A metric has a name that comes from its input measures. Metrics are persisted off-instance for two weeks, so even if you were to terminate the instance, the monitoring data could still be accessed. You retrieve metrics rather than measures from CloudWatch. These metrics can be averaged at an interval of one minute or multiples thereof.

The unit of a metric is typically bytes, seconds or percent. The *namespace* is used to differentiate metrics from AWS services such as EC2, the elastic load balancer or RDS. The *dimension* makes a metric more specific and could be an instance type or a particular instance ID.

If you click on one of the graphs displayed in the AWS console, you will see a new window. Here you can request the statistics of a metric (choose either samples, minimum, maximum, or sum), the collection period, and the time range.

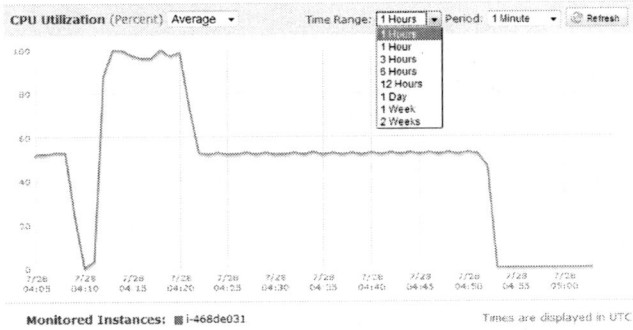

Figure 120: CloudWatch CPU Monitoring

Installation

CloudWatch does not only cost you extra money, it is also implemented as a separate service with its own command-line tools. So even though the current CloudWatch developer guide doesn't explicitly explain, you do have to download an extra zip file: under http://aws.amazon.com/cloudwatch click on "Developer Tools" to reach the download.

Download

After downloading, unzip the file, set the AWS_CLOUDWATCH_HOME environment variable, and add AWS_CLOUDWATCH_HOME/bin to the path as described in the included README file.

The following examples require you to have already set the credentials, as explained in chapter 3.4 of this book (without these credentials, the monitoring command-line interface commands will complain). In addition, you have to set the following two environment variables: EC2_CERT and EC2_PRIVATE_KEY.

Usage

Verify the installation with the mon-version command. This command should return the version of the installed command-line tools.

```
frank@ubuntu:~$ mon-version
Amazon CloudWatch CLI version 1.0.2.3 (API 2009-05-15)
```

To list available metrics that you can query, execute the following command. This lists the name of the measure attached to the metric in the first column, the corresponding namespace in the second column, and the dimension such as ImageId, InstanceId, InstanceType in the last column:

Command-line usage

```
frank@ubuntu:~$ mon-list-metrics
CPUUtilization          AWS/EC2   {ImageId=ami-cf4d67bb}
CPUUtilization          AWS/EC2
CPUUtilization          AWS/EC2   {ImageId=ami-cd517bb9}
CPUUtilization          AWS/EC2   {InstanceId=i-28a1cc5f}
CPUUtilization          AWS/EC2   {InstanceType=c1.medium}
CPUUtilization          AWS/EC2   {InstanceId=i-468de031}
DiskReadBytes           AWS/EC2   {InstanceType=m1.small}
(... output shortened)
```

CLOUDWATCH REGIONS

All users outside of the default US region should set EC2_REGION to their appropriate region, e.g. eu-west-1 for Europe.

To access monitoring data outside of the default region, and without setting the environment variable above, you have to add the -- region eu-west-1 switch to all monitoring commands.

If you don't set either EC2_REGION or --region the monitoring commands will not only return without data, but also without a message explaining what went wrong when used outside of the default region.

To obtain a short list of every metric with its associated namespace, run the CloudWatch command below. Please note, that you will only see metrics with the AWS/EBS namespace when monitoring data from volumes or EBS-backed instances is available. Also, the metrics from the elastic load balancer or the relational database service will only be shown if there is data available (i.e. when the service has been running in the last 2 weeks).

```
$ mon-list-metrics --region eu-west-1 | cut -c1-30    | uniq
  CPUUtilization              AWS/EC2
  DiskReadBytes               AWS/EC2
  DiskReadOps                 AWS/EC2
  DiskWriteBytes              AWS/EC2
  DiskWriteOps                AWS/EC2
  NetworkIn                   AWS/EC2
  NetworkOut                  AWS/EC2

  HealthyHostCount            AWS/ELB
  Latency                     AWS/ELB
  RequestCount                AWS/ELB
  UnHealthyHostCount          AWS/ELB

  VolumeIdleTime              AWS/EBS
  VolumeQueueLength           AWS/EBS
  VolumeReadBytes             AWS/EBS
  VolumeReadOps               AWS/EBS
  VolumeTotalReadTime         AWS/EBS
  VolumeTotalWriteTime        AWS/EBS
  VolumeWriteBytes            AWS/EBS
  VolumeWriteOps              AWS/EBS

  BinLogDiskUsage             AWS/RDS
  CPUUtilization              AWS/RDS
  DatabaseConnections         AWS/RDS
  FreeableMemory              AWS/RDS
  FreeStorageSpace            AWS/RDS
  ReadIOPS                    AWS/RDS
  ReadLatency                 AWS/RDS
  ReadThroughput              AWS/RDS
  ReplicaLag                  AWS/RDS
  SwapUsage                   AWS/RDS
  WriteIOPS                   AWS/RDS
  WriteLatency                AWS/RDS
  WriteThroughput             AWS/RDS
```

Now, using the command-line or API you can further investigate the metrics. For example, you could request the average and maximum CPU usage over 10 minute intervals using the following command:

```
frank@ubuntu:~$ mon-get-stats CPUUtilization   --period 600
--statistics "Average,Maximum" --namespace "AWS/EC2"

2010-07-28  14:22:00    10.0    0.11499999999999999    0.35    Percent
2010-07-28  14:32:00    10.0    0.16000000000000003    0.79    Percent
2010-07-28  14:42:00    10.0    0.07899999999999999    0.26    Percent
2010-07-28  14:52:00    10.0    0.07999999999999999    0.26    Percent
2010-07-28  15:02:00    10.0    33.351                 53.33   Percent
2010-07-28  15:12:00    3.0     0.03                   0.09    Percent
```

Adjacent to the date and the timestamp, the number of samples for that particular interval will be displayed, followed by the statistical values and their unit of measurement.

Assuming you have a set of machines running in the cloud, you can narrow the query down to one instance by adding:

`--dimensions "InstanceId=i-c07704a9"`.

Use the following command to calculate to total number of bytes written to disk by a particular instance, which have been calculated over 15 minute periods for the last hour:

```
frank@ubuntu:~$ mon-get-stats DiskWriteBytes  --period 900
--statistics Sum --namespace "AWS/EC2"

2010-07-28 14:27:00   15.0   2875392.0   Bytes
2010-07-28 14:42:00   15.0   2777088.0   Bytes
2010-07-28 14:57:00   15.0   2805760.0   Bytes
2010-07-28 15:12:00    9.0   1658880.0   Bytes
```

A similar query can be started for the number of bytes transferred out of the network:

```
frank@ubuntu:~$ mon-get-stats NetworkOut   --period 900 --statistics Sum
--namespace "AWS/EC2"
2010-07-28 14:34:00   15.0   0.0       Bytes
2010-07-28 14:49:00   15.0   3884.0    Bytes
2010-07-28 15:04:00   15.0   45004.0   Bytes
2010-07-28 15:19:00    9.0   0.0       Bytes
```

Alarms You can create up to 400 alarms per account using the mon-put-metric-alarm command. For further details take a look at the CloudWatch developer guide at the following site:

http://docs.amazonwebservices.com/AmazonCloudWatch/latest/DeveloperGuide/

Restrictions Amazon's CloudWatch does however come with a number of drawbacks and limitations.

- For a micro instance costing $0.025 per hour, you will pay another $0.015 per hour for detailed monitoring with CloudWatch (60% of the instance price). In other words, detailed monitoring will cost you $131 per year and instance.
- CloudWatch can only monitor a basic set of system parameters.
- Currently you cannot extend CloudWatch to include middleware or application specific parameters. Indeed, a service provider interface to extend the CloudWatch monitoring would be very useful, and a generic way to incorporate JMX based runtime values would be even better.

11.6 AWS Simple Notification Service

AWS Simple Notification Service (SNS) is a publish/subscribe service for notifications in the cloud. The scope of SNS is much broader than that of monitoring and it's a good starting point used in combination with the CloudWatch to implement custom monitoring and notification.

To use SNS, create a topic with the AWS management console or the SNS API. Clients interested in this topic subscribe to it, and whenever a notification is published to the topic, SNS will push it to all subscribers.

SNS supports a variety of transport protocols for the subscriptions:

- HTTP(S) using POST
- Email
- Email with JSON format
- SQS

Different subscribers can subscribe to a single topic using any of the listed transport protocols.

Topic names must be unique within an AWS account and their length is limited to 256 alphanumeric characters and hyphens. Within the AWS infrastructure there is no single point of failure for SNS: messages are stored redundantly across multiple availability zones. SNS attempts to deliver the notifications in order, however, due to network issues this cannot be guaranteed. The maximum message size is 8KB.

SNS is an attractive cloud service that delivers all the functionality necessary to develop a monitoring solution similar to the notifications of WebLogic Diagnostic Framework. Unfortunately, the AWS management console doesn't integrate SNS with CloudWatch yet. You have to use the CloudWatch command-line (or write your own code) to trigger an SNS notification if a CloudWatch metric is above a configured threshold.

Examples for using SNS

SNS is more general and can be used for tasks other than sending notifications based on monitoring data. Thanks to the email transport protocol for subscriptions it is rather easy to build your own newsletter system based on SNS.

Would you feel more relaxed if you knew that you would receive an email if your AWS fee has exceeded a certain amount? You can easily implement a process that retrieves your account usage and then triggers an SNS notification to an email subscriber if things get too expensive.

In general, you should regard SNS as a generic notification service that can be used by all kinds of applications in the AWS cloud so the applications can interact with each other.

Best effort Protocols such as email or HTTP are inherently unreliable, and there is no retry count for notifications that SNS couldn't push to the subscriber. The notification delivery semantics of SNS is best-effort: There is no guarantee that your notification will ever be delivered. Don't use SNS to build systems where the delivery of notifications is essential.

Usage

To create a new topic, use the AWS management console and click on the "Amazon SNS" tab. When using it for the very first time you have to sign in for this service.

Once this process is completed, click on "Create New Topic" and choose a name for the new topic:

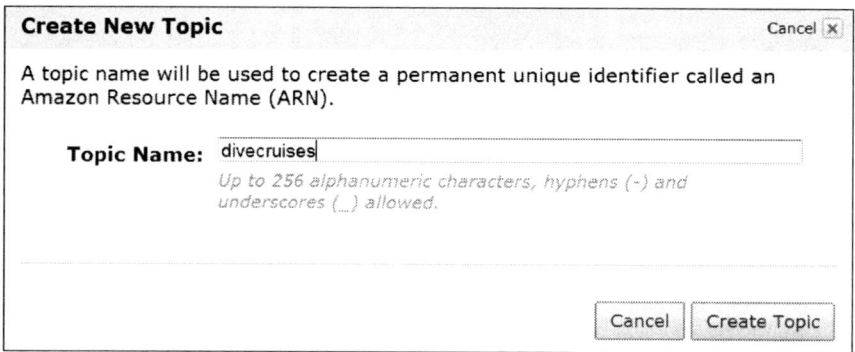

Figure 121: SNS Create Topic

The topic's name is used to construct a unique identifier called Amazon Resource Name (ARN), which is then displayed on the next screen:

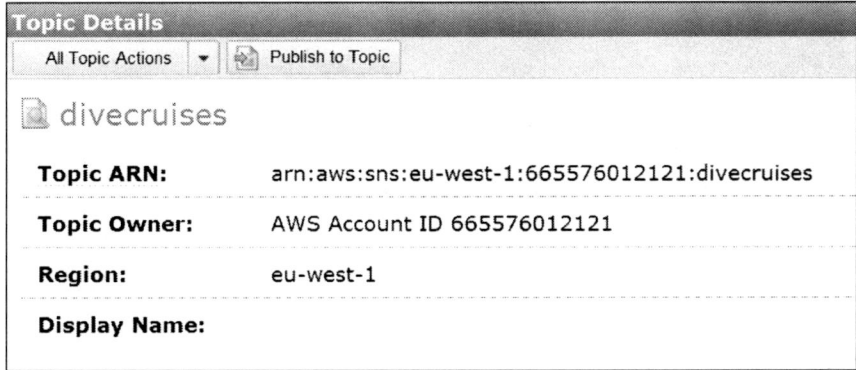

Figure 122: SNS Topic ARN

Then create a new subscription, choose the transport protocol Email, and provide the email address:

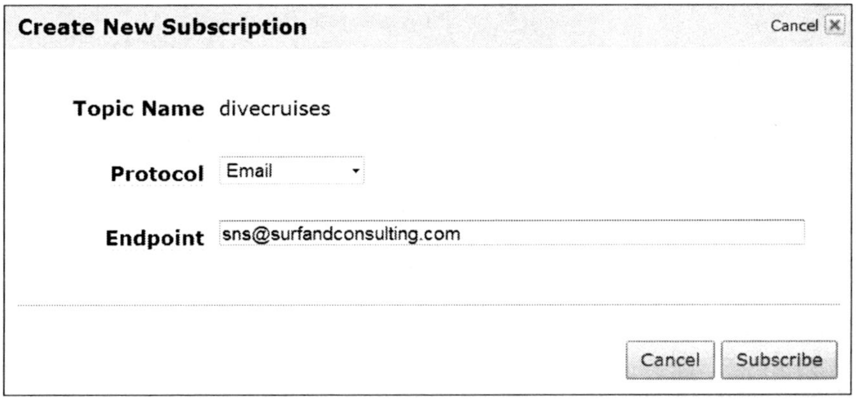

Figure 123: SNS Email Subscription

There is an opt-in process for email. To avoid spamming, the email subscription has to be confirmed. SNS sends an email to the new subscriber containing a link for the confirmation.

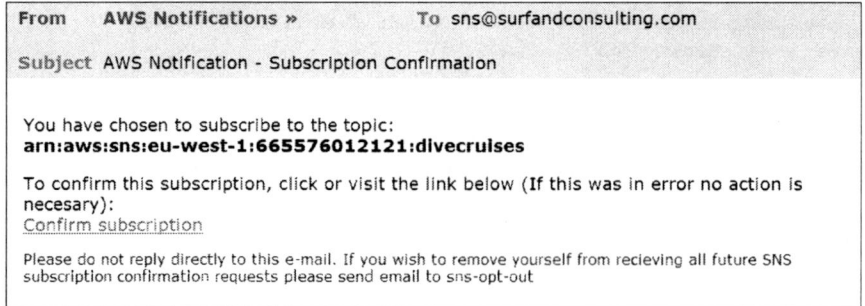

Figure 124: SNS Email Opt-In

The confirmation process takes you to the SNS web site where you can confirm your subscription or unsubscribe.

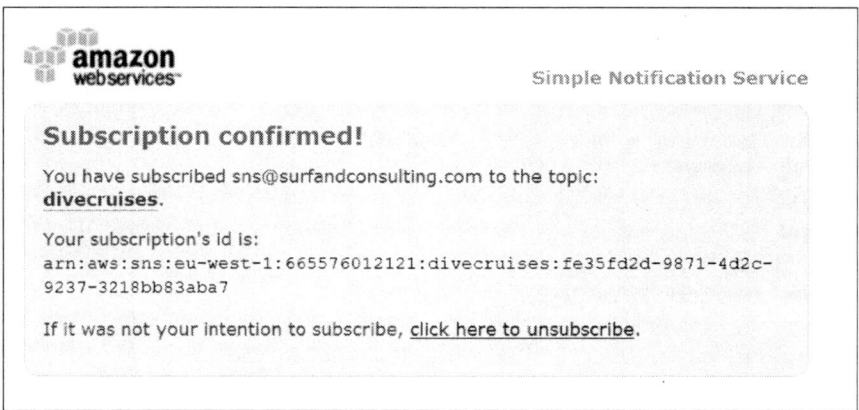

Figure 125: SNS Subscription Confirmation

For all other protocols except email there is no opt-in mechanism.

Now it is time to test the new subscription. Even a first test can be done with the AWS management console. Select the topic and click on "Publish to Topic".

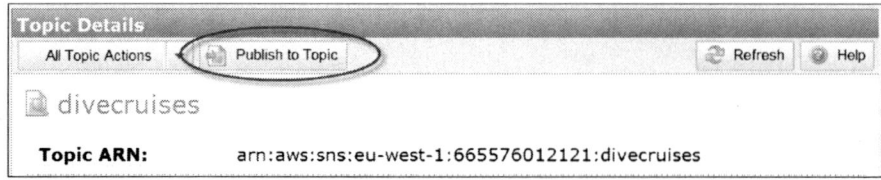

Figure 126: SNS Publish to Topic

Enter a subject and a message text for the notification, and submit the notification. Then check your email for a new notification. It should be displayed along with your subject and the message, including an unsubscribe link.

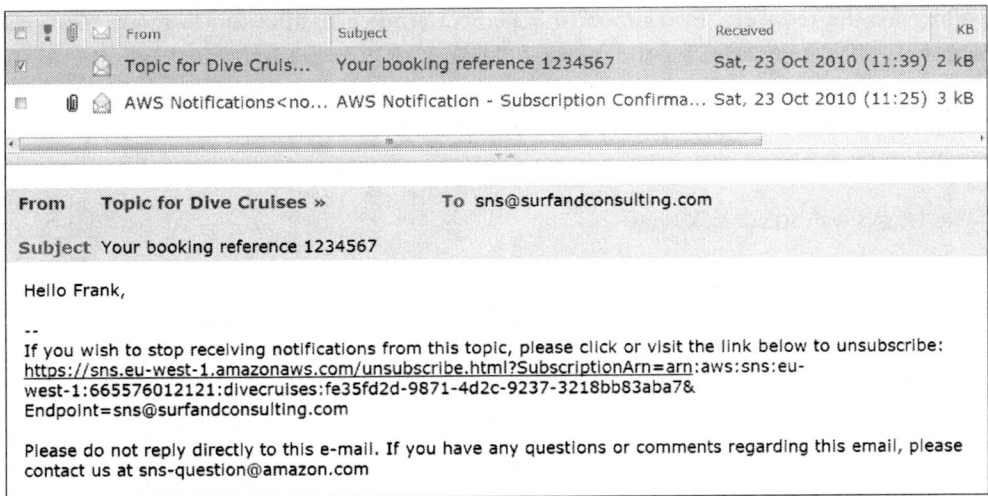

Figure 127: SNS Email Notification

Certainly you won't be using SNS from the Amazon management console, but from your applications or within custom tools.

SNS APIs

There are SNS software development kits for Java, .NET, and PHP available for downloading at the following Amazon site:

http://developer.amazonwebservices.com/connect/kbcategory.jspa?categoryID=314

SNS is also supported by the popular open source library Typica. For an example about how easy it is to SNS with Typica have a look at the following Java class:

http://typica.googlecode.com/svn/trunk/test/java/TestSNS.java

SNS versus SQS

Simple Notification Service and Simple Queue Service (see section **9.7**) are both messaging systems. SQS implements a one to one message pattern with at least once semantics and polling for the receivers. In contrast to SQS, SNS sends a notification to many receivers with best effort semantics for the message delivery. SQS is not integrated into the AWS management console. In contrast to SNS, where messages get lost if the receiver is not available, you can use SQS to decouple systems because the messages are stored persistently until they are retrieved.

Table 12: SNS with SQS Comparison

	SNS	SQS
Message pattern	1 to many	1 to one
Purpose	Notifications	Reliable Messaging
Message semantics	Best effort	At least once
Similar to	JMS topics	JMS queues
Message delivery	Pushed to receiver	Receiver poll
Maximum message	8 KB	64 KB

Integration with SQS

You can forward an SNS notification to an SQS queue. The publish method of SNS is synchronous, meaning that it only returns after the notification is pushed to the subscriber -which in this case means the message is stored in the SQS queue. Once the notification is placed in the queue you will benefit from the at-least once delivery semantics of SQS.

SQS is only used programmatically. To create an SQS subscription you have to subscribe to the SQS queue with the Amazon resource name of the queue. In addition, you have to set the access control policy of the queue to allow SNS to send notifications to the queue.

Integration with Oracle Service Bus

Did you ever wonder about how to bridge information from AWS to OFM? Connecting Oracle Service Bus with SNS directly, is possible with HTTP, or can be done indirectly over email. For a direct connection, create an OSB proxy service with the transport protocol HTTP, and register it as an SNS subscriber.

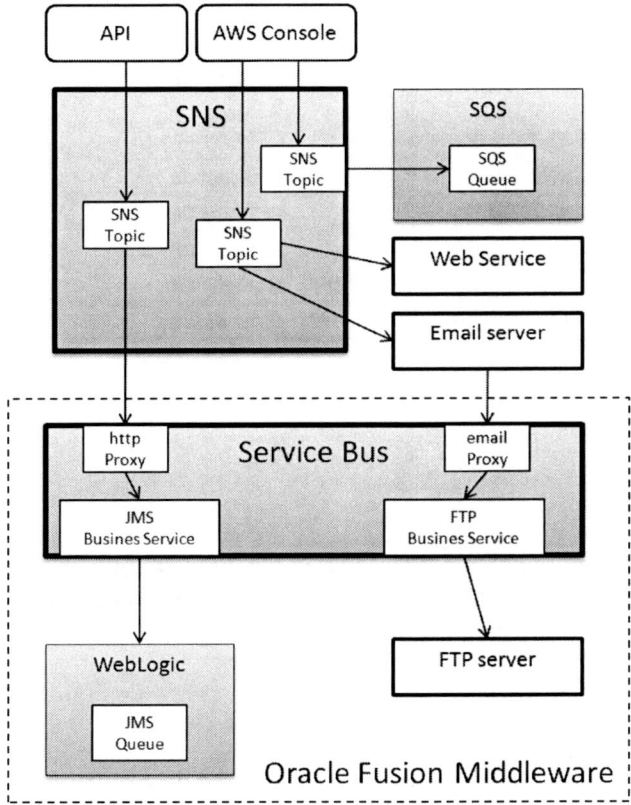

Figure 128: SNS with OSB Integration

Pricing

There is a free usage tier for 100,000 SNS requests, 100,000 SNS HTTP(S) notifications, and 1000 email notifications.

Beyond the free tier Amazon will charge you for the API requests and notifications.

- $0.06 per 100,000 API requests
- $0.06 per 100,000 HTTP(S) notifications.
- $2.00 per 100,000 Amazon SNS Email/Email-JSON notifications
- SQS notifications are free of charge

In addition, you have to pay for data transfer in and out of SNS, see Figure 129 for details. Within a single region there is no charge for transfer between SNS and other AWS. For cross-regional data transfers, the Internet data transfer pricing applies.

Data Transfer In	US & EU Regions	APAC Region
All Data Transfer	$0.10 per GB	$0.10 per GB

Data Transfer Out ***	US & EU Regions	APAC Region
First 1 GB per Month	$0.00 per GB	$0.00 per GB
Up to 10 TB per Month	$0.15 per GB	$0.19 per GB
Next 40 TB per Month	$0.11 per GB	$0.15 per GB
Next 100 TB per Month	$0.09 per GB	$0.13 per GB
Over 150 TB per Month	$0.08 per GB	$0.12 per GB

Figure 129: SNS Data Transfer Rates

11.7 Misc Tools

In order to establish a useful monitoring process, knowledge of the different tools available and their capabilities, is imperative. I'd therefore like to provide an overview of alternative solutions that are commonly used and should therefore be on your radar.

RRD Tool

RRD is an open source tool often used for data logging and displaying time series data. It stores data in a round-robin database (hence the name) and it retrieves the data to create graphs. The database never runs out of space because of its circular storage. You can either write your own custom monitoring shell scripts, or alternatively create whole applications using its Perl, Python, Ruby, TCL or PHP bindings.

As a starting point, take a look in the following gallery at all the aesthetically pleasing graphs that users created using RDD:

`http://oss.oetiker.ch/rrdtool/gallery/index.en.html`

Once you are confident with the output, check the technical details at the RRD site:

`http://oss.oetiker.ch/rrdtool`

Martin Pot has written a tutorial about how to use RRD to monitor Linux network traffic. He describes how to generate a graph displaying daily, weekly, monthly and yearly statistics, as shown below:

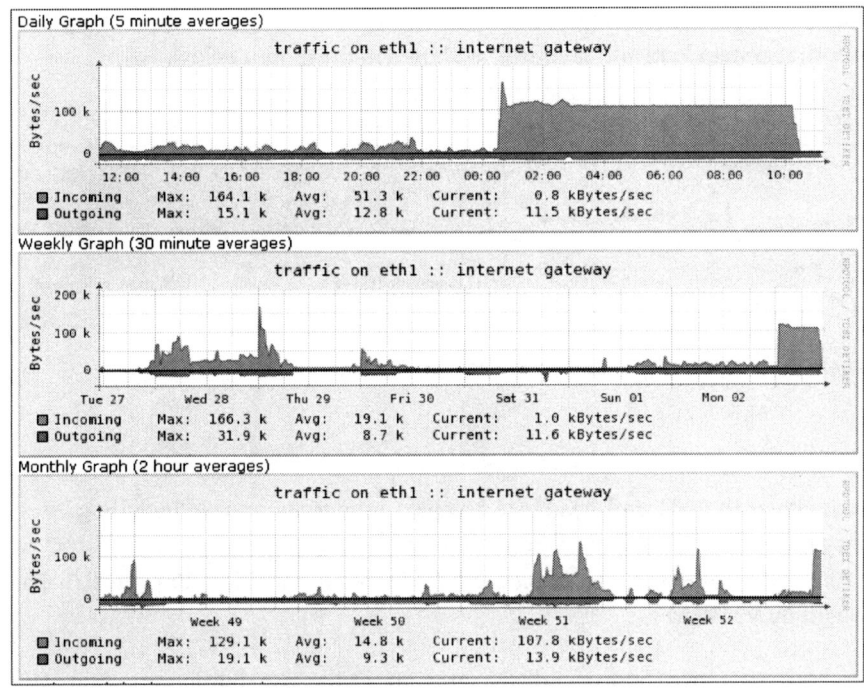

Figure 130: RDD Network Statistics

The complete article can be accessed at the following site:

http://martybugs.net/linux/rrdtool

Ganglia

Ganglia is a scalable and distributed monitoring system that is typically used in high-performance computing for clusters and grids. It was developed under a BSD-licensed open-source project that stemmed from the University of California, Berkeley Millennium Project. To note: according to John Allspaw, Flickr uses Ganglia. You can learn more about Ganglia usage in John's book about capacity planning.

Ganglia leverages technologies such as XML for data representation, XDR for compact, portable data transport and RRDtool for data storage and visualization, and can be seen live at Berkeley on the following site:

http://monitor.millennium.berkeley.edu

The link above takes you to the Ganglia site of the Millennium project, where Ganglia is used for monitoring system load and memory, as shown in the graphs below:

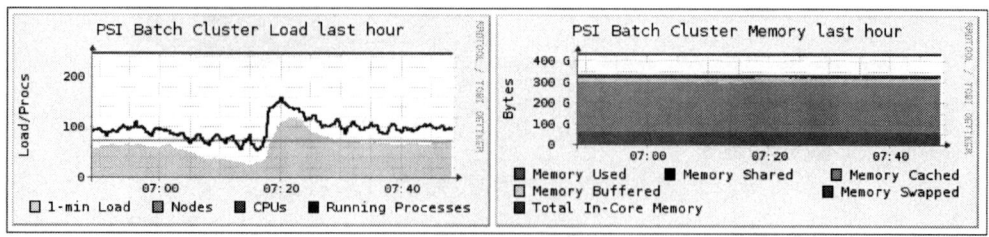

Figure 131: Ganglia at the University of Berkeley Millenium Project

Hyperic

Hyperic was launched in 2004 and has since received numerous awards including "Best Systems Management Tool" at LinuxWorld 2007 and "Top Open Source Project" at Sourceforge 2008. The company was bought by SpringSource in May 2009 (which has since been bought by VMWare).

Hyperic offer both an Open Source Edition and an Enterprise Edition of their HQ monitoring tool, both of which integrate smoothly with WebLogic. Please refer to their web site for further details:

http://www.hyperic.com

Nagios

Nagios is the de-facto, industry standard, open-source, monitoring tool. For Nagios, the equivalent of the developers "Hello World" program is the monitoring of a laser printer, yet it can also be used for network devices, for thousands of Unix servers or for WebLogic clusters. The screenshot in Figure 132 shows one of the Nagios status pages.

For further information about Nagios, I recommend you start by exploring the following site, then get some practical experience:

http://www.nagios.org

It is possible to see Nagios live, as there are online demos available to give you an initial impression at the following location:

http://demos.nagios.com/

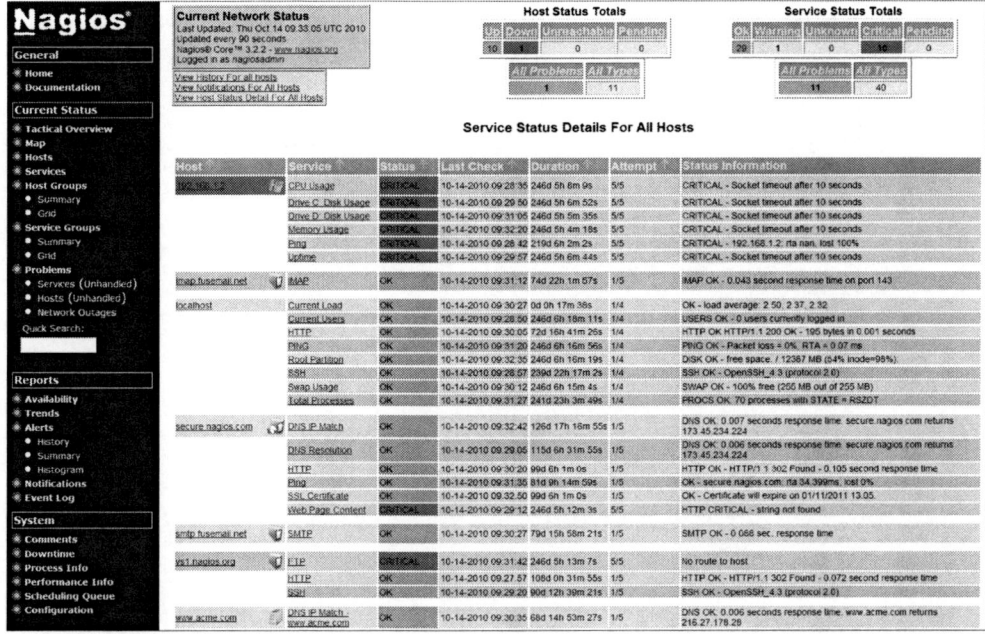

Figure 132: Nagios Monitoring

An interesting extension to Nagios is JMX4Perl, which also includes the JMXShell. Nagios uses the JMX4Perl plugin to efficiently retrieve JMX values from any kind of application server. JMX4Perl and JMXShell are covered in section 11.4.

Oracle Enterprise Manager Grid Control

Oracle Enterprise Manager (EM) is Oracle's answer not only to monitoring, but also to management, patching and performance tuning. EM requires a separate license when starting with a WebLogic deployment. It's a powerful and complex tool, but unfortunately, is more complicated to install than WebLogic.

In the area of monitoring, Oracle EM is competing with Nagios. Nagios is user-friendly and can be extended as an enterprise-wide solution to monitor everything. It is also worth noting that Nagios is free and open source. On the other hand, Oracle is certainly right to emphasize that a combined monitoring and management solution specifically tailored to their software stack is advantageous.

Oracle EM is unfortunately beyond the scope of this book. As with Nagios, I therefore recommend you get some hands-on experience. To overcome the installation burden, I would suggest obtaining a pre-installed Oracle VM image and running it on Oracle VM.

12 Oracle VM

No Oracle cloud computing book would be complete without taking a look at Oracle's own virtualization platform, Oracle VM, and seeing how it relates to current IaaS clouds. Actually, Oracle has made a giant leap forward from Larry's statement "Everything is cloud computing…" to its recent announcements to support the Amazon cloud.

In this chapter we'll have a look at Oracle VM, the WebLogic Server Virtual Edition and the Assembly Builder before analyzing the new Oracle / Amazon announcement.

Remember that although cloud computing uses virtualization technologies, virtualization per se is not cloud computing. Flip back to the definition of cloud computing in section 2.1 and compare it to virtualization again. Often virtualization platforms lack most of the criteria defined here.

12.1 Oracle Virtualization

Oracle is in the desktop and server virtualization market. Virtual Box and Sun Ray are Oracle's desktop virtualization products, Oracle VM is the server virtualization product.

Sun Ray

Sun Ray enables a secure virtual desktop solution with lean desktops, management programs as well as data centrally hosted on a server in the data center (not a bad architecture for a company that is selling the servers as well).

Desktop virtualization

Clients such as Sun Ray Clients, Windows PCs and Mac OS X can access the virtual desktop environment.

Oracle VM Virtual Box

Virtual Box offers desktop virtualization. Unlike Sun Ray, which is based on a central server, Virtual Box is used as an operating system on top of another operating system. You can install Virtual Box on Windows, Linux, Macintosh or OpenSolaris hosts, and then run any supported guest operating system within that Virtual box.

Virtual Box is distributed as open source software under the terms of the GNU General Public License (GPL).

You can download it including the documentation from the following location:

http://www.virtualbox.org

If you are wondering whether this has anything to do with cloud computing, the short answer is no. There are two reasons why I believe you should know about this solution anyway.

OS in OS — Firstly, it's free, open source and established software: Running a Linux operating system in Virtual Box on your Windows 7 computer is a good choice when starting with AWS. You will appreciate the benefits of Linux (having a comfortable command shell, ssh, scp and other useful tools) without leaving the comfort zone of your Windows system.

Software appliances — Secondly, there are software appliances for Virtual Box available, such as a fully configured, ready-to-use SOA/BPM 11g Suite. You can download it from the following location:

http://blogs.oracle.com/virtualization/2010/09/vm_templates_or_appliances_for.html

Oracle emphasizes that these appliances are for testing only, but they easily serve as a comfortable entry ticket to the complex SOA world. You can get a huge software stack without installation and configuration.

Oracle VM

Free — Oracle VM is an interesting product because it enables free server virtualization. To be more precise, only the download of the binaries and the sources is free - if you are interested in software updates, you need a paid support contract. You can download the product from the following location after agreeing to the export restrictions:

http://edelivery.oracle.com/oraclevm

No operating system — Oracle VM consists of VM Server (the Xen-based hypervisor) and VM Manager (a web-based management console). It installs directly onto the hardware: There is no operating system required for the installation of the hypervisor. By the way, this is the reason why it is a bit difficult to try Oracle VM at home; since it installs itself directly on your PC or laptop, it gets rid of your operating system - including all your data. Please read that last sentence again before you try installing Oracle VM at home.

Virtualization is a strategically important technology for Oracle. For example, it enables Oracle to deploy applications in a grid without depending on physical server configuration and installation.

Oracle VM is certified for the Oracle database including Oracle RAC (see section 7.5, page 154, for a discussion about using Oracle RAC in the cloud), middleware and applications.

Apart from the fact that it is free, the biggest advantage of Oracle VM is the availability of Oracle VM templates. These templates eliminate software installation and configuration. *Oracle VM templates*

In case you ever complained about lengthy and complicated installations that depend on many prerequisites: Deploying a VM template is a quick and easy way to get Oracle enterprise software up and running. It might be worth it to install Oracle VM just to take advantage of the available VM templates. To get to a list of templates provided by Oracle, click on "VM Template" at the following site:

http://www.oracle.com/technetwork/server-storage/vm/

One of Oracle's biggest competitors in the server virtualization market is VMware. VMware users amongst you will have already realized that Oracle VM competes with VMware's vSphere ESX offering. VMware vSphere is a very popular and well-established commercial product for server virtualization. *VMware vSphere ESX*

Both products install directly on the hardware, support the live migration of virtual instances and offer other advanced features such as load balancing.

12.2 Oracle WebLogic Virtual Edition

Oracle WebLogic Server Virtual Edition enables the deployment of an Oracle VM template that includes WebLogic server with JRockit Virtual Edition running directly on the hypervisor without a guest operating system.

Oracle JRockit Virtual Edition

Every virtual machine abstracts the underlying hardware and provides a standardized runtime environment. As an example, the Java Virtual Machine (JVM) is the runtime environment for Java byte code and abstracts the Java program from the underlying operating system.

Oracle has taken this a step further with Oracle JRockit Virtual Edition. It has removed the requirement for the underlying operating system and implemented those services that were provided by the operating system into the JRockit Virtual Edition itself.

Getting rid of the operating system is an inviting idea for several reasons:

- From a middleware perspective, the operating system is more of a necessity. Or, to put it more bluntly, it's something you have to deal with, but you don't really care about it. Many Java EE developers never think about the operating system.
- Eliminating the operating system eliminates the time for installing, tuning and maintaining it.
- Getting rid of the operating system can reduce the overhead and increase the performance because only the required services are implemented by the JVM.
- Virtual templates are smaller without the operating system, therefore they are faster to deploy and the running instances have a lower memory footprint.

Oracle claims a "30% improvement in overall throughput of the application compared to the traditional para-virtualized deployment, while achieving 83% performance of a physical deployment".

Figure 133 illustrates the deployment of WebLogic Server Virtual Edition, side-by-side with the Oracle VM Manager for the administration of Oracle VM, an Enterprise Manager template and another Oracle VM template. The whole stack is running the hardware without any operating system.

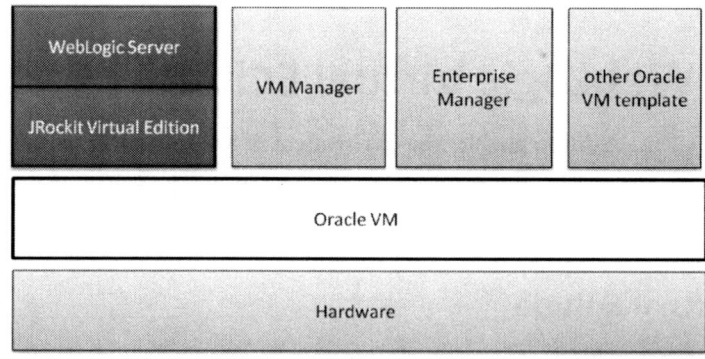

Figure 133: Oracle VM with WLS Virtual Edition

I recommend reading the white-paper with the performance data yourself, because it contains some more details. You can get it at the following location:

```
http://www.oracle.com/us/products/middleware/application-server/wls-virtualization-twp-067890.pdf
```

Oracle documentation

There are however, a few limitations due to the missing operating system layer:

- The Java Native Interface (JNI) is not supported because there cannot be any native code.
- Applications cannot use operating system calls.

Oracle Virtual Assembly Builder

Oracle Virtual Assembly Builder is a graphical tool used to create assemblies for Oracle VM. Assemblies consist of customizable appliances. These appliances are standardized building blocks listed in a catalogue, and can be connected to each other with the drag-and-drop interface of Assembly Builder.

You can create a set of bootable machine images that allow customization at the deployment time. There is also a command-line interface that can be used for the scripting of assemblies, the packaging and the deployment of the images.

The idea of assemblies is similar to the deployments in RightScale cloud management as described in section 8.

At the time of this writing, Virtual Assembly Builder cannot include any third-party products; therefore, it is not a good choice for heterogeneous environments. Only Oracle WebLogic, HTTP Server, Web Cache and database are supported (and only certain versions).

12.3 Oracle VM on AWS

It was big news when Amazon announced the support of Oracle VM images on AWS. At the time of this writing there is only little information available, but in general Amazon tends to announce features just a short time before they become available.

So far, the major problem with using Oracle VM in a smaller environment has been the requirement for dedicated hardware. This lack of hardware is one of the reasons why few people explore the preconfigured Oracle VM templates that come with products such as the Oracle SOA Suite.

With the new announcement this situation has changed. You will now be able to start your Oracle VM templates on EC2. Rather than buying dedicated hardware for an Oracle VM installation, you simply decide which EC2 instance type to use it on. So, after the long detour to virtualization, we are finally back to the cloud with its virtually unlimited resources and the pay on demand model.

According to the information available, Oracle will initially provide images containing Oracle Enterprise Linux, Oracle Database 11gR2, Oracle E-Business Suite, Oracle WebLogic Server and Oracle Universal Content Management.

Any product currently supported on Oracle VM will be supported when running Oracle VM based images on EC2. However, there is no support for Oracle RAC (see the discussion about the availability of Oracle RAC in section 7.5).

Licensing

Management of the Oracle VM images will be done with the AWS console and tools. There is no support for the Oracle VM Server Management on EC2. This is good to know, since you can use everything that you learned in this book, starting right with the AWS basics in chapter 3.

When you use the Oracle VM backed images you have to pay the AWS fees. For the licenses Oracle's standard partitioned processor licensing models will apply, since the Oracle software will run on Oracle VM with hard partitioning. Customers with Amazon Premium Support accounts will be able to contact either Amazon or Oracle for support.

Bibliography

Gorge Reese, "Cloud Application Architectures", O'Reilly, 2009

A classic, almost a must-have. Many things have changed since then, but it's still a good read.

John Allspaw, "The Art of Capacity Planning", O'Reilly, 2008

Another classic. Teaches a lot about scaling, ceilings and capacity.

Jeff Barr, "Host Your Web Site in The Cloud: Amazon EC2 Made Easy", SitePoint, 2010

A good book if you are considering hosting your website in the cloud. Not for the Java, Oracle or SOA/middleware folks, but for the PHP programmer.

There are more than one hundred links to articles, whitepapers, blog entries, and product sites mentioned throughout this book. You can conveniently access all of them from the following site:

http://cloudbook.munzandmore.com

Alphabetical Index

/proc/cpuinfo 36
/proc/meminfo 36
99designs 19
account 22
ADF 114
admin server 105
aiCache 217
ALBPM 114
ALER 117
Alestic 40, 78
algorithms 1
ALSB 110
Amazon Linux 23
Amazon Machine Image 21
Amazon Web Services 21
AMI 21, 23
AMI design 125
Andrew S. Tanenbaum 62
Animoto 18
AOP 246
APEX 135
architecture blueprint 132
archive 244
ARIS 116
Armageddon 189
as-cmd 221
as-create-auto-scaling-group 221
as-create-launch-config 221
as-create-or-update-trigger 222
as-delete-auto-scaling-group 228
as-delete-launch-config 228
as-delete-trigger 226
as-describe-auto-scaling-groups 225, 227
as-describe-launch-configs 225
as-describe-scaling-activities ... 222
aspect-oriented programming 246
as-set-desired-capacity 225
as-update-auto-scaling-group 226

asynchronous messaging 175
attributes 240
authentication 89
auto scaling 134, 219
automation 174
availability 119, 175, 188, 198
availability zone 25, 133, 176, 215
AWS account 185
AWS cloud service 186
AWS cloud services 132
AWS CloudFront 228
AWS Console 26
AWS Elastic Load Balancing 208
AWS Import/Export 62
AWS Linux 39
AWS regions 185
AWS Relational Database Service 139
AWS S3 buckets 59
AWS Simple Notification Service 259
AWS simple queue service 176
AWS Simple Queue Service 184
AWS SimpleDB 136
AWS virtualization 218
AWS_AUTO_SCALING_HOME 220
backup AMI 166
backup window 141
backups 165
bandwidth cap 76
basic monitoring 253
bc (Unix command) 223
BEA 110
billing address 22
BitTorrent 61
block device 51
blocking send 193
bookkeeping 17
BPEL 99
BPEL4People 99

Oracle VM 279

BPM	99
BPM Composer	116
brain research	1
Brian Adler	217
Bro	131
bucket	232
Business Process Execution Language	99
business service	112
C#/.NET	89
calculator	47
Canonical	40, 80
canonical data model	98
capacity constraint	191
capacity planning	201
CAPEX	5, 136
CDM	98
CDN	88, 228
CDN distribution	232
CentOS	38
certificate	212
CISCO	204
Cloud Files	87
Cloud Files APIs	89
Cloud Files Manager	92
cloud management	161, 168
Cloud Market	39
cloud storage	123
CloudBerry	58
CloudFront	133, 235
CloudWatch	144, 212, 237, 253
cluster	107
cluster compute instances	30
cluster graphics processing units	30
cluster shell	163
clustered domain	164
CNAME	140, 211
command-line	41
commodity of the shelf	198
common data model	98
Common Enterprise Meta Data Service	114
composites	102
compression	166
concept	12
configuration driven	97
configuration model	129
configurations	169
connect()	241
connection pool	195
connect-time failover	156
content distribution network	133
Content Distribution Network	88, 228
cooldown	222
cost report	173
cost versus user experience	201
costs	47
COTS	198
coupling	175
CPAN	251
CPU capacity	28
create a new image	68
create AMI	62
credentials	23
CUDA	30
curl	36
curve fitting	201
Cyberduck	93
Cygwin	79
dashboard	168
data center	25
data points	201
database	135, 165
database security group	146
dd (Unix command)	50
DDOS	189
decentralized load balancing	206
decoupled	175
deep monitoring	237
definition of cloud computing	5
delivery guarantee	115
deploy	108
deployment	177
deployments	113, 170
-describe-triggers	226
design	19, 132, 201
design tradeoff	188
desktop	66
development machine	105
diagnostic module	244
dig	204

dimension	254
disaster recovery	167
disk drive	55
distributed caches	230
distributed denial of service attack	189, 208
distributed file system	10
distributed JMS destinations	177
distributed processing	10
distributed system	175
distributed transactions	158
DNS	34
DNS caching	211
DNS lookups	212
DNS name	210
DNS round robin	203
domain	104
Domain Name Service	34
domain specific language	239
domainRuntime()	242
DSL	239
DSP	113
durability	55
dynamic scaling	199
EBS	51, 123
EBS snapshots	62
EBS-backed	27
EBS-backed instance	125
EC2	134, 276
EC2 commands	65
EC2 Compute Unit	28
ec2-authorize default	54
ec2-create-image	63, 68
ec2-create-volume	52, 68
ec2-describe-availability-zones	43
ec2-describe-images	43, 53, 65
ec2-describe-instances	66
ec2-describe-regions	43
ec2-describe-snapshots	68
ec2-describe-volumes	52, 67
ec2-get-password	54
ec2-modify-instance-attribute	67
ec2-run-instances	53, 65, 68, 253
ec2-stop-instances	67
Eclipse	103, 116
ECU	28
edge locations	230
EJB	202
Elastic Block Store	51
elastic compute cloud (EC2)	21
elastic IPs	34, 176
elasticity	120
ELB	208, 235
elb-configure-healthcheck	214, 215
elb-create-lb	213
elb-describe-instance-health	214
elb-describe-lbs	213, 215, 221
elb-register-instances-with-lb	214
electricity	5
EM	269
email	112
encrypting	50
encryption	165
Enterprise Manager Database Control	135
enterprise service bus	115
environment variables	42
ephemeral	50
Eric Hammond	40
Eucalyptus	7
event-driven	206
excessive load	175
execute thread	191, 195
export	42
external load balancer	202
F5 load balancer	204
Facebook	13, 92
failover	140, 205
features	5
FIFO	193
file	112
fine granular	197
firewall	76, 189
fixed IP address	34
Flickr	92
floating IP	182
framework	10
free usage tier	44
FreeNX	79
Freshbooks	17

full-baked AMIs 130
functional imaging.................................... 1
fvwm... 78
Ganglia 267
Gartner 8
get() 242
GitHub 206
Gmail 12
GNU General Public License 272
GoodData 116
Google App Engine 10
Google Docs 13
Gorge Reese 277
governance................................... 99, 117
GPU 30
grep 161
Hadoop 10
halt 38
HAProxy 170, 206
hardware load balancers 204
heap size 192
HIDS 131
horizontal scaling 197
host intrusion detection 131
HP 7
HPC 2
HPC instances 30
HTTP keep-alive 218
HTTP load balancing 108
HTTP proxy plugin servlet 205
HTTP sessions 107, 192
HuaaS 14
Human as a Service 14
Human Intelligence Task (HIT) 14
hybrid clouds 8
Hyperic 268
hypervisor 78
I/O capacity 146
IaaS providers 71
IBM 7
IDEs 103
Infrastructure as a Service (IaaS) 9
initial cluster configuration 205
InnoDB 139
inoffensive traffic 188

installation 104
instance storage 123
instance type 28
instances 21
instantaneous growth 188
integrated development environment
.... 103
International Data Corporation 175
Internet Technologies........................... 6
j4p.war 251
j4psh 252
Java 89
Java EE 168, 187
Java Management Extensions 239
Java Messaging Service 109
Java Transaction API 109
JConsole 189, 240, 252
JDBC data source 151
JDBC pinned to thread 195
JDBC URL 152, 180
JDeveloper 103
JDK 41
Jeff Barr 277
Jeff Bezos 21
JeOS 37
JetS3t 62
JMS 101, 109, 112, 183
JMS Path Service 183
JMS queues 186
JMS quota 193
JMS server 179
JMS Store-and-Forward Service 183
JMS topics 187
JMX 239
JMX clients 240
JMX4Perl 250
JNDI name 179
John Allspaw 277
JPD 113
JSON 86
JTA 109, 183, 184
JVMRuntime 242
Jython 239
key pair 32
KVM 9

Larry Ellison	11
latencies	230
legal issues	164
license agreements	36
licensing	164
Limelight Networks	88
linear scalability	197
Linux	76
load balancer	198
load balancing	157
load tests	199
local storage	50
location transparency	112
Mac OS X	271
maintenance window	142
manage costs	173
managed server	105, 163
managed server independence	106
management	200
MapReduce	11
mathematical function	201
MBeans	240
MD5	91
MDS	114
measures	254
Mechanical Turk	14
message buffer size	193
message expiration	185
message oriented middleware	176
metrics	254
micro instance	28, 29, 44
migratable target	183
Mike Cico	248
MOM	176
mon-get-stats	257
monitoring	119, 237
mon-list-metrics	256
monthly costs	47
mon-version	255
Mosso	71
MQ transport	113
MSI	106
multi data source	155
multi-availability zone instance	142
Multi-AZ Deployment	140
multicast	177
multicast test	178
multi-cloud	187
MultiCloud Image	169
MySQL database	139
MySQL replication	146
Nagios	250, 268
Nagios demo	268
namespace	254
NAT	34
National Institute of Standards and Technology (NIST)	5
Netbeans	116
Network Address Translation	34
network bandwidth	209
network intrusion detection system	131
new business models	8
NFS	162, 180
nginx	203
NIDS	131
NIST	10
nodemanager	106, 181
non-shared file	161
NoSuchBucket	59
number crunching	7
NX	66, 79
OASIS	95
objects	56, 87
OEPE	103
OESB	110
offensive traffic	188
OFM	101
OpenSolaris	23, 271
operating system	274
OPEX	6
opt-in process	261
Oracle AMIs	23
Oracle BPM	114
Oracle Business Process Analysis Suite	115
Oracle Coherence	109
Oracle database AMIs	135
Oracle Enterprise Linux	135
Oracle Enterprise Manager	269
Oracle Enterprise Pack for Eclipse	103

Oracle Enterprise Repository 117
Oracle Fusion Middleware 11, 95, 101
Oracle JRockit Virtual Edition 274
Oracle Linux 23
Oracle Mediator 102
Oracle Portal 114
Oracle RAC 273
Oracle Real Application Cluster 154
Oracle Recovery Manager 165
Oracle Secure Backup Cloud Module 165
Oracle Service Bus 110, 264
Oracle Service Registry 116
Oracle SOA Suite 102, 110
Oracle software provisioning 130
Oracle Virtual Assembly Builder 275
Oracle VM 21, 271
Oracle VM on EC2 136
Oracle VM templates on EC2 276
Oracle WebLogic Server Virtual Edition
 273
OSB 110
OSB cluster 114
OSSEC 131
OTN 164
out of memory 194
outage 55
parking 37
per use 6
performance 51
persistent store 180
personal data 22
photos 18
PHP 89
Picasa 92
plan for failure 119
Platform as a Service (PaaS) 10
portal 114
primary instance 142
primary session 108
private address 34
private cloud 7
private key 41
proactive 201
proxy service 111
public / private IP address 182

public address 34
public clouds 6
publish/subscribe 259
Python 89
queue length 191
RAC 154
Rackspace Cloud 71
Rackspace server image 82
RAID 51
RAID 10 .... 76, 123
rapid elasticity 6, 197
RDP 54
RDS 139
read replicas 146
Real Time Messaging Protocol 230
receiver 175
region 24
registry 100
reliable messaging 181
remote desktop 54
rendering 18
replica-aware 108
Replica-aware 108
replication 109
repository 101
Resizing an Instance 67
resource ceilings 199
REST 21, 82
REST API 61
REST service 36
restaurant 7
RightImages 169
RightScale 168, 217
RightScale console 171
RightScale ServerTemplates 169
RMAN 165
RMI 115
Roman Stanek 116
root apex 211
root device 27, 52
round robin 203
routing 232
RRD 266
rsync 166
RTMP 230

Ruby	89
runtime environment	10
runurl utility	128
S3 browser	56
S3 bucket	134
S3-backed	27
S3-stored backups	165
SalesForce.com	12
SAN	51
SCA	102, 114
scalability	120, 180, 188, 197
scanners	1
script repository	129
scripted AMI	130
sdbtool	137
SecludeIT	166
secondary session	108
security	131
security exception	54
security group	32, 131
self service	6
server migration	176
Service as a Service	14
service bus	13, 97
Service Component Architecture	102
service implementation	96
service level agreement	73
service migration	177
service migration framework	183
service orchestration	99
service oriented architecture	13
service virtualization	97
services	6
session stickiness	212
shared file system	161
shared-nothing architectures	197
Shlomo Swidler	210
shortcut file	54
shutdown	38
SimpleDB	136
singletons	183
SLA	74, 230, 237
slowloris	206
snapshot	63
Snort	131
SNS	259
SNS notifications	253
SOA	95
SOA stack	96
SOA strategy	100
SOA-DIRECT	113
SOAP	21, 100
SOAPUI	85
software vendors	7
spamming	22, 261
speedup	198
spiky load patterns	212
spot instances	46
SQS	184, 264
SQS queue	264
SQS subscription	264
ssh	34, 35, 79
SSL	190, 212
Stackoverflow	206
standby instance	142
static content	229
statistical multiplexing	9
statistics	254
sticky HTTP sessions	212
storage area network	51
stress test	199
subscribers	259
sudo	41
Sun Ray	271
sun.net.inetaddr.ttl	211
support	73
SUSE	23
symmetrical multi-processor	198
synchronization overhead	198
system architecture	95
system monitoring	238
Systinet	116
tags	31
Tangosol	109
Thorsten von Eicken	168
thread pool	191
threads	191
throughput	180
TIBCO	117
TightVNC	79

time to live	89	web services	21
tools	92	WebCenter Framework	114
topic	259	WebCenter Interaction	114
tracert	233	WebCenter Spaces	114
training environment	15	WebDAV	93
transaction recovery service	184	WebLogic	104, 235
transactional integrity	115	WebLogic admin server	164
TripWire	131	WebLogic cluster	176, 202
TRS	184	WebLogic domain	163
TTL	89	WebLogic JMS queue	176
Turnkey Linux	40	WebLogic Portal	114
Tuxedo	113	WebLogic Scripting Tool	239
Twitter	206	WebLogic web server plugin	206
Typica	138, 263	wget	41
Ubuntu	23, 40	whole-server migration	108, 183
Ubuntu Lucid desktop	65	Wikipedia	5, 13
UDDI	116	Willy Tarreau	207
unicast	177	Windows 2008	53
uniformly distributed destinations	114	Windows Server 2003	76
unused capacity	46	Windows Server 2008	43
upgrade	206	Windows Server 2008 R2	76
usage terms	72	WLDF console	249
user experience metric	200	WLDF dashboard	249
--user-data-file	127	WLDF diagnostic monitor	246
versioning	56	WLDF instrumentation	246
vertical scalability	198	WLDF notification	246
videos	18	WLDF watch	245
Virtual Box	271	WLS administration port	190
virtual desktop	271	wlsifconfig.sh script	182
virtual private networks	8	WLST	239
virtualization	8	work manager	191
virtualization bottleneck	218	worker threads	191
virtualization techniques	9	workflow engine	117
VM Manager	272	Workshop	103
VM Server	272	WSDL	83
VM template	273	X.509 certificate	41
VMware	21	XA158	
VNC	79	XaaS	14
volumes	52	Xen	9, 272
VPN	8, 15	Xeon processor	28
vSphere ESX	273	XML	86
WADL	83	YouTube	11, 92
web container	202	zero investment	8
web servers	229	Zeus Load Balancer	217